THE NEW SELF-DIRECTED WORK TEAMS

THE NEW SELF-DIRECTED WORK TEAMS

MASTERING THE CHALLENGE

SECOND EDITION

JACK D. ORSBURN

LINDA MORAN

McGraw-Hill
New York   San Francisco   Washington, D.C.   Auckland   Bogotá
Caracas   Lisbon   London   Madrid   Mexico City   Milan
Montreal   New Delhi   San Juan   Singapore
Sydney   Tokyo   Toronto

Library of Congress Cataloging-in-Publication Data

Orsburn, Jack D.
    The new self-directed work teams : mastering the challenge / by
    Jack D. Orsburn and Linda Moran. — 2nd ed.
        p.   cm.
    Rev. ed. of: Self-directed work teams. © 1990.
    Includes bibliographical references and index.
    ISBN 0-07-043414-X
    1. Self-directed work teams.   2. Self-directed work teams—United
States.   I. Moran, Linda.   II. Self-directed work teams.   III. Title.
    HD66.S45   1999
    658.4′036—dc21   99-30690
                                                                            CIP

McGraw-Hill

A Division of The McGraw·Hill Companies

1 2 3 4 5 6 7 8 9 0   DOC/DOC   9 0 9 8 7 6 5 4 3 2 1 0 9

ISBN: 0-07-043414-X

The sponsoring editor for this book was Kelli Christiansen and the production supervisor was Elizabeth J. Strange. It was set in Fairfield by Carol Barnstable of Carol
Graphics. Word processing was by Spring Point Publishing Services.

Printed and bound by R. R. Donnelley & Sons Company.

This publication is designed to provide accurate and authoritative information in regard to the subject matter covered. It is sold with the understanding that the author
nor the publisher is engaged in rendering legal, accounting, fugures/securities trad-
ing, or other professional service. If legal advice or other expert assistance is required,
the services of a competent professional person should be sought.

> —*From a Declaration of Principles jointly adopted by a Committee of
> the American Bar Association and a Committee of Publishers.*

McGraw-Hill books are available at special quantity discounts to use as premiums
and sales promotions, or for use in corporate training programs. For more information, please write to the Director of Special Sales, McGraw-Hill, 11 West 19th Street,
New York, NY 10011. Or contact your local bookstore.

This book is printed on recycled, acid-free paper containing a minimum of
50% recycled de-inked fiber.

CONTENTS

PREFACE

This book was written for the many people within organizations who need to learn about self-directed work teams:

- For the *executives* who want to get the straight story about the pitfalls and bottom-line payoffs of work teams directly from the men and women with first-hand experience implementing work teams.

- For the *line managers and supervisors* who are facing a move to work teams and want to understand the challenges and rewarding new roles this transition can open up for them.

- For the *organizational development, training, and human resources practitioners* who want an overview of the transition and a practical, step-by-step plan for helping to move work teams off the planning table and into the office and factory.

- For *team members* themselves, seeking to deepen their understanding of the powerful workplace transformation in which they are participating.

The book is divided into three parts. Part 1, "Facing the New Challenge," offers a perspective that can help you decide if self-direction is right for your organization. It divides into five stages the often confusing development process work teams go through as they grow from start-up to fully functioning maturity; and it describes for each stage the specific steps an organization must take to facilitate this development.

Part 2, "Special Work-Team Issues," explores several situational issues that advocates of work teams may have to contend with and provides guidelines for dealing with each issue. In particular, we want to thank the three authors who contributed chapters to this section: Seth McCutcheon, Managing Partner, Domicile, Raleigh, North Carolina ("The Philosophy of Teams"); Jerry Smolek, President, Smolek Associates, Indianapolis, Indiana ("Developing the Role of Supervisors and Managers"); and Annemarie Michaud, Executive Consultant, AchieveGlobal, Montreal, PQ, Canada ("Teams and Measurement").

Part 3, "Tools and Techniques for Implementing Work Teams," brings together 19 specific tools and techniques for getting self-directed work teams up and running. Within this section, members of the steering committee, the design team, the organizational development department, and the training department will find ideas and processes to facilitate their organization's transition to teams.

To those readers who can already feel themselves resisting work teams, the authors ask you to withhold final judgment until you read this book and take a fresh look at your organization. Within these pages are examples from some of the biggest and most successful American corporations—the Cornings, the Northern Telecoms, the General Electrics, and the TRWs—mainstream organizations that have created uniquely American work teams and made them work, in some cases for decades. Work teams in these organizations are far too entrenched and productive by now for anyone to call them faddish or experimental.

Self-directed work teams are a means to an end, not an end in themselves. For some organizations, the goal may be to improve the competitive quality of their products and services. For others, it may be realizing the full benefits of a just-in-time inventory system. Sometimes work teams are established to help the entire organization, or one part of it, carry out a marketing strategy. And of course, some organizations see work teams as their best chance to improve productivity and avoid going under.

Within these pages, self-directed work teams are discussed primarily as a vehicle for gaining the significant performance advantages of full employee involvement. This focus reflects the authors' deeply held conviction that no major organizational improvement effort—be it quality improvement, just-in-time inventory, or enhanced productivity—will ever really be successful unless everyone in the organization is empowered to contribute their very best.

Jack Orsburn
Linda Moran

EARLY LESSONS

It was the early 1980s. While American companies were weighted down with cumbersome organizational charts and many layers of management, foreign companies were redesigning their organizations to be agile and responsive to customer demands. And they were stealing away business right and left. These companies embraced the principles of W.E. Deming, who believed that each employee had an untapped potential and that all organizations could run leaner by creating higher levels of employee participation. If America was going to remain competitive, something had to be done, and fast.

Two significant changes took place in America that helped pave the way for the introduction of self-directed work teams. First was the tremendous pressure placed on businesses to perform. Yet capacity could not be increased by the traditional American remedies of more management layers and increased micromanaging. The cumbersome hierarchies were already stretched to the breaking point. In casting about for creative solutions, organizations began realizing that to meet the demands for shorter cycle time and higher customer satisfaction, people at lower organizational levels would have to become more responsible for the well-being of the organization. This realignment of responsibility began in manufacturing and slowly spread across the full spectrum of organizational activities, from product design to customer service.

The other factor that set the climate for self-directed teams was that organizations began making significant cuts in the work force in order to reduce overhead, mostly at the middle management level. This left the top of the organization with the job of setting vision and direction and the bottom of the organization with the task of fulfilling it. Without as many middle managers to translate the business requirements into activities, employees were being given more latitude and responsibility in how they went about their jobs.

If there were fewer management people, then a logical step was to get people at lower levels to become more involved in the decision-making process. One of the more promising approaches for pulling decision-making down through the organization was the self-directed work team, and throughout the 1980s, such teams stimulated lively interest as articles on self-directed teams began appearing with increased frequency in the journals. It was during this seminal period that Linda Moran, one of this book's coauthors, developed her first experiences with self-directed teams. The experiences of coauthor Jack Orsburn go back even further to 1965, when he was learning the craft of managing and supporting what were then called "autonomous teams" from pioneers like Herb Shepard, Richard Walton, Shell Davis, and Tom Wickes.

AN EFFECTIVE COLLABORATION

Orsburn entered factory life as a blue-collar worker. He started in manufacturing, put in long days on the factory floor, and knew firsthand the humiliation, frustration, and the waste of brain power that characterized factory life. Orsburn was driven to respond, and he did so in a most appropriate fashion. He went back to school and earned an M.A., and ultimately a Ph.D., in organizational development. Because he had worked his way through the ranks, he had a hands-on appreciation of life on the factory floor and the potential that teams offered. He also had an instinctive understanding of the unique problems encountered by teams. As he moved into higher management levels and then into consulting, Orsburn was able to use his combined theoretical and practical knowledge to develop and implement programs in which people had a greater opportunity to become self-directed. Over time, he developed a vast array of tools that he used to help teams with problem solving. By the time the first edition of this book appeared, he had direct responsibility for designing and implementing more than 100 self-directed work teams in a variety of manufacturing and service organizations, both as an internal staff member and as an external consultant.

Linda Moran earned her master's degree in organizational communication, and quickly moved into the organizational world as a consultant, primarily in the area of transitioning to self-directed work teams, management and supervisory effectiveness, continual quality/service improvement, and improved problem-solving processes. Many of the organizations Moran worked with were already making tentative excursions into the tenuous waters of self-directed work teams, and she had a ringside view of the successes and failures of these early experiments.

Orsburn and Moran crossed paths in the mid-1980s and quickly discovered their complementary interests and experience. For one year they even worked for the same training and consulting firm. After many intense discussions and common projects, it was apparent that they had amassed enough practical experience to publish a comprehensive guide to establishing and maintaining self-directed work teams. Their collaboration led to the first book on this fast growing aspect of American business.

A CHALLENGE TO THE HIERARCHY

What was apparent, even back in the '80s, was the difficulty in implementing self-directed work teams. These teams were a threat to anyone who grew up in the traditional corporate hierarchy because they went counter to the corporate culture, and it was the rare company like Kimberly Clark, Proctor & Gamble, TRW, and General Foods' pet food plant in Topeka that would continue to support teams, despite the upheavals they created. But American businesses found themselves with little choice. If they were to respond to industry's growing obsession with quality, they would have to find a way to make the teams work.

In doing so, managers began recognizing they had to give up the arrogant posture that they could do everything themselves.

They began focusing on quality improvement, on measuring results, and on building an organization that was agile and responsive to the customer. It also became clear that if managers were really going to drive quality, they had to allow the decisions to be made closer to the customer.

Easier said than done. For most organizations, self-directed work teams were an unruly challenge and could be difficult to manage. Standard management practices often failed to work. To run teams successfully, management needed both a broader understanding of how the teams functioned and a battery of tools and techniques that could be applied to almost any aspect of team operation. Management also needed a better understanding of precisely what constituted a self-directed work team.

DEVELOPING A CLEAR DEFINITION

The term "self-directed" breeds misunderstanding because it implies that it is only the team members who set direction. For this reason, organizations have often shied away from considering self-directed teams. Instead of looking beyond the terminology to the concept behind the team, organizations have gotten lost in the language. They've said, "Our teams are not going to be self-directed; they're going to be something else," and then they've come up with their own terminology. Consequently, it would be useful to spell out precisely what "self-directed" means.

In our lexicon, "self-directed" means to follow the basics of team discipline and to be in agreement regarding the size of the team; its goals, mission, and metrics; the way the team functions; and the way team members share responsibilities. Whereas a project team is responsible for completing a particular project, and a quality circle is responsible for specific tasks such as identifying breakdowns in the quality process, the self-directed work team is responsible for an entire segment of work that is core to the business.

The team is not responsible for the "what." This is defined by management, which spells out the productive purpose of the team and what outcomes (or outputs) are required. The team, as it matures, takes on ever-increasing responsibility for the "how"—that is, how the outcomes will be achieved, who will do what tasks in what order of priority, and how the goals will be met.

Generally, if the knowledge and skills do not reside in one individual, or if a high level of interdependence is required, a self-directed work team becomes a more promising alternative to the individual manager because the skills and knowledge of many team members can be brought to bear on the situation. But management has to first review a whole list of questions and issues to decide if self-directed teams are truly appropriate; and it must consider such things as the industry, the management, the willingness to invest in resources, and the complexity of the work.

GETTING MANY MINDS INVOLVED

Ten years ago, a self-directed work team may have consisted of an entire department or a function working without a supervisor. Today, self-directed teams are more cross-functional and more fluid and less likely to interface with a single manager.

For example, a mortgage processing team might pass information to another mortgage processing team. Or the team may look at the flow of work and see an opportunity to help out a team in another part of the organization. Self-directed teams are not dependent on a manager to tell them how to do their work or how to schedule it. They're able to look at the expectations of the customer and the flow of the business and make certain decisions themselves. Previously, teams would not be looking at that same breadth of information nor making those same kinds of decisions.

Organizations are recognizing that no longer can there be systems organized around individuals; there must now be systems that support and reinforce teams. Creating these systems can be one of the organization's biggest challenges, because teams push on all the other systems within the organization.

PUTTING THEORIES TO THE TEST

The first edition of this book introduced the emerging phenomenon of self-directed work teams and attempted to present the subject in a way that would give organizations the confidence to be innovative. The fact that many managements took up the challenge attests to the active interest that existed in the promising potential of self-directed teams. Now that almost ten years have passed, we are pleased to report that virtually all the information in the first edition has proved itself. We are more convinced than ever that when the manager and the organization get it right, the benefits of self-directed work teams are impressive. Plants employing self-directed work teams often demonstrate 20 to 40 percent greater productivity, and those who work in self-directed teams report a higher level of job satisfaction and greater sense of dignity in what they do.

At the same time, we have learned much more about the unique difficulties and challenges faced by self-directed work teams. We have a more realistic appraisal of the personal challenges they face and a much clearer understanding of why teams work or don't work in particular corporate settings.

SAMPLING A BROADER UNIVERSE

One of the questions we couldn't answer a decade ago was how broadly the concept of self-directed work teams could be applied across the entire organizational spectrum. Self-directed teams had worked in manufacturing, but would they work in health care environments? In high tech? In service environments? The information in the first edition came primarily from manufacturing, as did most of the examples in the book. The rare service examples were taken mostly from the white-collar "paper mills."

We also couldn't determine with any certainty how the teams would function in less forward-looking organizations. Because self-directed teams were not yet a widespread phenomenon, the organizations that first experimented with them tended to be more innovative, more open to possibilities, more willing to take a chance. Some were start-ups that did not have to contend with an existing hierarchy. Many were captained by inspirational and courageous leaders who liked to manage on the cutting edge. But would our concepts apply to less extraordinary companies run by more "ordinary" people over a broad range of industries, or to companies that were in different life cycles? At the time, we had few opportunities to test this out.

What we particularly lacked was a clear sense of the longer-term problems—specifically, the kinds of struggles that teams were likely to encounter over time and the various factors that cause teams to fail. To gain this information, we needed to observe a sufficiently large number of self-directed teams over a broad enough time frame to be able to identify patterns and make diagnoses. We needed more examples of team-based organizations where entire systems were changed to support teams versus the more common practice of jury-rigging the existing systems to accommodate the teams. This new edition fills in the missing pieces. The information is more validated. Our database is broader and deeper. And we can refer to the track record of self-directed teams at all levels and in all industries.

LESSONS FROM THE EARLY PIONEERS

The wealth of information developed over the last decade has served to discredit some of the myths that contributed to the early failures of self-directed work-teams.

Myth. *Self-directed teams do not have to be linked to the larger organization.* Typically, we found there would be one or two areas of an organization with self-directed work teams, but few organizations had "linked teams" or "teams working with teams" in a facility. Isolated teams often led to disappointing results because they couldn't be directly linked to the business outcome.

Myth. *Managers are not needed to play an integral role in the team's success.* In fact, quite the opposite is true. As we came to see, managers are very much needed to make the transition and help keep self-directed teams up and running. The new team is really a babe in the woods—free to go anywhere but quite uncertain of how to do it. What's the best path? Where are the potholes? The team may have a general idea of how to proceed, but in the beginning, team members often lack the day-to-day know-how that makes people proficient at what they do. This is where coaching and nurturing by the manager become of critical importance.

What we saw in those early pioneering organizations was the need for a *gradual* transfer of responsibility. So often, the manager says to the team, "Here's what I've been doing. Now that you're a team, *you* do it," and marches off to take care of other business, unmindful of the issues the team is wrestling with. The reason this happens is that managers live in a command/control world where direction and purpose cascade from above and where the responsibility of those below is to execute and not to question. Consequently, managers often have little understanding of how to coach and support the team and how to remain sensitive to the team's nonverbal cues.

Myth.   *Teams can flourish without strong support from management.* The reality is that the success of teams has more to do with how they're supported than with their strengths or weaknesses as performing units. New teams are very fragile. Not only are they struggling to establish and define their own identity; they are also running counter to the normal functioning of the corporate hierarchy. Consequently, team members often feel that they're rowing upstream; and without support from management, the teams can be easily swept further and further away from their objectives.

Myth.   *A new team culture can be instantly created.* We found that it takes longer to make the shift to self-directed teams than we had imagined—typically about 18 months. People first have to get through culture shock. The learning has to be internalized so that situations automatically default to a team-oriented way of thinking and reacting. As much as possible, the system has to become self-reinforcing. If these things do not occur, when difficulties arise, people are likely to slip back into the old system.

People at all levels require time to undergo a philosophical and personal change as well as to bring about the necessary organizational changes. The corporate culture takes time to evolve as individuals take on more and more responsibility. Because self-directed teams change the rules of the game, this change in team culture does not happen overnight.

Myth.   *Self-directed teams are at heart just like other kinds of teams.* At heart, self-directed teams are *quite different* from other teams, and the more we studied the teams in a variety of settings, the more these differences became apparent.

The typical ad hoc work team is formed to solve a problem, find a solution, or design a product. Once the goal is accomplished, the team is disbanded. Such a team is easier to manage from a traditional point of view. The team has only a short-term focus, and there are usually no significant changes in how the work is done. That's the way the early quality circles functioned. They would look at an issue, determine the problem, present recommendations to a management group, and disband.

The introduction of self-directed work teams represented a conceptual shift. These teams were created as a way to get more done with fewer organizational layers and fewer people. These were permanent teams responsible for performing a unit of work. Unlike quality circles or ordinary work teams which functioned as parallel structures to the business and had a short-term focus and no permanent team dynamic, self-directed work teams were permanent structures for organizing the work. Consequently, the nature of the changes was much more complex.

Myth.   *The growth of teams has to be carefully orchestrated.* In the early days we lulled ourselves into believing that team learning followed a very developmental, mechanistic, linear progression. But this idea of a linear progression is a fantasy. We learned from the early pioneers that self-directed work teams need to build on the energy of change that resides within the team. The team's growth cannot be orchestrated from without.

Bringing to bear the authority of the hierarchy does little good, and, in fact, often hinders the team's evolution.

The growth of the team happens organically, and for that reason, there must be a continuing opportunity for incidental learning. Incidental learning consists of all the little things we learn about our job—or in this case, about team functioning. It's the day-to-day insights and discoveries about what works and what doesn't. It's what gives us a sense that something is right or wrong, even before it registers on our conscious awareness. It's not something you can see, touch, quantify. Such random learning happens simultaneously and in parallel, and the learning patterns are often not directly observable until much later. Incidental learning takes time to evolve, and while it's maturing, the team's growth can seem undirected and chaotic.

We have come to recognize that the patterns of evolution and organization in team development are often not immediately apparent, and that it is more evident and understandable when viewed within the context of chaos theory. Chaos theory proposes that so-called chaotic events have meaning and organization only when viewed from a broad enough perspective and over a great enough time frame. Chaos theory suggests that while teams are struggling to define who they are and are working out effective ways of functioning, it may *seem* like everything has gone to hell in a handbasket. The strife, the struggles, the confusion, the growing pains—these are all signs that can be interpreted negatively by the nervous manager who has to answer for the results. Many teams have been disbanded because managers didn't understand that the teams' struggles were following a natural progression, and they, the managers, were not willing to believe that the purpose and direction of these events would, over time, have a successful resolution.

But as chaos theory shows, there *is* an order that usually emerges, given sufficient time and nuturing, and organizations that have pursued self-directed teams intelligently and realistically and have given them sufficient time to mature have seen powerful results.

Myth. *Organizations will welcome self-directed teams with open arms.* We were unprepared for the kind of resistance that surfaced in one company after another when self-directed teams were introduced. This was startling, because a decade ago we didn't even see the resistance. We thought that self-directed teams were such a good idea that when people saw the benefits, they'd automatically and enthusiastically embrace them. We didn't recognize how threatened people could become and how negatively the hierarchy was likely to respond.

Managers resisted the teams because they believed that they, the managers, were entitled to do all the thinking for the teams, and withheld information and other vital resources. Furthermore, they found themselves drawn into activities that were unfamiliar or considered beneath them. Many managers thought that self-directed work teams were a good idea as long as those in charge could stay at stratospheric levels and make changes for those down below. But changes have to be made at higher levels as well.

For example, if someone on the team were out ill, the manager might be called upon to take over that person's work. This was a big stretch because managers were often forced to display their lack of knowledge in particular areas. Normally, there would be sufficient layers of management between them—supervisors, foremen, assistant managers—so they wouldn't have to directly involve themselves in front-line activities. Now, however, they could no longer hide behind their titles. If they hadn't stayed up to date on new equipment, technologies, and industry information, such lack of knowledge would become painfully obvious. For this reason, managers were often reluctant to reveal their weaknesses; and either consciously or unconsciously, they would end up sabotaging efforts to get teams up and running by failing to provide them with the proper direction and guidance.

What has become obvious is the powerful information gap that frequently exists on the part of management. Those at higher levels must develop a greater understanding of how self-directed work teams function and recognize that there are many complex issues that have to be understood, worked through, and resolved if teams are to succeed. For example, we identified five stages that self-directed teams move through before they became fully self-sufficient and productive, but what we saw time and again was that teams would be pressured to move directly from Stage 1 to Stage 5. Like trying to cross a brook with some of the stepping-stones missing, teams would get to a certain place and then become stuck. They could only evolve so far. As a result, everyone would end up frustrated and disappointed with the results.

Switching to self-directed work teams involves more than just acquiring a little additional knowledge and training. Self-directed teams call for a philosophical change that often has a gut-wrenching impact on the self-image of both manager and team member. It also calls for a great deal of faith on the part of everyone associated with the change. Managers and team members alike must hold realistic expectations of the capabilities of the teams and how the conversion is likely to unfold. Like Thomas Edison, who plodded tediously though hundreds of substances before he finally came up with the right filament for the light bulb, the manager has to hold the course in the face of constant chaos and breakdowns and believe that the process will work.

We've learned that a self-directed work-team environment demands more than many people are willing to give, and that halfhearted experiments are usually doomed. For teams to succeed, they need the support of all the players.

CONTRIBUTING TO THE LEARNING ORGANIZATION

Something else we were able to see over the last decade is the critical contribution that self-directed teams can make to the learning organization. Peter Senge observes that the driving force for organizational growth is not structural change and redefining roles and responsibilities but the acquisition and productive use of information. He believes that an organization's vision grows as a by-product of individual visions, which in turn are a by-product of ongoing, day-to-day conversations in the hallways, the cafeteria, and in other communications crossroads. Information changes too rapidly to burden an elite few with having to learn it all. Self-directed teams become essential building blocks in the learning organization because of the more active role they play in managing organizational process.

"In the traditional model," says Margaret Wheatley in *Leadership and the New Science,* "we leave the interpretation of information to senior or expert people. Although they may be aware, to some extent, that they are interpreting the data, choosing some aspects of it, and ignoring others, few have been aware of how much potential data they lose through acts of observation. A few people, charged with interpreting the data, are in fact, observing only very few of the potentialities contained within that data."[1]

Self-directed teams expand the potential of the learning organization. Because self-directed teams assume more responsibility, team members are privy to information that the typical employee does not have access to; and they have an opportunity to discuss and explore the material and contribute their ideas. "Instead of losing so many of the potentialities contained within the data . . .," Wheatley observes, "the multiplicity of interactions can elicit many of those potentials, giving a genuine richness to the data that is lost when we restrict information access to only a few people. An organization swimming in many interpretations can then discuss, combine, and build on them. The outcome of such a process has to be a much more diverse and richer sense of what is going on and what needs to be done."[2]

Back in the late eighties, however, the ideas of Wheatley and Senge were not yet mainstream. We spent considerable time thinking about the skills needed for people to accomplish tasks, but we paid little attention to the learning that had to simultaneously occur. We have since understood that if acquiring new skills is to be meaningful, if employees are to be able to fully internalize and take ownership of what they have learned, then learning must precede the acquisition of those skills. Without this learning, the locus of responsibility for change remains outside the individual, the skills become mechanical, and the employee's discretionary effort is never fully awakened.

SELF-DIRECTED TEAMS ARE NOT FOR EVERYBODY

Finally, what emerged from our observations is that there are specific and often unique responsibilities for which self-directed teams are not the best solution. For example, self-directed teams are usually unsuitable when you do not need interdependence in order to satisfy the customer requirement, complete a process, or build the product. A good illustration would be a collection agency that requires just one person to contact the customer.

Self-directed teams are also inappropriate for organizations where challenging deeply embedded work rules would create too great an upheaval, or where the learning process would involve undue risk. An example of the latter occurred when a continuous process chemical plant sought advice on moving to self-directed teams. A study of the organization indicated that each individual task, such as turning a valve or adding a chemical, involved serious risk of catastrophic errors. Individuals had to pass a certification process that often took years to accomplish. Teamwork and networking were needed, but self-direction would have been inappropriate.

Another example in which self-directed teams would be inappropriate includes the organization where a single creative genius has intentionally recruited and placed role players with specific abilities into a finely tuned throughput process.

For 75 percent of the organizations, however, self-directed teams offer substantial benefits and can lead to solid, measurable gains in productivity, profit, and customer satisfaction. For example, Dick Jarman, president of Butler Manufacturing's Building Division, said that when his division adopted the self-directed work-team model in 1995, it gave them a sharper focus and led to a 39 percent increase in engineering output, three years of record profits, and 18 percent improved on-time reliability.

The Graphics Group of Palm Beach County's Performance Enterprise Program reported similar improvements. The first year that self-directed teams were introduced, revenues increased by 26 percent while price increases accounted for only 5 percent. The second year showed continued increases, and the end of 1995–1996 showed a 195 percent revenue increase over the three years with only an aggregate price increase of 15 percent. Customer satisfaction also tripled from a low of 29 percent in 1991 to more than 95 percent in quality and timeliness in 1996.

Dr. Dave Lehman, vice president of manufacturing, and Joanne Stang, general manager of human resources, at Solar Turbines Incorporated of San Diego, California, have been strong advocates of self-directed teams across functions and across levels since 1990. Teams have been successful in all manufacturing production areas and in many less traditional venues, such as in product testing with engineers and technicians, in security, in maintenance, in package assembly, and in new-product introduction.

Solar Turbines was awarded the Malcolm Baldrige award in 1998 on the company's first application. This is a unique accomplishment, and both Lehman and Stang acknowledge that the many benefits derived from their teaming efforts contributed significantly.

Another advocate is John Sprague, VP in charge of the Experian consumer service center in Allen, Texas. The consumer service center works with consumers and with creditor organizations to resolve credit issues and provide credit data. Back in 1994, when it was still TRW, Sprague took over a call center facility with low morale, a phenomenally high turnover rate, fractionated service functions, and a marginal compliance record. Sprague did many things, including providing better technology, treating people with dignity, integrating the fractionated functions, and making himself available as a coach and adviser. Within months, he also began the move toward self-directed work teams throughout the operation.

Within a year, Allen, Texas, became a benchmark site for other call center operations around the country and the world. Sprague is convinced that teaming was a key ingredient.

Those who are willing to actively support the teams while they work through their initial struggles discover that the good qualities of a maturing team, like a fine cabernet, become more apparent with age. Al Ilg, a city manager in Windsor, Connecticut, who recently retired after 30 years and was one of the early advocates of self-directed teams, has not modified his beliefs since we quoted him in the first edition. Ilg is fully convinced after eight years' experience with self-directed teams that they are the only way to go. Despite his regular skirmishes with town council members who were more comfortable with a hierarchical structure ("We need to have someone in charge that we can talk to"), he feels that the concept of self-directed work teams has more than proved itself in the amount of discretionary effort it unleashes and the higher level of job satisfaction and lower rate of turnover.

THE NEW CHAPTERS

A few words about the chapters that have been added to this edition.

Chapter 10, "The Philosophy of Teams." There is not just a structural change when organizations make a successful transition to self-directed teams. A philosophical shift also has to occur. This chapter explores the way ideas about work, workers, and management have evolved over the last century and the different mindset that is necessary to sustain a culture that supports self-directed teams.

Chapter 11, "Developing the Role of Supervisors and Managers." Many companies move to self-directed work teams by abruptly eliminating the supervisors and managers and calling what remains a team. This chapter talks about the necessary and vital role that supervisors and managers play in making the transition to self-directed teams. It looks at why their continued support and direction are not only necessary, but absolutely essential, if the transition to self-directed work teams is to succeed.

Chapter 12, "When Process Improvement Is Necessary." Management frequently installs a team with the expectation that employees will do things the same old way, but simply do them better. Teams, on the other hand, are most effective when they can get involved in how the total throughput of goods and services can be improved. This means that managers need to know how to encourage team members to become involved in process improvement. This chapter looks at what managers can provide to the teams so that continuous process improvement is sustained.

Chapter 14, "Teams and Measurement." Generating data on team performance is the only way to make sure that improvements from team activities can be sustained. Teams need to know where they've been, where they are, and where they're going, and they need the proper measures to serve as directional markers. This chapter addresses common questions about the measurements needed for both start-up teams and mature teams. It looks at the relationship between team decision making and measurements as well as the roles the manager and team leader play in helping to generate the necessary metrics.

Now that we have fine-tuned the first edition, sharpened the insights, and provided additional information, it is time to look at the power and potential of self-directed work teams: how they function, how they fail, and what you can do to make them succeed.

NOTES

1. Margaret Wheatley, *Leadership and the New Science* (San Francisco: Berrett-Koehler Publishers, 1992), p. 65.
2. Ibid., p. 66.

ACKNOWLEDGMENTS

I want to recognize the contributions of the many who have contributed to the understandings—sometimes the wisdom—that are the essence of this book. There are hundreds of organizations and thousands of individuals with whom we at Orsburn Team Works have learned together over the last 30 years. A few organizations, and some of their leaders, have contributed notably in the last eight years to the contents of this revision, and they merit special notice.

Tom Stich and I have collaborated in developing high-involvement cultures as he moved from United Technologies to Solar Turbines to Hexcel Corporation. Together we refined the design-team process to combine broad involvement and deep effectiveness. That part of the contents of this book, and the excellence of several organizations, shows the mark of Tom's intellect and involvement.

Dr. Dave Lehmann is vice president of manufacturing and Joann Stang is general manager of human resources for Solar Turbines Incorporated in San Diego. They have been deeply dedicated to the development of a team-based organization since the early 1990s, and we have learned with them in the process. The good work that resulted from their sponsorship contributed to Solar's receipt of the 1998 Malcolm Baldrige Quality Award—on the first attempt! Much of what we have learned since the first edition of this book is the result of this very special relationship with Dave and Joann.

John Sprague is the vice president in charge of the Experian (formerly TRW Information Systems) call center in Allen, Texas. John's influence on this revision is pervasive and hard to isolate to specific learnings. In particular, the way he interacted with his work teams to challenge them to be truly creative and empowered has been a fine example of the learning organization.

Morgan Wolfe was the field manager and Dan Trull was team development facilitator for the Vastar Resources "South Pass 60" offshore petroleum production platform complex. Their contributions included the refinement of the approach to organization change discussed herein—that is, the sponsor group with two action arms, the design team for planning the future, and the process improvement council for keeping current.

Mark Peterson and Ken Bunkowski are plant managers at Hexcel's 2-plant shared resource site at Salt Lake City. Their positive leadership with their people combined the benefits of involvement and ownership resulting from the establishment of horizontal work teams with the structure and discipline provided by the concepts of Lean Enterprise. It has influenced the concept of empowerment included in this book, and is really the competitive edge in work teams' future.

To Dr. Cyndi Orsburn goes my final and most significant acknowledgment of appreciation for the learnings to be passed on to you. Cyndi is my business partner, best friend, and marriage partner for life. In addition to the contributions made directly through her position with Orsburn Team Works, Inc., she has contributed immeasurably to the professional and personal insights that are the foundation of whatever I, personally, can offer to the rest of the world.

Jack Orsburn

I want to express my deep appreciation to the many people who have believed wholeheartedly in the effectiveness of work teams and who have contributed their time and energy to help update the original *Self-Directed Work Teams* book and keep it reflective of current philosophies and practices.

Jeffrey Krames offered suggestions on how to make the book more relevant to organizations in different countries and continents, and Kelli Christiansen of McGraw-Hill used masterful negotiation skills and humor to successfully shepherd us through the many phases of this project.

Ed Musselwhite and Jack Zenger, coauthors on the first version, remain trusted and valued mentors.

My AchieveGlobal teammates helped me to develop strong work teams for my clients and to communicate what was learned to a broad audience. Kathleen Hurson offered support and understanding of the challenges of updating a book in which many of the original references to people and organizations had to be revisited. Barry Schwenkmeyer provided invaluable perspective on what has happened at the front line over the past 10 years. Lilanthi Ravishanker and Lilia Schwartz were of invaluable help in finding the most current and relevant research. And Rosie Morales, who oversaw every phase of the project, kept all of us from getting lost in the details.

My colleagues Seth McCutcheon, AnneMarie Michaud, and Jerry Smolek had a profound impact on this book and on the lives of thousands of work-team members and leaders. Their passion, experience, and insight make them three of the most capable guides for the journey to effective teams.

My thanks also go to John C. Harrison, who wrote a new introduction and edited the pieces by our new contributors.

I am deeply grateful to my clients, who return my loyalty as I help them transition to teams. Their courage and commitment to change continue to inspire my admiration.

Finally, I want to thank my family, who believed in my commitment to work teams and to making a difference in the lives of leaders and team members. To Joseph and Meg, who wondered why mommy was working when they were sleeping, perhaps you will one day have the opportunity to realize your talents and intelligence in a team-based organization. And to Joe, thanks for being a patient husband who was always willing to listen perceptively to team problems and challenge my assumptions, and for continuing to share my passion for team-based organizations.

Linda Moran

FACING
THE NEW
CHALLENGE

A TOOL FOR THE TWENTY-FIRST CENTURY

According to General Electric Chief Executive Officer Jack Welch, a primary cause of stagnant productivity in this country is the oppressive weight of corporate bureaucracy— what in a 1989 *Fortune* profile he called "the cramping artifacts that pile up in the dusty attics of century-old companies: reports, meetings, rituals, approvals, and forests of paper that seem necessary until they are removed."[1] Since his rise to prominence in the early 1980s, Welch has set about resolutely clearing the GE corporate attic—raising hackles as well as dust—as part of his plan to boost productivity by 5 to 6 percent every year.

A second powerful drag on U.S. productivity is employee alienation and flagging motivation in the workplace. In a national poll conducted by Daniel Yankelovich for *Psychology Today*, American workers clearly indicated that as far as they're concerned, the work ethic is alive and well.[2] Respondents said they want to work hard, want to contribute to a satisfying group effort, and do get a sense of accomplishment from doing the best job they can. Ironically, though, many of these same people say they habitually perform only to the minimum level necessary to keep their jobs. The most commonly cited reason for half-hearted effort: long-term resentment about the way their work is structured, managed, and rewarded.

INNOVATION IN OUR OWN BACKYARD

None of this is news to most U.S. executives. In fact, all over the country they are giving serious thought to new—even startling—ways to reduce bureaucracy, increase employee motivation, and foster continuous improvement.

One controversial tool generating intense interest is the self-directed work team. But recent cover stories aside—in *Fortune*,[3] for example—self-direction is no Johnny-come-lately. During the past decade, a number of major American companies have quietly launched and nurtured self-directed work teams, and have reaped substantial rewards with little or no fanfare. Xerox, Procter & Gamble, Tektronix, GM, Blue Cross of California, TRW, Shenandoah Life, and many others have realized the enormous power of the fully trained, fully committed team that is fully responsible for turning out a final product or service. Here are some typical results:

- Using work teams, Halliburton Energy Services dropped manufacturing cycles from 103.7 days to 28.5 days. On-time delivery improved from 64 percent to 94 percent, and spoilage as a percentage of output dropped from 1.62 percent to 0.46 percent.[4]

- At the Quaker Oats Company plant in Danville, Illinois, empowered work teams drove down manufacturing costs 37 percent, improved first-pass yields for snack products 37 percent (and now average 99.6 percent), and reduced standard order-to-shipment lead times by 30 percent.[5]

- Not only did the move to self-directed work teams and empowered work teams at Dana Corporation's Parish Light Vehicle Structures Division plant in Hopkinsville, Kentucky, help improve statistics across the board (e.g., total inventory dropped 23 percent, product-development cycle plummeted 40 percent, and work-in-process inventory fell from 20 days to 1 day), but the number of accidents also dropped from 94 in 1990 to just 2 by mid-1998.[6]

- There was a dramatic two-year increase in WIP turns of 165 percent at Borg-Warner Automotive Automatic Transmission Systems Corp., and a reduction in days of inventory on hand of 64.3 percent ("We're usually producing today what we're going to ship tomorrow").[7]

- At TRW Canada, where 100 percent of the work force moved to self-directed work teams and where teams are expected to operate as their own small businesses, maintenance performed as the result of equipment breakdown fell from 90 to under 15 percent.[8]

- Tektronix Inc. reports that one self-directed work team now turns out as many products in three days as it once took an entire assembly line to produce in 14 days.[9]

- According to the recent *Fortune* cover story, "At General Mills in Lodi, California, teams . . . schedule, operate, and maintain machinery so effectively that the factory runs with no managers during the night shift. . . . Since General Mills introduced teams to the plant, productivity has risen up to 40 percent."[10]

- Aid Association for Lutherans (AAL) raised productivity by 20 percent and cut case processing time by 75 percent.[11]

- Shenandoah Life processes 50 percent more applications and customer services requests using work teams, with 10 percent fewer people.[12]

Results like these, common in companies willing to stick out the sometimes painful period of transition, emphasize the unique ability of self-directed work teams to shrink bureaucracy and revive employee motivation with a single competitive strategy.

WHAT *IS* A SELF-DIRECTED WORK TEAM?

A self-directed work team is a highly trained group of employees, from 6 to 18, on average, fully responsible for turning out a well-defined segment of finished work. The segment could be a final product, like a refrigerator or ball bearing; or a service, like a fully processed insurance claim. It could also be a complete but intermediate product or service, like a finished refrigerator motor, an aircraft fuselage, or the circuit plans for a television set. Because every member of the team shares equal responsibility for this finished segment of work, self-directed teams represent the conceptual opposite of the assembly line, where each worker assumes responsibility for a narrow technical function.

Although work-team members demonstrate classic teamwork, they're much more than simply good team players. For one thing, they have more resources at their command than traditional teams do: a wider range of cross-functional skills within the team itself, much greater decision-making authority, and better access to the information they need for making sound decisions. Work teams plan, set priorities, organize, coordinate with others, measure, and take corrective action—all once considered the exclusive province of supervisors and managers. They solve problems, schedule and assign work, and in many cases handle personnel issues like absenteeism or even team member selection and evaluation. To make sure all this happens smoothly, each team member receives extensive training in the administrative, interpersonal, and technical skills required to maintain a self-managing group.

Here are a few examples of work teams in action:

- An insurance company team takes responsibility for all phases of customer service (applications, claims, and payments) in a given geographic area. Traditionally, a separate group performs each of these activities.

- An electronics assembly team preps components, stuffs and solders circuit boards, tests and repairs boards, sets and monitors inventory levels, inspects, ships, receives, and processes paperwork. Not all team members perform all tasks, but they've all mastered several and understand the rest.

- A team of six assembles, paints, and tests automobile engines on traveling stands wheeled from station to station. Supporting the team are conventional work groups that do machining and purchasing at the front end and shipping and billing at the back.

CONVENTIONAL WORK GROUPS AND SELF-DIRECTED TEAMS

Since self-directed teams are accountable for producing a finished product or service, they differ in several "revolutionary" ways from conventional groups accountable only for performing specified tasks:

JOB CATEGORIES

Companies using conventional groups divide work into narrow jobs employees can handle with minimal training and effort. But because hundreds of people may contribute to an overall process, individual employees often see little relationship between their own efforts and the finished product. This detachment plus the narrowness of their jobs add up to the apathy and alienation so many companies experience. In contrast, each member of a self-directed work team performs many activities, and managers leave the team alone, so long as the team's product or service meets or exceeds established expectations. When a conventional machine shop converts to self-direction, for example, ten or so job categories may collapse into one or two. All team members then get appropriate cross-training so they can share in the challenging, as well as the routine, activities.

AUTHORITY

Since members of a self-directed team perform many of the tasks usually handled by supervisors—communicating, planning, monitoring, scheduling, problem solving—every team needs the authority to initiate a broad range of actions. The first level of supervision over the teams usually functions at a distance to enable rather than directly control team activities. In companies where a supervisor or manager remains in close daily contact with each team, that person's title often changes to "facilitator" to reflect a new, nontraditional role. Further, because the conventional activities of some support groups (e.g., cost accounting, quality assurance, or maintenance) turn out to inhibit rather than promote team productivity, many teams absorb some of those functions as well. And even when support groups play their role more or less as before, the teams have more say about the specific services these groups provide.

REWARD SYSTEM

While executives and managers retain authority over strategies of "why" and "what" for the business, the teams assume substantial authority over the tactics of "how." To realize the benefits of self-directed teams, a company has to reinforce individual behaviors that promote the flexibility of the team as a whole, usually by paying team members for mastering a range of skills required to reach team performance goals. Pay for knowledge (instead of pay for seniority and pay for a single narrow skill) promotes the flexibility teams need to respond quickly to changing conditions. Pay may increase as a team member acquires new skills, or may decrease if old skills begin to erode. Many companies also institute gain-sharing or profit-sharing programs to encourage team members to keep finding new ways to improve productivity.

Table 1-1 summarizes these fundamental differences between conventional work groups and self-directed teams.

Many U.S. companies, like some of their European and Japanese counterparts, have found that shifting ownership of the work processes to the employees themselves promotes employee commitment and, as a result, promotes continuous improvement of quality and productivity. "It's not all wonderful stuff," says Roger Gasaway, plant manager at GE's super-productive Salisbury plant . "But we've found that when you treat people like adults, 95 percent act like adults."

THE PARANOIA AND THE PROMISE

To the many people with a hip-pocket interest in the status quo, at any level, these fundamental changes in the way work gets done can look pretty threatening. Many fear that their expertise will no longer be valued, that they will no longer perform important duties, or even that they will no longer have a job. When they hear about self-directed teams, people typically suspect

TABLE 1-1. Self-Directed Teams: The Key Differences

Issue	Conventional Group	Self-Directed Team
Job categories	Many narrow categories	One or two broad categories
Authority	Supervisor directly controls daily activities	Through group decisions, team controls daily activities
Reward system	Tied to type of job, individual performance, and seniority	Tied to team performance and individual breadth of skills

that the company will use them to justify "downsizing," and indeed, some companies do reassign people and restructure to eliminate entire organizational layers. The most successful companies, however, use self-directed teams for "downloading." As the first-line teams assume responsibility for daily operations, support personnel and managers all the way up to the CEO are able to delegate, or "download," some of their duties to the level just below them. In effect, work teams release their managers to perform duties now exercised by managers at the level above, who in turn release those above them, and so on. At the top, the executives gain additional time for strategic planning, highly profitable time, because operational functions are now managed by the people who understand them best.

Once they get through the unavoidable trauma of transition, most people find themselves playing a new, vital role in the long-term health of the company. Mid-managers, for example, now have time to act on new or long-neglected opportunities, such as:

- Coaching the teams.
- Developing an overall strategy for the teams.
- Interfacing between the teams and the larger organization.
- Championing innovative ideas.
- Paying more attention to the technology side of the business.

- Attending to team resource needs.
- Working with vendors and customers.
- Making critical improvements long left on the back burner.

Former supervisors, now often facilitators or team leaders, learn new skills and take pride in helping the teams achieve rising standards of quality and productivity. And front-line employees demonstrate energy and commitment all but unheard of in conventional operations. The result is improved overall performance, which typically translates as increased job security and increased opportunity for anyone who learns to contribute in new ways.

THE ROAD TO SELF-DIRECTION

The cautious Princeton economist Alan S. Blinder sees great promise in a conspicuous but widely ignored way to accelerate "our miserably slow pace of productivity improvement."[13] At a 1989 conference that Blinder organized for the Brookings Institution (the prestigious Washington, D.C., think-tank), researchers presented five major studies and summarized 15 others on productivity in the American workplace. "To me," Blinder says in an essay in *Business Week*, "all this [research] adds up to a stronger and rather different message than I had expected. . . . Institutionalized participation by workers can raise productivity as well as increase the effectiveness of other productivity-enhancing measures." Blinder's judgment and a wealth of recent research confirm the practical experience of innovative companies all over the country:

> Self-directed work teams improve productivity, because deep employee involvement builds intense commitment to corporate success.

That realization, obvious as it seems, was a long time coming. Formal involvement programs caught the public eye only in the 1960s, when many American workers started demanding a bigger say over how they were managed. One early response, the "Quality of Work Life" movement, began by devising ways to make work more enjoyable: recreation facilities, spruced-up work areas, and the like. Even if these efforts begged the question of participation, they signaled the end of a frigid epoch in labor-management relations. Later decades brought more effective measures—jointly established work standards, work climate surveys, and multilevel task forces—but in this country the notion of workers as thoughtful, responsible contributors is only now coming into its own.

Many people think self-directed work teams were initially an import from Japan; in fact, they were pioneered in Britain and Sweden during the 1950s. (Volvo, for example, is now so advanced that, in their new Uddevalla plant, self-directed work teams assemble entire cars.) In the United States, Procter & Gamble and a few other forward-thinking companies implemented work teams in the early 1960s with profitable results. Much later, the Japanese introduced their own highly successful teams, which emphasize quality, safety, and productivity. In the States, as Table 1-2 shows, it took a brutal decade in the global marketplace, as well as the spectacular success of Japanese teams, to build a mainstream following for self-directed teams.

These days, no U.S. company is totally unaffected by the movement toward increased involvement. Even so, very few companies are willing to grant workers the power to say yes, the power to make something happen. Certainly, more companies allow employees to say no, but being allowed to halt production to fix a problem is quite different from being empowered to improve production. Blinder is one more in a growing chorus of

TABLE 1-2. Major Companies Using Self-Directed Work Teams[14]

COMPANY	YEAR STARTED	COMPANY	YEAR STARTED
Boeing	1987	GE	1985
Caterpillar	1986	General Motors	1975
Cummins Engine	1973	Procter & Gamble	1962
Ford	1982		

researchers, consultants, and top executives saying more or less the same thing: To carve their niche in the world marketplace, U.S. companies must give employees the authority and resources to carry out positive actions in the technical areas they know best.

Multilevel participation is an idea whose time has come. One of the most promising tools is the self-directed work team.

THE PAYOFFS OF SELF-DIRECTION

What do companies hope to gain through self-directed work teams? The answer varies depending on strategic goals, but companies typically cite one or more of the following critical benefits:

PRODUCTIVITY

An article in *Fast Company* documented how in 1995 while the billion-dollar world market for hearing aids had been flat for the previous five years, Denmark's Oticon with revenues of $160 million was able to more than double in size thanks to work teams and process innovations.[15] And while that degree of improvement is the exception, most companies moving to teams report 20 to 40 percent gains in productivity after 18 months. To cite another common occurrence, factories routinely report an 800 percent reduction in set-up and tear-down time—say, from a day-and-a-half to an hour-and-a-half—because self-directed teams find shortcuts that have absolutely no deleterious effect on productivity or the quality of finished work. Anything that brings gains like these is something that no responsible manager can dismiss out of hand.

STREAMLINING

Since first-line teams assume many of the functions formerly exercised by supervisors, mid-managers, and support staff, self-direction creates new options for flattening the organization—by redeveloping supervisors as facilitators or team members, or through attrition. Work teams also provide a simple way to trim other forms of redundant bureaucracy: Anything that does not support the teams is a candidate for elimination. For example, a number of companies reduce the flow of paper with a process they call "work-out." Every piece of paperwork handled by the teams is reviewed periodically. If it's not directly useful to the teams, it's modified, eliminated, or dealt with in some other way.

FLEXIBILITY

Economists have been saying for years that to succeed in a world market, companies must be capable of producing small batches of tailored products on a tight schedule to meet growing demands in emerging markets. This practice—a creed really, among the dominant foreign competitors—calls for innovative technical procedures and workers who move easily from job to job. Because self-directed work teams have the skills, the information, and the motivation to adapt to change, the company as a whole can respond quickly to changing conditions in both the organization and the marketplace.

QUALITY

Self-directed work teams help drive a quality improvement effort into every fiber of the organization. When teams assume more operational responsibility, they develop a deep affinity for the technical nuances of their work. As a result, it becomes a matter of professional pride with them to seek and act on opportunities for quality improvement. Analyzing their own work processes in search of improvements is a way of life for work teams. And since team members perform both technical and administrative functions, they gain the experience they need to improve the interface between those functions.

COMMITMENT

Company after company implementing self-directed teams has found that increased involvement breeds increased commitment to corporatewide goals. Commitment tends to remain high as well, partly because companies reward skills and contributions, not just seniority, and partly because team members take enormous satisfaction in managing their piece of the business. At the forge division of Eaton Corporation, for example, managers were stymied when their primary customer (another division) urgently requested 48-hour turnaround on a huge order. Hoping at best for a few volunteers to work overtime, managers briefly explained on the plant floor what the problem meant to the customer, to the forge division, and to Eaton as a whole. "We expected a trickle," noted Eaton Corporation's human resources manager Paul Logue, Jr., "but we got a torrent." The teams contacted the second shift, mapped out a schedule, made assignments, went to a 12-hour work day, and delivered the parts early.

CUSTOMER SATISFACTION

The energy and flexibility of self-directed work teams promote customer satisfaction through quick response and improved quality. Customer satisfaction, of course, brings repeat business, which in turn brings growth, increased market share, and expanded opportunities for both employees and the community. What self-direction means to the customer is clearly illustrated by two groups of teams in a midwestern plant producing engines for heavy-duty trucks. One group of conventional teams worked assembly-line style, each installing one component of the finished engines. Another group of self-directed teams worked autonomously, each assembling entire engines from start to finish. Although the conventional teams met standards in every way, managers soon realized the work of these groups didn't match up to the higher standards achieved by the self-directed teams. When someone inadvertently shipped the conventional teams' engines to people who normally received engines produced by the self-directed teams, these formerly privileged customers besieged the plant with bitter complaints about "the sudden decline in quality."

HOW EMPLOYEES BECOME
SELF-DIRECTED TEAMS

Picture the far-too-typical U.S. organization: Executives get bogged down in tactical decisions, managers retain most of the control, supervisors make most of the operational decisions, and workers do only as much as it takes to meet externally imposed performance standards. Now picture the same organization with fully vested work teams: Executives focus on strategic decisions, and managers and team facilitators clear the way for motivated workers to exceed ambitious team standards they've set for themselves. This second is a pretty picture, but the transformation implies profound changes that many executives, managers, and supervisors find deeply unsettling. So, like Hamlet, many would rather bear the ills they have, than fly to others they know not of.

The antidote to this quandary is foresight. If executives and other decision makers can visualize the path toward self-direction, challenging as it may seem, they're far more likely to endorse the journey. Indeed, when a company gives up and turns back, it's usually because naive guides failed to forewarn people about the predictable perils of transition.

No Train, No Gain

It takes a group of employees from two to five years to become a mature self-directed work team. During that period, teams normally experience both progress and regression as they struggle to escape the comfort and safety of their old ways. Without proper skills and understanding, virtually any team will bog down permanently in mid-process. That's why—both during and after the transition to full self-direction—an organization must provide intensive training in three critical areas:

Technical Skills.   Technical cross-training, which allows team members to move from job to job within the team itself, is the foundation for the flexibility and productivity of the team as a whole. After a thorough review of all of the tasks performed by the team, individual team members receive training in the specific skills that will broaden their personal contributions to the overall effort.

Administrative Skills.   Self-directed teams, as the name implies, perform many tasks formerly handled by supervisors. At first, the teams will need training in record-keeping, reporting procedures, and other aspects of working with the larger organization. Later, depending on the team's charter, they will need to learn procedures for budgeting, scheduling, monitoring, and even hiring and evaluating team members.

Interpersonal Skills.   With their broader responsibilities, members of a self-directed work team must communicate more effectively than conventional workers, both one on one and in groups, with each other and with people outside the team. Conventional workers rely on the boss to ensure good communication, set priorities, and handle interpersonal conflict. The peers who make up a self-directed team must handle these critical, often explosive matters on their own, and since these skills rarely come naturally, team members will need skill-building training in several areas. Day-to-day interactions can be chaotic unless team members master the basics of listening and giving feedback. Cooperative decision making within and among teams demands the skills of group problem solving, influencing others, and resolving conflicts. In short, every team member must learn to collaborate in getting the right information, sending the right information, and using that information to increase productivity.

THE STAGES OF TRANSITION TO SELF-DIRECTED TEAMS

The engine that drives the transition is ongoing training in the three skill areas—technical, administrative, and interpersonal. Not only does training give team members the operational know-how they need to turn out a finished product or service, it also helps them to cope with five predictable stages[16] in their long-term progress toward mature self-direction:

Stage 1: Start-Up.

Stage 2: State of Confusion.

Stage 3: Leader-Centered Teams.

Stage 4: Tightly Formed Teams.

Stage 5: Self-Directed Teams.

What follows is a map of this five-stage transition to fully self-directed teams—a quick sketch (to be filled out in later chapters) that will give you some idea of the magnitude, the excitement, and the inevitable perils of the actual journey.

STAGE 1: START-UP

The charged atmosphere and high hopes of this honeymoon phase last a few months at most. Prior to start-up, an executive steering committee has established the feasibility of teams and developed a mission statement, and a multilevel design team has fleshed out a plan, selected the initial work-team sites, done their pre-work with mid-managers and employees, and fired the starting gun. Then, at start-up, the optimistic teams and wary supervisors begin figuring out, and acting out, what they believe to be their new roles. Even people with serious reservations, often members of support groups, either pitch in cautiously or toe the line under the watchful eyes of senior managers. "Most of us wanted this thing to work," says one facilitator in a North Carolina nuclear fuels plant. "But even with the awareness training—which was very good—I'd say we had a pretty vague idea of what we were getting into."

The dominant feature of start-up is intensive training for all involved. Team members learn the ABCs of communication and group dynamics, begin using administrative procedures, and expand their repertoire of technical skills. Supervisors, who may see themselves as having the most to lose, also receive focused training and, if they've been carefully selected, generally do their best to facilitate, rather than control, the operational and decision-making efforts of the teams. (For more on Stage 1, see Chapter 4.)

STAGE 2: STATE OF CONFUSION

After the initial enthusiasm, a period of confusion is predictable, normal, and perhaps necessary. Informing people of what to expect during this stage reduces the agony, but even then foot-dragging and outright obstruction can exacerbate the problems teams have in adapting to their new roles. With the supervisor fading as a clear authority figure, new teams often have difficulty reaching cooperative decisions. An older team member, now retired from a New England insurance company, was a mainstay for her team during this period: "I'd seen the same kind of thing before, just after the big war started. People get scared, confused. They work like crazy but they're not quite sure if they're doing the right thing. The horrible part is nobody can tell if what they're doing is gonna make things better or worse."

Some teams fret about higher work standards or wait sullenly for hypothetical disasters. Job security is Topic A, and many speculate about the "real reasons" for the move to self-direction. Now is the time when nonteam members may openly express their opposition, and unions (if any) may predict the return of the sweat shop. Struggling managers contemplate their shrinking role in day-to-day operations and wonder if executives will delegate enough responsibilities to fill the void. More than one group secretly hopes the transition will collapse. (For more on Stage 2, see Chapter 5.)

STAGE 3: LEADER-CENTERED TEAMS

If managers and facilitators continue to demonstrate their faith in the ability of teams to manage themselves, positive signs appear. Support groups begin responding more quickly and openly to requests from the teams. Confidence grows as teams master new skills, find better ways to accomplish the work, and meet ambitious goals. Lines between salaried and hourly people begin to blur. Finally, one team member steps forward as the primary source of direction and information within each team. Far from making a power play, this person usually emerges because the team wants one of their own to interface with the organization, clarify work assignments, and referee internal disputes.

"The teams want a coach," says a long-time team leader in a midwestern clothing factory. "Somebody that can draw everybody else into group decisions—which is what you have to do as a team. And they sure don't want any 'deputy boss.'"

The chief danger in Stage 3 is the team that becomes too reliant on its internal leader. So, to make sure everyone continues to learn and eventually exercise leadership skills, teams often rotate the leadership role or allow anyone to exercise leadership functions as needed (e.g., to deal with someone doing substandard work).

Also significant at this stage: Conflict declines between the teams and their managers; norms evolve for team meetings, assignments, and interactions with the organization; managers withdraw further from daily operations to work on external matters affecting team performance; and productivity expands dramatically. (For more on Stage 3, see Chapter 6.)

STAGE 4: TIGHTLY FORMED TEAMS

This next stage of the transition is deceptive because teams appear to be flying high. They manage their own scheduling, clearly express their needs, and meet challenging goals with limited resources. But at least one major kink remains: an intense team loyalty that can mask internal unrest and outright dysfunction. "Our main problem at this point was the teams' hiding a poorly performing member to protect the person from outside discipline," says an area manager in a California computer components company. "They also had trouble accepting a new team member or—even worse—letting a long-time person go who, for some reason, had to move to another team." Another common Stage 4 phenomenon: The teams become extremely defensive if the organization fails to meet their needs for information or resources.

These fierce loyalties often give rise to fierce competition among the teams. While friendly rivalry enhances productivity and job satisfaction, overzealous teams can withhold information and assistance in order to undermine the efforts of other teams. At this point, managers must refocus the teams on cross-team and organizationwide goals, often through councils of elected team members who review issues of mutual concern. (For more on Stage 4, see Chapter 7.)

Stage 5: Self-Directed Teams

After the firestorm of narrow loyalties comes the period of true self-direction. Mature teams develop a powerful commitment to achieving corporate and team goals, even if those goals require reconfiguration of the teams themselves. "We really couldn't believe what was happening," reports a vice president in a midwestern consumer goods company. "People on the floor were talking about world markets, customer needs, competitors' products, making process improvements—all the things managers are supposed to think about. Now they're like a satellite, in orbit, and sending back information all the time. They just keep going without much help from people on the ground." During Stage 5, all team members routinely acquire new skills, take on new technical tasks, seek out and respond to internal customer needs, improve support systems, handle administrative duties, and refine work processes, using detailed information about contracts, competitors, and external customers.

For the manager, mature teams are a new kind of challenge. Teams have now learned to think for themselves about strategically vital information, so they need to understand the rationale behind important management decisions. Further, to maintain the competitive advantage of multilevel involvement, managers must continuously seek new ways to foster the commitment, trust, and responsible involvement of team members. The system does not evolve into a perpetual motion machine. It must be constantly energized with training and information. (For more on Stage 5, see Chapter 8.)

THE REQUIREMENTS FOR SUCCESS

The enormous benefits of self-direction are possible only through dramatic organizational change. The fact is, no proven shortcuts have yet been found, for unless teams get the resources and authority they need, they'll never gain the flexibility and commitment from which all benefits ultimately flow. Therefore, any organization considering self-directed teams should first make sure that all of the following elements are in place:

TOP-LEVEL COMMITMENT

Organizations considering work teams need a dedicated and courageous champion (often, but not always, the top executive) who protects the endeavor and ensures the availability of all necessary resources. This person must be committed enough to withstand the stormy early stages of transition and clear-headed enough to earn the support of the potentially fractious groups involved.

MANAGEMENT-EMPLOYEE TRUST

Executives and managers need to trust that, given time, employees will actively support the massive changes necessary for success. Employees need to know that management is serious about wanting people to take risks and express their opinions, and not just using a new trick to get more work out of fewer people.

WILLINGNESS TO TAKE RISKS

The risks of self-direction can be very personal. Executives and managers must be willing to risk a complex and costly organizational innovation that will restructure their daily activities and probably disrupt their sleeping patterns as well. Workers and supervisors must be willing to trade their traditional jobs for less clear-cut, more demanding roles as team members, team leaders, and facilitators.

WILLINGNESS TO SHARE INFORMATION

If teams are to make decisions that support organizational goals, they will need detailed information about overall operations, including financial information. In other words, to manage themselves, work teams need management information.

ENOUGH TIME AND RESOURCES

Work teams take time—years, really—to mature, so management needs to recognize that the rewards of self-direction depend on massive planning, intensive training and retraining, prompt access to resources, and often the physical redesigning of plants and offices.

COMMITMENT TO TRAINING

Self-directed work teams stand or fall on the training they receive. Since people now have to put aside personal privilege and contribute to the group effort, self-direction represents a big change for anyone accustomed to blindly giving, following, or resisting orders. People therefore need intensive long-term training in the interpersonal, administrative, and technical skills that will counteract habits and attitudes left over from years of employment in a much more narrow environment.

OPERATIONS CONDUCIVE TO WORK TEAMS

Although any operation can benefit from increased employee involvement, the very deep involvement of self-directed teams requires an operation that includes a range of employee tasks, with some complex enough that improved skills and commitment can lead to improved productivity.

UNION PARTICIPATION

In any unionized operation, executives must take early and continued steps to make the union an active partner in the transition to teams. For its part, the union must demonstrate willingness to work for the overall health of the organization. And both union and management must find common ground in the shared understanding that a more competitive company is the best guarantor of job security.

ACCESS TO HELP

Organizations going to self-directed work teams will need experienced help throughout the transition, and they must make sure at the outset that they know where to find it. This is a journey that benefits from guides who know the territory.

THE FLIP SIDE OF VISION IS CAUTION

While the potential benefits are enormous, self-direction is no walkover, and in the words of Bismarck, "A little caution outflanks a large cavalry." Anyone considering work teams is, therefore, strongly advised to see them as one among several proven ways to improve productivity, quality, and morale through structured employee involvement.

These pages distill many years of practical experience in helping organizations to realize the benefits of employee involvement. Not every company went the whole nine yards. Some stopped short of true self-direction. Some went beyond, to include employees as full members of strategic planning groups. Some, like Dorothy, found happiness right back home in Kansas. No judgments were or will be offered about anyone's choice, for a pluralistic society demands a pluralistic approach to corporate structure.

To help you choose the best route for your organization, Part 1 of this book surveys the major options for employee involvement and outlines a detailed strategy for implementing the self-directed team, one of the purest and potentially most rewarding forms of participation; Part 2 explores in depth a number of special issues in implementing work teams; and Part 3 describes the practical tools that planners, managers, and teams will need in order to make a success of self-direction.

Teamwork is both the subject and the genesis of this book. But the central purpose of the book is to help readers fathom the difference between orthodox teamwork and the self-directed work team. Teamwork once made the American way of business the economic prototype for the better part of the planet. Self-directed work teams could well make that happen all over again.

NOTES

1. Stratford P. Sherman, "The Mind of Jack Welch," *Fortune,* 27 March 1989, 38–50.

2. Daniel Yankelovich, "The Work Ethic Is Under-Employed," *Psychology Today,* May 1982, 5, 6, 8.

3. Brian Dumaine, "Who Needs a Boss?" *Fortune,* 7 May 1990, 52–55, 58, 60.

4. John Teresko, Halliburton Energy Services, *Industry Week:* Profiles in Excellence. Available on-line..

5. Jill Jusko, Quaker Oats Co., Danville, IL. *Industry Week:* Best Plants 1998. Available on-line http://www.industryweek.com/iwinprint/best plants/98winners.htlm.

6. Glenn Hasek, Dana Corp., Hopkinsville, KY. *Industry Week:* Best Plants 1998. Available on-line http://www.industryweek.com/iwinprint/best plants/98winners.htlm.

7. G. Taninecz, Borg-Warner Automotive. *Industry Week:* Best Plants 1998. Available online http://www.industryweek.com/iwinprint/best plants/98winners.htlm.

8. Tim Stevens, TRW Canada LTD., Tillsonburg, Ont. *Industry Week:* Best Plants 1998. Available online http://www.industryweek.com/iwin print/bestplants/98winners.htlm.

9. John Hoerr, Michael A. Pollock, David E. Whiteside, "Management Discovers the Human Side of Automation," *Business Week,* 29 September 1986, 74.

10. Brian Dumaine, "Who Needs a Boss?" *Fortune,* 7 May 1990, 55.

11. F. Paul Clipp, "Focusing Self-Managing Work Teams," *Quality Digest,* April 1990, 20–22, 24–29.

12. John Hoerr, Michael A. Pollock, David E. Whiteside, "Management Discovers the Human Side of Automation," *Business Week,* 29 September 1986, 70.

13. Alan S. Blinder, "Want to Boost Productivity? Try Giving Workers a Say," *Business Week,* 17 April 1989, 10.

14. John Hoerr, "The Payoff from Teamwork," *Business Week,* 10 July 1989, 58.

15. *Fast Company,* no. 3, 77.

16. Linda Moran and Ed Musselwhite, *Self-Directed Workteams: A Lot More Than Just Teamwork* (San Jose, Calif.: Zenger-Miller, Inc., 1988), 13–18.

CAN WORK TEAMS
WORK HERE?

In his office at the Specialty Records cassette and CD plant in Olyphant, Pennsylvania, Training Manager Bill Sharp talks about his grandfather: "When I was 14 or so—probably 50 years ago—I used to spend time with him over at the silk mill he managed. After work he'd take me down to the American Legion hall for a soda. And I was always surprised by how many mill workers would go out of their way to thank him for something he did."

Sharp lets his gaze drift to the window. "Those people are especially vivid because they'd usually offer to buy me another soda."

He brings his attention back into the room. "One day, I asked my grandfather point blank why people enjoyed working at the mill so much. He just said, 'Because no one works for me, Bill. We all work together.'"

The belief behind that remark—namely, that employees have valuable ideas, and that you unleash tremendous energy when you help them put their ideas into action—is the one absolutely essential ingredient for self-directed teams. At Specialty Records, in a silk mill, or anywhere else.

Maybe your company already practices some form of what people now call "participative management." If so, the conditions may already be right for self-directed teams. If your company adheres to the classic military model—that leaders lead, and soldiers follow—that doesn't necessarily mean self-directed teams can't be made to work (although it probably means you must travel a longer road). Chances are, you're somewhere in between. But in any case, before you decide to proceed or not to proceed with teams, you'll need to take a very careful look at the company as a whole. That's the only way to find out if, over the next two to five years, your company can be made to resemble in certain ways the silk mill run by Bill Sharp's grandfather.

WHERE DO YOU STAND NOW?

Although the term *participative management* points conversation in the right direction, it really doesn't define either the intentions of managers or the actions of employees. The phrase certainly implies that employees somehow get involved in decision making. But even if your company recognizes the value of involvement, you need to decide if self-direction really suits your employees and your strategic goals.

The following checklist is an informal, nonscientific self-assessment to help you begin thinking about the kinds of participative management, if any, now operative in your organization. Getting a handle on what's going on now, the extent and the specific forms of employee involvement, is an essential first step in exploring the feasibility of self-directed teams (a very pure form of involvement) in your environment. To begin that exploration, make a check mark in the box shown on page 27 for each statement that applies to your company.

As you see, the statements are arranged in order of increasing employee involvement. Each of these statements, in fact, corresponds to one of eight levels of involvement (item 7, for example, refers to self-directed work teams operating in parts of an organization). Among those items you checked, the item with the highest number corresponds to the deepest level of current employee involvement in your company. Keep in mind, though, that these eight levels do not constitute a step-by-step sequence that moves you toward self-directed teams. Some companies do implement less risky forms of involvement before they go to self-direction. Other companies, however, go directly to teams with no intermediate steps. And regardless of which items you checked, your present

**Employee Involvement in Your Company:
An Informal Checklist**

☐ **1.** Managers make decisions on their own, announce them, then respond to any questions employees may have.

☐ **2.** Managers usually make the decisions, but only after seeking the views of employees.

☐ **3.** Managers often form temporary employee groups to recommend solutions for specified problems.

☐ **4.** Managers meet with employee groups regularly—once a week or so—to help them identify problems and recommend solutions.

☐ **5.** Managers establish and participate in cross-functional employee problem-solving teams.

☐ **6.** Ongoing work groups assume expanded responsibility for a particular issue, like cost reduction.

☐ **7.** Employees within an area function full-time with minimal direct supervision.

☐ **8.** Traditional supervisory roles do not exist; all or most employees participate in cross-functional self-managing teams.

level neither guarantees nor bars the success of self-direction in your company. Your responses to the eight statements simply give you a rough idea of where you stand now and provide a personal backdrop for looking in more depth at the eight levels.

EIGHT LEVELS OF EMPLOYEE INVOLVEMENT

To understand the uniqueness of self-directed teams and to get a sense of the other available options, you'll need to look more closely at the eight increasing levels of employee involvement described in the checklist. Before you formally begin to explore whether self-directed teams are right for your company, you should have at least a passing acquaintance with this range of participation.

LEVEL 1: INFORMATION SHARING

At the lowest level, managers make all important operational decisions, inform employees, and then clarify what is required by responding to questions. Information sharing encourages conformance to policies, procedures, and standards through a formal explanation of both the letter and the background of management decisions.

LEVEL 2: DIALOGUE

After open discussion between managers and employees, managers make the final decisions. Typically, a group that works together regularly meets for an hour once a month with their boss, other managers, and/or specialists. This group freely considers current issues, but only the managers or specialists take action to address serious problems. At level 2, managers hope to encourage acceptance of largely predetermined policies, procedures, and standards.

LEVEL 3: SPECIAL PROBLEM SOLVING

Here, managers assign selected employees to explore a limited issue or problem and recommend a course of action. This ad hoc, often cross-functional, team or "task force" meets weekly or monthly to consider a one-time, predefined problem. By encouraging contributions from people with specialized knowledge and skills, managers hope to solve a nagging problem once and for all. Once they complete work on the problem, the group disbands.

LEVEL 4: INTRA-GROUP PROBLEM SOLVING

At this level, managers solicit employee suggestions for solving operational problems within a given area. Sometimes called a "quality circle," a small, ongoing group of employees from a single work area meets for an hour or so each week with a supervisor, who in turn refers employee recommendations through management channels for approval. In this way, managers hope to generate ideas and strengthen commitment to improvement within the functional area represented by the group.

LEVEL 5: INTER-GROUP PROBLEM SOLVING

Experienced cross-functional problem solvers meet regularly with a manager to work on problems overlapping three or more units. Here, managers hope to solve chronic problems through cooperation among the normally separate functional areas of the company.

LEVEL 6: FOCUSED PROBLEM SOLVING

Level 6, often an immediate precursor to self-direction, expands the best feature of levels 4 and 5—group problem solving in well-understood operational areas—by integrating it into the daily activities of a conventional work group. What's different here is that managers empower the group to make decisions and take action affecting an important organizational issue (such as service quality, just-in-time delivery, or cost reduction). With a degree of autonomy unknown at levels 1 through 5, an "improvement team" focused on product quality, for example, might gather data on customer needs, analyze work systems, identify opportunities for improvement, and implement changes, all without direct supervision. Managers continue to exercise broad control, but their main job is to foster concentration on nuts-and-bolts matters within the targeted area. Like levels 1 through 5, level 6 requires no drastic changes in the conventional management system. The success of these teams, however, depends on unusually flexible, credible managers who can yield control within a system that still holds them accountable. Many Japanese companies routinely operate at level 6, with problem solving focused on safety, quality, and production goals.

LEVEL 7: SELF-DIRECTION

At this point, whether self-directed work teams are limited to a few selected sites or are broadly dispersed across the company, employee involvement becomes an integral part of the management system. As you saw in Chapter 1, the multiskilled members of a self-directed work team turn out a well-defined segment of work, and themselves manage their own efforts. To encourage operational accountability, managers hold these teams accountable for all procedures and results. This deep employee involvement requires considerable training and a cautious step-by-step approach that avoids tricky matters like compensation and peer discipline until the teams are mature enough to handle them. The two to five years of a typical transition to mature work teams require substantial commitment and patience (not to mention courage) from both managers and team members.

LEVEL 8: THE COLLABORATIVE ORGANIZATION

Together, self-directed teams, traditional work groups, and individual contributors have forged a continually evolving, agile, customer-focused business unit. Many of the teams are cross-functional in composition (long teams), and it is not unusual for teams to exchange members to meet specific production needs. One or more leadership councils serve a linking role and manage the white-space functions within this ever-changing, process-improving, focused chaos.

At level 8, virtually every employee belongs to a self-directed team, starting with a highly interactive executive group. At level 7, a few work teams can be accommodated without far-reaching changes in the overall management structure. But here, the company must realign all systems to support the teams, and managers (themselves often members of self-directed teams) must devote major effort to helping other employees manage themselves and develop a sense of ownership. Such a company is sometimes called a "team concept organization."

A word of caution: Don't mistake this company-wide self-direction for codetermination, the European practice of making employee representatives equal members, along with top executives, of strategic planning boards. Unlike self-direction, codetermination has no necessary effect on employee involvement in daily operations (which grows in these European companies only if blue-collar board members push for it). So, although codetermination would be a radical step in this country, it would not in itself promote overall employee involvement as effectively as the activities outlined at levels 1 through 8.

Table 2-1 shows a quick summary of the eight levels. At each level through level 6, involvement is an adjunct to the formal operating structure, not an integral part of it. Employees participate in

TABLE 2-1. Levels of Employee Involvement

	LEVEL	ACTION	PRIMARY OUTCOME
1	Information sharing	Managers decide, then inform employees	Conformance
2	Dialogue	Managers get employee input, then decide	Acceptance
3	Special problem solving	Managers assign a one-time problem to selected employees	Contribution
4	Intra-group problem solving	Intact group meets weekly to solve local problems	Commitment
5	Inter-group problem solving	Cross-functional group meets to solve mutual problems	Cooperation
6	Focused problem solving	Intact group deepens daily involvement in a specific issue	Concentration
7	Self-direction	Teams at selected sites function full time with minimal supervision	Accountability
8	The collaborative organization	Executives facilitate self-management in an all-team company	Agility

decision making for at most a few hours a month, and as a result they often become frustrated when their restricted involvement hampers serious effort, when managers don't implement their ideas, or when they feel they've been assembled to rubber stamp management decisions. In contrast, levels 7 and 8 require a partial or full restructuring of organizational systems to support full-time self-management by the teams.

KNOWING YOUR OPTIONS

In considering self-direction, as with any important decision, you can't make a wise choice unless you know what's possible. Some companies operate quite profitably at level 1, thank you, with no intention of going further. Some decide that quality circles (level 4) are the best route for them. Others take a step-wise approach—by gradually moving employees to deeper levels of involvement—to minimize possible adverse reaction to change. And when conditions are right, many companies zero in immediately on self-direction (level 7). Although new company, or "greenfield," sites commonly go directly to the collaborative organization (level 8) and hire accordingly, it's less common for existing conventional sites to do the same. Most established operating units aren't prepared to marshall the necessary organization-wide resources or to expose the whole organization to such a sudden, radical change. (For more information on levels 1 through 6, see "Employee Involvement: Alternatives to Self- Direction," pages 247–256.)

Once you've come to grips with the major options for employee involvement, you'll be in a good position to pose the central question of the entire exploratory phase: Will self-directed work teams make this organization more productive, more competitive in its market, and a more satisfying place to work? To answer that question, most organizations take the following steps:

- Establish leadership.
- Develop a steering committee.
- Conduct a feasibility study.
- Make the go/no-go decision.

The remainder of this chapter looks carefully at these four steps in exploring the feasibility of self-directed work teams for your company.

ESTABLISH LEADERSHIP

The fact is, no transition to self-directed teams can succeed without the sustained efforts of a spirited leader—ideally but not always the top executive—who foresees the goal, forms and educates a steering committee, and leads the full corporate effort from inception to maturity. Some of these leaders see self-direction as the natural extension of a lifelong belief in employee involvement. Other outstanding leaders, like Borg-Warner executive Joe Cox, arrive at self-direction by a tortuous route indeed.

Joe Cox wasn't always an innovator. Early in his career, he was a manager in the Hessian colonel mold: firm in his views and quick to apply his verbal riding crop to anyone who didn't agree with him. The metamorphosis of Joe Cox came about gradually, almost by accident, during two general manager stints in Canada and Australia.

To get up to speed at the struggling operation he was assigned to in Canada, Cox decided to spend time every week walking and asking questions on the shop floor. "One machinist, a guy named Jack Thompson, never failed to doff his cap and call me 'Mr. Cox.' I don't think he ever got used to the fact that I actually *wanted* his opinion." Through people like Jack Thompson, however, Cox began to realize the profound value of simply asking people for their ideas.

But it was only on his next assignment, in a failing century-old Australian operation with original equipment and original philosophy still intact, that he found out what it takes to bring about lasting change. Decades of autocratic rule had robbed these employees of the will to change. So even when Cox wrapped their own best ideas in detailed instructions, the package had absolutely no effect on actual performance. Then, with no small misgivings, Cox radically altered his approach: "I used to spend a third of my time with people on *what* to do and two-thirds on *how* to do it. In Australia, I started spending a *fifth* of my time on what to do and three-fifths on *why* it's important. The rest of the time I just watched." The net result: People developed an appetite for change, and in four years return on investment climbed from 3 percent to 26 percent. This experience gave Cox a lifelong respect for the power of employee involvement.

When Cox returned to the States, Borg-Warner gave him major capital and virtual carte blanche as president of Centrilift in Claremore, Oklahoma, a new division to be spun off in oil field equipment. Cox knew he wanted significant employee involvement, but since he'd cut his teeth in the old school, he wasn't sure, even after Canada and Australia, how to make it happen. About that time, at a Borg-Warner seminar in Chicago, Cox heard about self-directed teams in a keynote speech by Chairman of the Board Jim Beré. What the chairman had to say struck a chord in Cox that resonated all the way back to Canada: Employee involvement is the foundation of corporate achievement. That's when Cox knew he had both the mechanism—self-directed teams—and the backing he needed to do the right thing with his new opportunity.

Whether a leader comes ready-made and already convinced of the value of self-direction or whether, like Cox, he or she learns that lesson through practical experience, all successful leaders share four vital characteristics:

1. A belief that most employees want to be responsible.
2. A willingness to demonstrate the philosophy they urge others to adopt.
3. The ability to articulate a coherent vision of the changed environment.
4. The imagination and authority to overcome obstacles to change.

Like Cox and Jim Beré at Borg-Warner, these people recognize that self-direction is just good horse sense. They also recognize that horse sense is only idle barn talk until high-level people with serious clout decide to put themselves on the line.

DEVELOP A STEERING COMMITTEE

Organizations should consider whether or not they need a steering committee. Some organizations use a few champions to assume leadership responsibilities. These people often assume steering committee tasks. Other organizations merge a steering committee with a design team. Steering committees may not be necessary when the organization has:

- Experience with successful change efforts.
- A clear understanding of where and when to implement teams.
- Teams that are clearly linked to the business strategy.
- Managers who understand the importance of teams in achieving the business objectives.

If your organization does not reflect the conditions listed above, then a steering committee might be in order. These people need thorough preparation and a clearly defined mission. The exploratory phase is the time for low-key discussion, site visits, data-gathering, and analysis. It's not the time for raising employees' expectations or fears by showcasing the actions of the steering committee.

WHO'S ON THE COMMITTEE?

Although the size and make-up of the steering committee depend on its precise mission and the available talent, effective committee members, like their leaders, have several things in common:

1. A basic respect for the idea of employee involvement.
2. An inquiring mind.
3. A flair for creative thinking.

4. The ability to pinpoint critical elements in a large body of information.
5. The ability to interact effectively with all levels of the organization.

To make sure you've got the right people for the job, you may want to start small and build the committee gradually. At Borg-Warner, Joe Cox initially had only two people—the manufacturing vice president (for technical issues) and the human resource manager (for people issues). In contrast, one plant manager in a Texas chemical facility started with a committee of ten: one member of his direct staff and nine managers from production and support areas. Sheldon Davis, as vice president of human resources, the prime mover in TRW's early transitions to work teams, assembled the top human resource executives from the major divisions. Often leaders recruit union representatives and especially well-suited first-line employees.

PREPARING THE COMMITTEE

Members of your steering committee will probably need substantial awareness building, which often begins during extended conversations with the leader about the philosophy and practical benefits of employee involvement. Seminars, like the one Joe Cox attended in Chicago, can also help. But by far the most useful orientation is actually visiting sites that use self-directed teams (as well as sites operating at other levels of employee involvement). Almost every steering committee that tours a functioning work-team site returns with a rock-hard vision of what self-direction is all about. They've been to the mountain, and they'll probably have to guard against jumping to conclusions about what's needed back home, a danger generally avoided with visits to several sites. The point is, to thoroughly assess your company's readiness for self-direction, the steering committee needs firsthand experience of the tangible benefits, day-to-day realities, and deep cultural changes that come with the package. (For more information on forming and preparing a steering committee, see "The Steering Committee," pages 257–264.)

If, after the site visits, the steering committee decides to explore the feasibility of self-directed teams or other involvement options, it needs to work out a succinct statement of purpose for a thorough feasibility study. At Borg-Warner, the purpose of the feasibility study was narrow: "Find out how to make self-directed teams function successfully in this plant." TRW took a broader approach: "Determine the most potent vehicle to diffuse the total team concept." Some companies prefer a still broader statement: "Determine which levels of involvement are best suited to our people, products, and manufacturing process." Without the focus provided in a mutually understood purpose, committee members have no clear way to sort the wheat from the chaff, and they can easily find themselves overwhelmed by the sheer volume of data they collect.

ON CONSULTANTS

A key question at this early stage of exploration is whether or not to use a consultant. It may be that conversation, reading, seminars, site visits, personal experience, and native intelligence give your committee members everything they need to oversee a thorough feasibility study. More likely, especially if they've worked only in conventional organizations, they'll need help compensating for their own blind spots. An experienced consultant can point out the pitfalls, provide periodic feedback on progress, and in general help you avoid reinventing the work team. If, like most companies, you decide to bring in a consultant, be aware that finding a good one takes time. By all means, check out the available expertise within your company, ask your visitation sites to recommend external people, and put out feelers through your personal network. Pete Kremlick, a Marlin-Rockwell plant manager (whose committee recommended only limited employee participation), cites four cardinal rules for working with consultants:

1. Avoid consultants who assume they can manage the transition in place of the executives or instead of having a steering committee.

2. Develop an up-front contract specifically defining the consultant's role.

3. Encourage frankness in sharing ideas and experiences.

4. Don't turn the company over to any consultant, no matter how experienced.

CONDUCT A FEASIBILITY STUDY: SIX KEY QUESTIONS

The steering committee is now ready to study the feasibility of self-directed teams within a specific operating unit. Exactly which unit you choose depends on your circumstances. If you're a small division or independent company, you will probably assess the entire enterprise. At Borg-Warner, for example, Joe Cox and his committee studied the spin-off business in total, not the division they had just separated from, or the corporate body they now reported to. If you're operating at the corporate level in a multidivision company, you'll probably select the operating unit most likely to succeed. Lacking other internal selection criteria, you can use "Six Key Feasibility Questions" (following) for a quick-and-dirty assessment of several operating units under consideration; the most promising unit then becomes the subject of your full-scale assessment.

To assess the feasibility of self-directed teams in a specified operating unit, every steering committee must develop detailed answers to at least the six questions in the box on the next page.

Since none of these key questions can be answered with total certainty, no assessment, no matter how thorough, can guarantee the right decision. The fact remains, however, that a careful feasibility study (often taking several months) is the only way to find out if conditions favor self-direction, and to focus your efforts on changing the conditions that don't. Ask yourself:

1. *Are the work processes compatible with self-directed work teams?* To answer this question, examine the various processes (manual, mechanical, electronic, intellectual, interpersonal, and so on) by which goods or services are produced. Can these functions be enhanced through increased initiative, flexibility, and cooperation among the people who perform them? If the

---

Six Key Feasibility Questions

1. Are the work processes compatible with self-directed work teams?

2. Are employees willing and able to make self-direction work?

3. Can managers master and apply the hands-off leadership style required by self-directed teams?

4. Is the market healthy or promising enough to support improved productivity without reducing the work force?

5. Will the organization's policies and culture in both corporate and field locations support the transition to teams?

6. Will the community support the transition to teams?

---

answer is unequivocally no—if, for instance, automation handles 95 percent of the work—start looking at options other than teams.

Good candidates for teams are groups of 6 to 18 people who share "the Three T's"—*technology* (same tools or ideas), *territory* (same location), and *time* (same shift). If the technical skills employed within this group are relatively easy to learn and if day-to-day demand for one skill rises while it falls for another, you have fertile soil indeed.

One Kansas plant, for example, found Three T's galore. The steering committee grouped all 68 production people into five self-directed teams, with the 47 other employees (including the plant manager) in five office teams. Long term, the steering committee recommended cross-training between the shop and office groups. At the other extreme, a Connecticut company producing clothing fasteners found that, given their technology, the most they wanted was better dialogue with workers. The equipment for making buttons, rivets, and clasps had not changed for generations, and each unique machine required an artisan to pass on his or her skill to an apprentice, usually a relative. Subtle skills like these, requiring extended observation and practice, don't lend themselves to the cross-training so essential to self-directed teams.

In addition, as Richard Hackman reminds us,[1] the teams cannot be effective if they are organized around processes that are not interdependent. Often organizations do not examine how the teams must work with one another on a common process. For teams to be effective, the teams must have sufficient reason to interact with one another.

2. *Are employees willing and able to make self-direction work?* To find out if employees are willing to accept the responsibilities of managing their own activities, steering committees often begin by brainstorming a rough list of behaviors and attitudes, both helpful and otherwise, among potential work-team members. Interviews and questionnaires (sometimes completed anonymously) usually confirm or discount predictions and sometimes reveal unforeseen problems or strengths. In a Houston rubber goods factory, for example, the steering committee used extensive interviews to find out if technicians would share their knowledge with semiskilled coworkers—an especially troublesome issue, it turned out, because gender and ethnicity largely defined the internal caste system. Prejudicial attitudes don't automatically rule out a group of employees as potential team members, but pernicious behaviors like discrimination must be addressed with focused training prior to start-up.

Whether employees are able to make self-direction work boils down to assessing their aptitude for the range of tasks to be performed by the team. Strong work-team candidates have the intellectual and physical capacity to perform at least 80 percent of every required task, whether it's technical, administrative, or interpersonal. For example, work-team members usually need to be literate enough to share in the administrative side of self-management: keeping records, completing forms, preparing reports, and the like. And while employees need not be superb interpersonal communicators at the start, they should demonstrate an up-front capacity for cooperative problem solving. Finally, prospective team members must be able to tolerate the protracted ambiguity associated with the early stages of the transition to teams.

3. *Can managers master and apply the hands-off leadership style required by self-directed teams?* Many U.S. companies inhabit the rigid world of the pyramid chart, a domain, as one wag observed, "with its sacred cows, sacred pastures, and sacred fences penetrated only by sacred cattle trails." In such places, despite lip service to employee involvement, tradition dictates that managers make decisions and employees follow orders. For self-direction to work, however, that would need to change. Teams need the autonomy and information to make their own decisions, a change that requires a facilitative leadership style most managers have yet to master. The steering committee therefore has to assess (1) the extent to which managers already encourage employee involvement, (2) their aptitude for hands-off management skills, and (3) the likelihood that they will in fact yield operational authority to employees.

The essential question about employees is, "Can they handle increased involvement?" The corresponding question about managers is, "Will they permit increased involvement?" First-line managers can make or break self-direction because they have the power and proximity to encourage or squelch true participation. Are your managers basically sympathetic to the notion of involvement? If not, are their attitudes likely to change in response to concerted skills training and the example of top executives? If the answer to either of those questions is an honest yes, it's a safe bet they can make self-direction work.

Companies already operating at a fairly deep level of involvement can often decide the issue by looking at recent history. Companies operating with less involvement will have to be more circumspect, conducting exhaustive surveys and interviews, bringing in outside expertise, and perhaps trying out a few low-risk forms of participation. Joe Cox and his committee, for example, discovered a widespread management belief that employees must be coerced and controlled. "We don't care what silly game the executives play," said one typical manager. "We know how to run this place right, and we'll find a way to do it." Comments like that led the committee to look at two main options: either a massive training effort or physically relocating and leaving the present managers behind.

The moral here is that if you're looking for 21st century productivity from your self-directed teams, you can't leave them to
the mercy of 19th century managers.

4. *Is the market healthy or promising enough to support improved productivity without reducing the work force?* To ensure
the success of self-direction, the market for the goods or services you produce must be capable of rewarding increased productivity. A weak market, in fact, is one of the two most
common reasons for the demise of otherwise successful self-
directed teams (the other is a takeover by a parent company hostile to indigenous self-direction). The ounce of prevention in
this case is careful early analysis of the present and potential
market for what your company does. Ideally, you'll find a flour-
ishing market that can absorb the increased productivity normally fostered by self-directed teams.

With a static or shrinking market, productive teams can exceed external demand and make it necessary to lay people off—
an unfortunate turn of events whether calculated or not. The
company that implements teams to justify reducing its work
force will find itself sooner or later with disillusioned teams and
declining productivity. For that matter, any company that over-
estimates its market, even if it initiated teams with the noblest
intentions, usually ends up with the same sad result.

A GE plant in Holland, Michigan, formerly part of the Motor Business Group, was a case in point. A few years ago, the
plant found itself in bad straits, struggling to match the low cost
and high quality of foreign-made products. When managers told
the work force they wanted to implement self-directed teams in
order to avoid moving the business overseas, employee response
was nothing less than miraculous. Within six months—an in-
credibly short period—executives started to see a return on their
investment. Within 18 months, the teams had turned the business around, and the plant appeared well on its way to dominat-
ing the market. Then the primary Holland customer calmly
informed plant executives that, due to a change in specifications, it no longer needed the GE motors. So, with no more market, the plant closed. Work teams can help you dominate an

existing market, but in themselves they can't resuscitate a dead one.

5. *Will the organization's policies and culture in both corporate and field locations support the transition to teams?* Answering this broad question means finding out whether policies and procedures (e.g., as summarized in employee handbooks) encourage trust between organizational levels. If these relationships reflect a strong "us–them" attitude, or if the company emphasizes efficiency at the expense of job satisfaction, employees may have difficulty buying into the notion that work teams will in any way improve their lot.

Especially critical to self-direction is a culture in which executives are willing to communicate strategic plans to the people charged with putting those plans into action: Without a firm linkage between strategic and operational planning, self-direction can quickly turn to self-destruction. How open to the idea of teams are staff in important support functions like accounting, inventory control, and maintenance? How does multilevel communication typically operate, and will that system support self-direction? If these and similar questions reveal adverse conditions, a company is well advised to take developmental action prior to implementing teams.

Another critical question is, "Will corporate management support the transition to teams?" If your answer is a clear yes, or if you're blessed with an autonomous local leader willing to tolerate the initial stress of transition, you can afford to ignore this issue. Otherwise, you'll need to get the support of higher levels in the hierarchy (either division, corporate, or both) with substantial awareness-building all the way up to top executives. Corporate support is nice to have when the sun shines, but it's vital when a typhoon hits and you need to secure your resources. In the early days at TRW, for instance, Sheldon Davis got started by forming a high-level corporate council to coordinate the organization-wide transition to teams. Members of the council attended frequent workshops on self-direction, built a cadre of proven consultants, and offered assistance to constituent companies implementing teams.

Joe Cox unfortunately lost most of his corporate support when Centrilift was acquired by a new parent that lacked the commitment of a Borg-Warner to work teams. The ultimate demise of the teams was predictable: To do their job on the ground, work teams must be provided strong air cover from above.

Corporate mergers have long been the nemesis to otherwise successful teams, but Joe has found that there is life after a corporate merger. He bought into two smaller companies in Claremore, Oklahoma—Hydro Hoist and Rotational Technologies, Inc.—and is doing what he has long done so well. He is championing a high-involvement culture in which the people feel a pride of ownership, and the business is profitable and growing dramatically. He now calls the shots, and need not worry about someone walking in and discontinuing an effective and satisfying culture change.

6. *Will the community support the transition to teams?* While most communities either welcome or ignore the start-up of self-directed teams, there's a small chance that certain local people may object to self-direction as a threat to their values. In a small town in the Midwest, for example, several community leaders created a clamor with allegations that "a bunch of communists" were trying to destroy the bedrock values of local family life. At the other extreme, local and state leaders in Georgia (in three separate cases) gave their total support to self-directed teams—in part by recruiting and training employees with the appropriate talents and disposition. Examples are not always so vivid, to be sure, but you should check out the potential for active resistance and take early steps to build positive awareness.

Explore any avenues of cooperation with the community that suit your circumstances. Some companies, for instance, coordinate training with local high schools or colleges, perhaps arranging for on-site technical and leadership training or commissioning special courses for work-team members. Whenever you're dealing with local citizens, the key is to emphasize the fit between long-range community goals and the new values of deep employee involvement.

Another vital community issue is getting the support of employees' families. Early in their transition to teams, Mission Manufacturing in Houston, Texas, made a concerted effort to do away with perks and status symbols for supervisors, including the title itself. John, the supervisor of the work unit chosen as the pilot group, was a natural for his new role as facilitator; unfortunately, his spouse mistakenly saw the new title as a demotion. Nothing John said could change her mind, so she remained openly hostile toward Mission until Paul Maine, Mission's corporate consultant, spent some time with her explaining John's critical role in the new scheme. Stories like this—not uncommon when family members have only a sketchy understanding of self-direction—point up the need to involve the families in a carefully planned, two-way session early in the transition.

EMPLOYEE RESISTANCE TO THE FEASIBILITY STUDY

Every steering committee should prepare itself for employees and managers who may try to hide or color important information during the feasibility study. In basically healthy companies, resistance is usually minimal. In companies experiencing pain (e.g., morale problems, declining productivity, or loss of market share), managers and employees often refuse to divulge information that they fear may incriminate them. They also may downplay the symptoms for fear of the cure, or refuse to admit that what made the company successful in the past is no longer working. The committee also needs to recognize that because they're treading on tender psychological territory, the collective sense of corporate identity, they must show a basic respect for the culture that people have worked years to create.

A thorough feasibility study inevitably appears threatening to some, and only a polished bedside manner can unmask the pretense that all is well. If you condemn what you find, you won't find much. If you encourage honesty in the interest of long-term health, you'll get the information you need to decide if the cure is self-directed teams. (For detailed guidelines, see "The Feasibility Study," pages 265–272.)

MAKE THE GO/NO-GO DECISION

By this point in their exploration, the leader and steering committee have already had many discussions about the meaning of specific findings. Each person has a private view about the feasibility of self-directed teams, and each view deserves a fair hearing. The main task now is to keep the discussion focused on the pivotal go and no-go signals that will help the group reach a collective decision. Strong go signals include the following:

- The top executive champions employee involvement, encourages dignity and trust throughout the company, and acts as a mentor to other potential leaders.

- The steering committee has the business skills, the people skills, and the commitment to guide a long-term transition to self-directed teams.

- Mid-managers either encourage involvement already or appear willing to learn and use appropriate skills in a spirit of multilevel cooperation.

- Employees have the desire for new responsibilities and the capacity to master multiple skills.

- Work processes are such that motivated workers can in fact improve quality and productivity.

- There are clear metrics that are aligned with the business. These metrics can be used by the team members so that they can get immediate, accurate feedback about their performance.

- Corporate executives and the community are likely to support the transition.

- The estimated gains in productivity appear to justify the estimated cost of training and redesign.

- A stable or growing market will absorb and reward increased productivity.

- The company is willing to stick out a two- to five-year transition to mature teams.

The leadership team may want to consider alternatives to self-directed teams if it finds any of the following serious no-go signals:

- The feasibility study reveals an alarmingly low level of existing employee involvement.
- Employee learning capacity is so narrow that it dictates far more time in cross-training than originally thought.
- Employees don't want any more responsibility because they already feel too stretched by their current jobs.
- Employees have little desire for more say about operating practices.
- Mid-managers uniformly and actively oppose employee involvement.
- There is insufficient capital for essential training and technology.
- The work processes are so rudimentary that self-directed teams won't bring significant gains in productivity.
- The organization does not have information accessible to the team members. This information would prepare the teams to work in a focused way that enables them to meet their business requirements.
- The market is such that increased productivity is unlikely to improve the operation's ability to compete.

THAT IS THE QUESTION

Particularly if the weight of evidence favors self-direction, the leadership team has one further question to ask: "Do we really *want* self-directed teams?"

Implementing work teams is something like raising a child. We're talking about a fundamental change of life-style here. We're talking about years of personal commitment, uneasy nights, and unglamorous—often thankless—effort.

We're also talking about a calculated risk. To make the right decision, committee members need to recognize that reality. And if they decide to go with teams, they need to embrace it.

The outcome of these deliberations should be a firm decision to go or not to go with self-directed teams at this time, along with specific reasons for that decision. If you decide to go with teams, you can prepare by following the process outlined in Chapter 3. If you decide against them, explore some alternatives. The very fact that you've looked into the feasibility of teams probably means that somebody in the system sees value in expanded employee involvement. Think about options like round-table meetings (level 2) or quality circles (level 4) not as less desirable, but as more appropriate to the conditions you've found. Many companies temporarily implement these more moderate measures to prepare people for deeper involvement later on. Other companies make them permanent. The whole point of exploration is not to decide between self-direction and nothing at all. The point is to identify the kind of employee involvement that will make your organization as productive, as competitive, and as satisfying as it can be.

NOTE

1. R. J. Hackman, "Why Teams Don't Work," *Leader to Leader*, no. 7, Winter 1998, 24–31.

CHARTING THE VOYAGE

The intensive planning that precedes the official launch of self-directed teams is an exhilarating experience for most companies. The steering committee has decided that self-directed teams are a good potential fit. Enthusiasm starts to spread as new people get involved. Planners begin making the detailed choices that give operational shape to the teams. And almost everyone begins to feel the same butterflies and great expectations that precede any other long voyage. What people need during this period is a clear sense of where to focus, of what's important now and what can wait.

Usually lasting about three months, the planning phase initiates the long-term expansion of employee involvement. First, the leadership team drafts a mission statement, sets parameters, and chooses sites to host the first teams. Then, to ensure a smooth transition from theory to practice, the committee selects and prepares a new decision-making group, the *design team*, whose members have the detailed operational knowledge to sketch out the first iteration of a full-scale implementation plan.

One caution is not to overplan. A good model of this plan was followed by the army. Instead of planning to the last detail, the army created an environment in which people could interpret the plan and make modifications based on their needs. This approach allows enough flexibility to make modifications to the plan based on the needs of the organization.

So, whether your transition involves a single operating unit, a division, or the whole corporation, the critical steps in planning to launch self-directed work teams remain the same:

- Clarify the mission and parameters.
- Select the initial work-team sites.
- Establish and prepare the design team.
- Adopt a framework for planning.
- Draft a preliminary plan.

CLARIFY THE MISSION AND PARAMETERS

The "statement of purpose" developed earlier (see page 37) applied only to what the leadership team wanted to learn from their feasibility study. Now, exploration complete, that same group (plus any other key people they need to involve) constructs a public statement of the central purpose of increased employee involvement. By summarizing the long-range benefits the company hopes to gain through involvement, this formal statement establishes common ground for the efforts of executives, managers, supervisors, teams, and technical support staff. A related set of "parameters" establishes guidelines for the operational decisions of the design team.

MISSION IMPLAUSIBLE?

"Mission statements," "executive visions," and similar pronouncements have little effect on what people actually do if the actions of executives fail to match their words. It's vital, therefore, that the leadership team agree on a mission statement they can live with in the most literal way—through their concrete daily behaviors. From the employees' point of view, the only plausible mission statement is one that has an observable, day-to-day effect on the people who made it.

Since the "mission" expressed in the statement is actually the overriding purpose or purposes for going to teams in the first place, statements vary widely from company to company. Is the company struggling or basically healthy? Are employees and managers mainly concerned about job security, equal treatment, sharing in operational decisions, or something else? Are people jaded about corporate-wide "improvement programs?" Will the transition affect the entire company or only isolated units? Questions like these help you sift through data from the feasibility study and develop a mission statement uniquely suited to your environment.

All mission statements attempt to stimulate and focus the energies of the people involved. Most statements—depending on business conditions, employee needs, prevailing attitudes, and other issues—express one or more of six major purposes for a transition to teams (see Table 3-1).

The impact of a mission statement depends on its plausibility and on its match with current organizational needs and with employees' perception of what is desirable. That's why the key to drafting an effective statement is not so much in identifying the "right purpose," as in allowing the right people to follow an open process in formulating a shared vision. The leadership teams find this process invigorating when discussion centers not on what is saleable, but on what the full committee believes will meet critical needs, improve operations, and fire the imagination of employees. (For specific guidelines and examples, see "Developing a Mission Statement," pages 273–276.)

How Public Should You Be?

The intended effect of any mission statement, to ignite interest and focus a collective effort, seems to invite proclamation. And most companies, in fact, do want widespread awareness of the coming shift to teams. Initially, however, some companies keep a low profile, sharing the mission statement and related matters only with people directly involved with the first teams. Why do executives decide to keep things quiet? If other "visions" have appeared and faded, they may want to avoid the perception that work teams are this year's fad. They may want to forestall resistance by one faction or another, or maybe they just want to keep the first teams out of the corporate fishbowl. Whatever the reasons, these companies hold off on companywide awareness

TABLE 3-1. Six Kinds of Mission Statements

PURPOSE OF THE TRANSITION	SAMPLE STATEMENT*	TYPICAL EFFECT OF THE STATEMENT	CAVEAT
Continuous improvement	"We're going to be a better company tomorrow than we are today."	Can help bring on an initial burst of energy	Must define "better" in measurable terms
Employee entitlement	"All our people deserve to share in the rewards of superior corporate performance."	Can foster efforts to please "benevolent" employer	Can lead to squabbles about who gets what
Bottom-line results	"We promise a 15 percent return to all who invest in our future."	Can appeal to the need for security	Narrow financial focus may perpetuate autocratic management style
Competitive edge	"We will lead our industry into the 21st century."	Can build on the natural desire to be a winner	May also arouse fears about losing
Customer satisfaction	"We will meet the needs of our customers, work force, and investors."	Can expand ongoing efforts to focus on the customer	Despair sets in if the company fails to meet the needs of the teams
Social	"Our efforts will improve the lot of all humanity."	Can arouse patriotic or humanitarian zeal	Without specifics, can sound like platitudes

* Note: These oversimplified examples are intended only to illustrate the statement type.

building until the initial teams find their footing. Then they can point to solid local results at the same time they announce the mission statement and other specifics.

Hoping to avoid possible internal skepticism, a refrigerator plant in the Midwest took the low-key approach to teams. Executives decided not to mention self-direction and not to "hoopla" their mission statement (although they did discuss the mission itself with the people directly involved). Gradually, the operation eliminated executive perks, moved equipment, and reconfigured people into teams. Once the teams were up and running, executives proposed the mission statement to the whole plant, outlined the positive results that teams had brought about, and proceeded with the widespread support of employees.

Unfortunately, the transition later stalled when the plant manager and human resources manager were transferred. The lesson here is that because they kept things quiet, these two champions couldn't instill ownership of self-direction in enough employees throughout the plant. So, when the transition was decapitated, so to speak, no one remained to see the teams through to maturity.

SETTING PARAMETERS

With agreement on a mission statement, the steering committee can now list the operational limits, or *parameters*, within which self-directed teams have to operate. Identifying parameters is critical now because the design team (once it's formed) will have an easier time if they have clear boundaries for their efforts. Parameters, which differ from company to company depending on operational and fiscal constraints, might include mandates for:

- The size and number of initial teams.
- Roll-out dates.
- Consulting services and training at all sites.
- Forms of recordkeeping.
- White-collar as well as blue-collar teams.
- Employees at all levels to be work-team candidates.
- Problems to be solved at the level where they occur.
- Problems not to be handled by the teams.

Whatever the parameters, they must support the structure and purpose of self-directed teams. For example, a stipulation that employees may earn increased pay for learning only those skills needed by their primary team, and not for skills needed by other teams, could retard the cross-training between teams that promotes shopwide cooperation and gives team members a high degree of flexibility.

SELECT THE INITIAL WORK-TEAM SITES

The leadership team normally identifies the initial work-team sites because, having led the exploration effort, they are aware of which parts of the company best meet the baseline criteria for success. Note that at this time the steering committee is not looking for individual work-team members; it's looking only for the areas (divisions, departments, functional areas) where self-direction is likely to succeed. Later, the design team will oversee selection of work-team members from within those areas. Most steering committees identify several sites and implement several teams at once to avoid skewing results with too small a sample or too much pressure on a small number of teams. To decide if a proposed site favors self-direction, the steering committee should review data from the feasibility study and answer the five following questions:

1. *Do the products or services produced at this site involve multiple job categories?* The best sites take in a range of jobs of varying complexity, so cross-training gives team members the opportunity to improve productivity and grow professionally. Learning new tasks also keeps people motivated and encourages a sense of ownership in the team's collective product or service. If the teams handle challenging as well as simple tasks, new members can make immediate contributions without fear of being stuck forever in a "dumb" job.

2. *Can this site achieve improved productivity?* Expanded productivity, whether or not it's your primary goal, is a central benefit of self-directed teams. Look for an area where teams are likely to increase productivity in a relatively short period. If it

takes too long for initial teams to achieve significant improvement, they may lose their enthusiasm and unfairly acquire a country-club image among outsiders.

3. *Will this site welcome self-directed teams?* An area is a good risk for initial teams only if a large majority of employees and managers favor self-direction. The principle here is simple: Anyone who openly supports an idea will usually work hard to make it succeed; anyone who feels forced into a nontraditional role will feel little remorse in scuttling what appeared to them a bad idea from the start.

4. *Does this site have a history of success?* To work out the early kinks and pave the way for less promising groups, choose initial sites in historically high-achieving parts of the organization. Starting with high-potential groups also avoids the implication that teams are in any way punitive.

5. *Are people at this site open to nontechnical skills training?* At some sites, a large proportion of employees may resist training in interpersonal skills (giving feedback, for example, or resolving conflicts) because they believe it infringes on the "natural" way people interact. A promising site for self-directed teams is one where most people understand the value of these skills and welcome such training as a chance for professional growth.

HEADS UP FOR POLITICAL FOOTBALLS

Events at a well-known heating and air conditioning company clearly illustrate what can happen when executives ignore these five critical selection criteria. Based on a thorough feasibility study, the corporate-level steering committee decided independently that work teams made sense for the company. But even though the committee was aware of the five questions outlined above, no one was willing to ask them. They looked at site after site, and no one asked, "Will the people working there benefit from teams?" or "Could their products be made more efficiently in a team environment?" Eventually, two camps formed within the committee, each with the power of veto and each united by one of two selection criteria:

- Which division heads do we want to reward by making them more visible in the organization?
- Which operations do we need to "fix?"

Not surprisingly, site selection dragged on, mainly because the committee hadn't agreed on criteria in the best interests of the teams, the sites, and the long-term transition. Responsibility for proposing sites bounced from one executive to another, the issue turned red hot, and local site managers decided they wanted no part of self-direction. A year passed, nothing happened, and meanwhile back at corporate, everyone kept saying that work teams were the way to go.

"DON'T MEAN A THING IF IT AIN'T GOT THAT SWING"

Duke Ellington's pithy couplet summarizes a second critical lesson illustrated in site selection at this same company. Early on, the steering committee actually agreed on a particular site in order to reward the division head for past performance. However, this person didn't really "own" self-direction and felt no immediate need to make it happen. Then the division got a new head, who emphasized financial reporting rather than teamwork, and self-direction moved even further down the list of divisional priorities. The point is that *initial sites must have local champions,* people who get passionate about self-direction and wield the influence to make it happen. Otherwise, implementing teams is a matter of conformance, not commitment, and other priorities— perfectly legitimate priorities from someone's point of view— tend to take precedence.

ESTABLISH AND PREPARE THE DESIGN TEAM

With initial sites identified, the leadership team (which will oversee all of the sites) can now appoint, train, and empower the design team or teams (a steering committee might need several design teams in different areas, even of the same plant). A design team is a select group of managers, supervisors, and employees, often from the chosen sites, who will research the nitty-gritty staffing and operational questions that must be answered prior to start-up:

- How do we select initial work-team members?
- How do we prepare team members and managers for start-up?
- What changes in work processes and management systems do we need in order to ensure the success of these first teams?
- What needs to happen at each stage of implementation to make sure the transition proceeds smoothly?

DESIGN TEAM COMPOSITION

To ensure a wide range of know-how and to involve representatives from every area affected by self-direction, the design team usually includes 8 to 15 people at and above the supervisory level in different functional areas; in essence, a cross section of three or four levels of the people involved in the transition. Some companies also include employees (future work-team members); those companies that don't include them will need to get them involved later, during start-up. So important is this design work that one midwestern plant assigned several top engineers to the team for a year—full-time.

The steering committee selects design-team members (including at least one executive) on the basis of their knowledge of operations, influence at their respective levels, ability to work with others, and affinity for the notion of employee involvement. A strong design team includes at least one representative for every major aspect of the implementation: production (e.g., the vice president of manufacturing), technical (e.g., the chief engineer), financial (e.g., an accounting supervisor), quality (e.g., a quality engineer), human resources (e.g., the training manager), support functions (e.g., a clerical supervisor), and systems (e.g., an MIS manager). Depending on its composition, the design team is usually headed up by the highest ranking member, by a human resource person, or by an outside facilitator. The executive member of the team, like the human resources vice president in the early TRW implementations, plays the role of champion, monitor, and consultant, but usually doesn't get involved in the hands-on design work.

The design team investigates operational details and recommends an overall strategy for the transition to teams. Later, as the work teams gain the experience to make their own planning decisions, the design team evolves to meet the changing needs of the work teams. Like many design teams, the TRW corporate team remained intact for years to keep watch over the transition as a whole and recommend corrective measures involving different sites, organizational levels, or functional areas. At other companies, design teams sometimes refine themselves out of existence by gradually passing their expertise and authority on to the developing work teams.

GETTING THE DESIGN TEAM UP TO SPEED

Preparing the design team for its immediate task—planning the transition to self-direction—usually involves informal coaching by the steering committee, visits to sites successfully using self-directed teams, and classroom training. Design teams typically spend at least 10 to 25 percent of their working time for three months (including about five days of up-front training and site visits) in preparing a preliminary plan for implementing teams.

Throughout the planning phase, members of the steering committee need to meet regularly with the design team—to help them understand the mission and its underlying philosophy, to review research to date, or just to bounce ideas off one another. These meetings benefit both groups. The design team gets the background it needs to function independently and also gains confidence through regular contact with the executive group. The steering committee develops a practical appreciation of what it will take to implement work teams within the established parameters.

Site visits are even more valuable for the design team than they were for the steering committee. These visits stimulate discussion, yield a wealth of information about how work teams actually operate, and build the shared history that spawns shared commitment to a specific kind of change. During their visits, however, the design team should keep in mind the advice of Tom Wickes, a TRW human resource executive: "The problem [with site visits] is learning to see the *art* of implementing teams. Sure, you have to find out *what* was done. You've also got to find out *how* it was done." Acquiring that kind of knowledge involves more than simply observing how teams operate elsewhere. Design-team members need to ask about the process that planners followed in deciding how to structure and prepare their teams. Then, back in their own environment, the design team can follow a similar process, although that process will probably result in different decisions because they will be looking at their own unique conditions.

Two or three days of up-front classroom training are not uncommon for a design team. (For further details, see "Design-Team Training," pages 277–284). Major training topics include:

- The mission statement and parameters.
- The structure and functions of work teams.
- The reasons for the shift to teams.
- The role of the design team.
- The social and technical changes required by teams.
- The feasibility study.
- Initial sites.
- Preparing people and systems for the transition.
- The components of the preliminary plan.
- The five-stage transition work teams.

This last topic—the same five stages outlined in Chapter 1 (see pages 16–20)—provides the conceptual framework for the entire transition to teams. As such, this framework deserves further discussion here as the foundation for the planning work the design team will soon begin.

ADOPT A FRAMEWORK FOR PLANNING

As you recall, Chapter 1 describes five stages that virtually every group of employees undergoes in becoming a self-directed team. To plan for the inevitable rough spots and keep everyone on course, the design team must foresee the specific conditions that will arise at each stage. Table 3-2 outlines these conditions.

More importantly, the design team needs to understand *the transfer of decision-making authority that gives rise to these conditions*. Only then can team members plan a coherent overall strategy and later identify effective mid-course corrections.

THE TRANSFER OF DECISION-MAKING AUTHORITY

In conventional companies, decision-making authority rests firmly in the hands of the managers who create systems and procedures, set performance standards, control and measure results, and take corrective action. Workers in conventional companies, who lack the authority, skills, and information to make important decisions about their own work, simply carry out limited steps in a grand system they rarely comprehend.

The most distinctive (and unsettling) feature of the transition to self-directed teams is a *gradual transfer of operational decision-making authority from managers to work teams*. During the five stages of a typical two- to five-year transition, work teams acquire new skills, use new information, and assume ever-increasing authority to make decisions affecting day-to-day

TABLE 3-2. Conditions during the Transition to Self-Directed Work Teams

STAGE	USUAL CONDITION
1. Start-up	Optimism
2. State of confusion	Role upheaval
3. Leader-centered teams	Reliance on the team leader
4. Tightly formed teams	Fierce loyalty to the team
5. Self-directed teams	Cooperative self-management

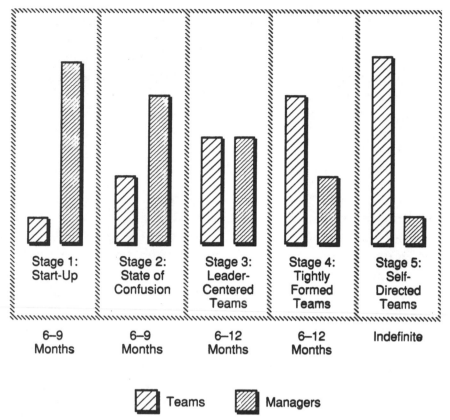

FIGURE 3-1.   A Planning Framework (The Transfer Of Decision-Making Authority)

operations. The chart in Figure 3-1 represents this increase in decision-making authority for the teams, as well as the corresponding decrease for managers.

No transition to self-directed teams is wholly without upheaval, but the least traumatic scenario runs something like this: In Stage 1, the distribution of authority has changed only slightly from that of a conventional company. In Stage 2, both teams and managers struggle to hit on the right degree of team autonomy in relation to the teams' capabilities at that point. In Stage 3, as the teams find their equilibrium through strong peer leadership, managers learn how to delegate authority in proportion to the growing abilities of the teams. In Stage 4, the confident teams largely control daily operations, and managers concentrate on helping them to make their decisions in the context of overall corporate goals. Finally, in Stage 5, fully self-directed teams take total responsibility for meeting jointly established work standards; by then, managers function mainly as coaches, facilitators, sponsors, and intermediaries among the teams.

THE JOY OF STAYING IN SYNC

To reduce the anxiety of transition, managers must cooperate in this long-term transfer of authority by giving the teams what they need at any point in their evolution. The teams, for their part, must let their managers know, through actions and words, when they're ready to take on new kinds of decisions. So, from the design team's point of view, the key to a smooth transition is to prepare managers and teams to move from stage to stage at the same time. In each stage of a smooth-running transition, the teams are making all operational decisions within the range of their skills and understanding, and line managers are providing the right kind of support in the right proportion. As a result, the teams have exactly the degree of decision-making authority they need at every point in their development.

NOT TOO MUCH, NOT TOO LITTLE

Apart from the inevitable trauma of any dramatic change, some companies experience additional problems when managers transfer either too much or too little decision-making authority for the teams at a given stage of development. Some companies have found that managers who see self-direction as a threat try to sabotage the teams by intentionally giving them far more authority than they know how to handle. For example, they might treat teams in a state of confusion (Stage 2) as if they already had the skills and experience of fully self-directed teams (Stage 5), which is something like giving a six-year-old the keys to the family car. In the best case, the teams simply fail to get rolling; in the worst, they create havoc. Then these managers who deep down really want to return to their old ways can say, "You told us to let them manage themselves, and look what a mess they're making of it."

At the other extreme, resistant managers sometimes intentionally lag behind the teams by refusing to give them the authority they have now grown mature enough to handle. Managers might freeze up in Stage 4, for instance, unable or unwilling to delegate sufficient authority to teams capable of full self-management. Unless the design team rectifies that sort of problem, the work teams will break down and the transition will fail.

For the teams to proceed with the least possible vexation— in fact, for the transition to proceed at all—everyone has to remain in sync by moving together from one stage to the next. Only then can the teams get the support they need to meet the special challenges of each developmental stage. When managers delegate too much authority, the teams drown. When they delegate too little, the teams wither.

WHAT'S IN A FRAMEWORK?

To develop a realistic transition plan and to identify appropriate corrective measures at any stage of implementation, the design team must make their decisions in the context of the planning framework. Every transition to self-directed teams requires the gradual transfer of decision-making authority from managers to teams. And although some turmoil goes with the territory (especially during Stages 2 and 4), the design team can avoid many problems by initiating training and systems changes that keep managers and teams moving together from one stage to the next. During training, this planning framework also can raise awareness of the inherent difficulties of the transition, thereby making it easier for employees and managers to cope with them.

DRAFT A PRELIMINARY PLAN

Armed with this conceptual framework, the design team develops a tentative plan for implementing the first wave of self-directed teams. This plan summarizes the best thinking of both the steering committee and the design team, and it provides a starting point for even wider participation. It's a "preliminary" plan because the design team will later modify it in cooperation with work-team members (who at this point haven't been selected). Getting work-team members involved not only improves the initial plan with the addition of their detailed operational knowledge, but also begins building the trust and ownership of the people who will have to make the plan work.

At minimum, a preliminary plan includes initial recommendations in the following six areas:

1. *The Work-Team Member Selection Process.* The steering committee has identified the sites that could host the first work teams. Now the design team needs to work out a method for finding the best people to comprise those teams.

2. *Roles and Responsibilities.* At start-up, people need to know their roles in the transition to teams. Precise duties will depend partly on evolving norms that can't be completely foreseen, but the design team must spell out these roles up front as best they can. The following basic definitions apply for most companies:

- *Team members* perform multiple technical and administrative tasks, participate in group problem solving, and gradually assume total responsibility for producing a specified product or service.

- *Team leaders* perform all the duties of team members, plus conduct team meetings and coordinate with a variety of groups outside the team.

- *Facilitators* are non-team members, usually former supervisors, who regularly work with a number of teams to promote effective group decision making.

- *Technical support teams,* including people with expertise in areas like engineering, human resources, and maintenance, provide assistance as needed to all self-directed teams; some support teams are also self-directed teams.

- *Managers,* as described earlier, tune in to the changing needs of the teams and assist the teams to assume gradually expanding responsibilities. They are not members of the teams, but they do spend a good deal of their time working with the teams, especially during Stages 1 through 3.

• *Executives* set strategic directions, oversee economic matters, reinforce positive actions by managers and teams, and insist on the restructuring of any systems that inhibit self-direction. Executives retain control of the "what" (the strategy) while the teams gradually assume control of the "how" (operational procedures).

3. *Training.* The distress people experience in the transition is inversely proportional to the quality and timing of the training they receive. Everyone involved will need new skills, and often new attitudes, to succeed in their new roles, and the kind of training each group receives must correspond to its needs at each stage. A typical training sequence begins in Stage 1 with area-wide awareness training and continues with basic interpersonal skills for team members, managers, and facilitators. Technical cross-training and administrative training begin for team members. By Stage 2 team members have learned to use a basic problem-solving method that helps them work together more effectively; managers have acquired additional skills for supporting the teams. By Stage 3, team members have learned intermediate leadership skills (so everyone can take on leadership duties) and group problem solving. By Stage 4, teams have received training that increases their flexibility within the team as well their ability to work across team boundaries. And by Stage 5, team members have learned market-related skills like identifying customer needs, supporting innovation, interpreting financial analyses, and evaluating team member productivity. A word of caution: Everyone needs time to integrate the basics before moving on to more challenging skills, so training must remain a continuous cycle of learning, use of skills, reinforcement, and new learning.

4. *Work Processes.* A preliminary plan should list the specific work processes that the various teams will perform. Notably, the design team should decide now whether to have "short teams," "long teams," or both. A short team handles a group of tasks traditionally performed by a department (e.g., customer service or electrical assembly). For example, a short team might produce a finished electric motor to be used in an appliance completed elsewhere in the operation. But unlike a department, where entry level people move up only as attrition or volume permits, short teams cross-train most team members in most skills. A long team, in contrast, performs a complete operation from beginning to end. Long teams that build entire motorcycles at Harley-Davidson, for example, contributed greatly to that company's comeback against competitors like Suzuki, Yamaha, and BMW.

Either way, short teams or long, most preliminary plans do no more than list and briefly describe the processes to be examined. Even if some members of the design team are capable of analyzing and reshaping the work, they should hold off until the work-team members get involved. This is the area where employees usually have the most to contribute, and the design team can build immediate commitment to the plan by including employees' ideas.

5. *Systems.* Self-directed teams will not flourish in the rocky soil of most rigid management systems. To take root and flower, teams need permission to experiment, even if that sometimes means bending the rules. Perhaps a new team is having difficulty filling out procurement forms. The system may have to tolerate that minor infraction while the team concentrates on matters more central to its survival. Even something as simple as establishing a petty cash fund for each team says that managers are willing to bypass convention, within reason, in order to give the teams what they need. Small exceptions like these build trust between managers and teams, and in the long run that trust is worth its weight in far more than petty cash.

To develop their recommendations, the design team must look at every system—operational, social, planning, tracking, and communication—and ask: Will this system promote responsible involvement among work-team members? If it won't, they need to change it or make room for exceptions. Who handles procurement? Would teams function better if they did it themselves? Questions like these about planning, quality, communication, budgeting, forecasting, compensation, performance review—every conceivable system—reveal many of the systemic changes the design team should recommend in the preliminary plan.

6. *Schedule.* Most preliminary plans include a two- to three-year master schedule with roll-out and milestone dates. Some design teams later renegotiate these dates with the steering committee after getting a sense of what the newly selected work teams believe they can realistically accomplish.

At this point, the design team submits the preliminary plan to the steering committee for approval, and with that approval the initial planning phase comes to an end. The steering committee has drafted the mission statement, set the parameters, identified the initial sites, and empowered the design team. The design team, in turn, has done its homework and drafted a preliminary plan. Now it is time for the design team, in close concert with the steering committee, to prepare employees, managers, and operational systems for their specific roles in the collective effort.

PRIMING THE PUMP

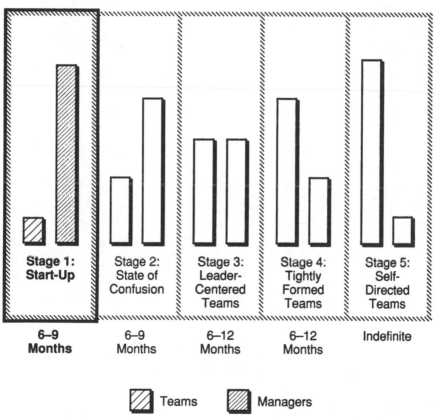

Stage 1: Start-Up	Stage 2: State of Confusion	Stage 3: Leader-Centered Teams	Stage 4: Tightly Formed Teams	Stage 5: Self-Directed Teams
6–9 Months	6–9 Months	6–12 Months	6–12 Months	Indefinite

Teams   Managers

A Planning Framework (The Transfer Of Decision-Making Authority)

Paul Logue, Jr., human resources manager in the forge division of Eaton Corporation at South Bend, mentioned that they followed the four basic practices of trust, involvement, communication, and mutual respect.

High-sounding words. And what do they buy you in South Bend, Indiana? In his unmistakable Boston accent, Logue continues: "We have one manager on the second shift, the shift coordinator, who represents all the departments—engineering, maintenance, production, and quality. He went for a cataract operation two days before Christmas, so we assigned two work-team members to take over his duties. Well, it was a real cold night, and one of them stayed to make sure everyone got their car started and got home. He could have gone home himself, but instead, he did one more walk-around. In the pump room, he noticed a reservoir was getting awfully high, about to overflow. He checked it out and found a valve had frozen. That means the water couldn't circulate to keep the furnaces from burning up. If he hadn't done that extra walk-around, if he hadn't crawled down into the pump to free up that valve, we'd have spent Christmas trying to undo hundreds of thousands of dollars in damage."

What Logue is talking about here is the kind of participation inspired by "trust, involvement, communication, and mutual respect." The Eaton teams are well into their transition, but as Logue points out, "You begin building employee commitment from the word go," during Stage 1, *Start-Up,* the first formal stage in the transition to self-directed teams. How do you prime the pump of responsible participation? Strangely enough, the answer to that question lies deep in a British coal mine.

LESSONS FROM THE COAL MINE

Modern self-directed teams are one outgrowth of the recognition that productivity flows neither from people nor technology alone, but from the union of the two. In the 1950s, when researchers with the Tavistock Institute studied productivity in British coal mines, they found that morale problems were much more than simply "people problems." They found that both morale and performance were shaped by the technology of production. These landmark findings gave rise to "socio-technical systems" (STS)—a ponderous name for a common-sense way to look at work—and led to the early experiments with self-direction in companies like Volvo, Procter & Gamble, and Best Foods. From a prodigious body of STS research, four key lessons can provide a solid foundation for any work-team start-up:

LESSON #1: KEEP SEARCHING FOR THE PERFECT FIT

The main idea behind STS is simply this: High productivity is possible only when there's a close match between the methods of production and the way people work together. These two elements, the technical and the social, are like marriage partners; each has to adapt or the marriage may not work. STS research also found that highly productive teams are constantly redesigning both their technical methods and their social patterns to create an ever-closer fit between the two (though never a perfect fit). From there, it was a short step to self-directed teams, which make continuing redesign the foundation for ever-increasing productivity.

LESSON #2: YOU CAN'T LEGISLATE PRODUCTIVITY

An overly detailed transition plan renders employees' good ideas obsolete before they are ever expressed. Certainly planners have to specify overall goals—for example, "help the teams manage themselves" in the case of managers, or "process mortgage loan applications from start to finish" in the case of a particular work team. But for the teams to achieve those goals through their own creative efforts, they need plenty of room to redefine both their technical work and their day-to-day social behaviors. One Houston bank, for example, specified every skill that team members were supposed to learn for the next five years. Only much later did managers realize they weren't meeting the real-world training needs of the developing teams and that productivity was suffering as a result.

LESSON #3: LET THEM SKIN THEIR OWN CATS

While some methods are better than others, there's rarely one best way to achieve a given result (a disquieting notion to many people). Managers therefore must encourage responsible participation in the knowledge that self-directed teams will find their own ways to meet or exceed established work standards.

LESSON #4: TO EVERY WALL, A DOOR

Work teams need boundaries. They have to be able to say, "This is us, and this is what we do." At the same time, they need easy access to the outside world—to managers, technical support groups, other teams, and the information that allows them to manage themselves. That's why planners have to make sure new teams learn what STS people call "boundary management"— that is, how to connect with the larger organization without losing their identity as a distinct team.

This practical advice from STS bears directly on the central challenge of the first stage in the transition to self-directed teams: finding an appropriate early balance between team autonomy and management control. If managers control too much or simply command the teams to manage themselves, a transition often stalls out. If managers help the teams to see early events as the first of many important lessons, the transition usually gets off to a smashing start. Jerry Smolek, a key figure behind self-direction in 11 GE Motor Business plants, saw start-up as "the first of many successive approximations of the ideal environment. It has to be OK for people to fail. That's the only way they'll gain the confidence to make a go of it."

On the principle of "well begun is half done," this chapter spells out the steps that get your initial teams rolling in Stage 1 toward self-direction:

* Conduct awareness training.
* Select initial work-team members.
* Specify team boundaries.
* Revise the preliminary plan.

- Begin training for team members.
- Prepare the managers.
- Encourage responsible participation.

All of these steps have one common purpose: to give your initial teams the best possible chance to survive.

CONDUCT AWARENESS TRAINING

"Work teams are in trouble if people see them as an experi-ment," said Robert Hauserman, vice president of human resources at TRW. "They're in double trouble if they're seen as the property of human resources. And if they're seen as a human resources experiment, they're doomed."

So how do you avoid that particular kiss of death? *Cascade information about the transition, using executives, line managers, and supervisors to conduct awareness training for the level just below them.* First, the steering committee leader conducts an awareness session for other executives, who then conduct similar training for middle managers, middle managers for supervisors, and supervisors for first-line employees. Cascading awareness pays off in several important ways:

- Bosses tend to develop personal ownership of the transition as they prepare for and lead the awareness sessions.
- Each level learns about the transition from the most immediate authority for that level.
- A multilevel pool of committed facilitators is now available to train people who get involved later in the transition.

Cascading awareness contributes to multilevel trust by demonstrating the declared intention of executives to share important information. It also reduces the potential for resistance and helps in the team member selection process. (For complete guidelines on awareness training, a critical step in your transition to self-directed teams, see "Designing and Implementing Awareness Training," pages 285–289.)

SESSION CONTENT

The format of awareness sessions varies considerably, depending on the audience, the scope of implementation, and other conditions. Most companies develop several level-specific formats with overlapping content in at least the following areas:

The Mission Statement. If you decide to use your mission statement to unite and motivate employees, awareness training is the place to begin. The top local executive often positions and reads the statement, explains its rationale, expresses his or her commitment, and asks for reactions.

The Structure and Functions of Self-Directed Teams. Don't assume the words "self-directed teams" carry meaning for employees. Describe work teams using concrete examples, and explain how daily operations may change in a self-directed environment.

The Reasons for the Shift to Teams. Whatever the reasons, employees will understand them best in the context of your overall industry: what competitors and vendors are doing, what customers expect, and whatever special conditions make teams a good move for the company. Many companies outline economic conditions and long-range objectives, then position self-directed teams as the best way to get there. Make sure your explanation is not only plausible, but complete and don't minimize the challenges of the transition. This is no time to plant the seeds of distrust.

The Transition to Teams. Present the preliminary plan, ask for reactions, and explain how employees will participate later in finishing out the plan. Identify milestones like training, moving equipment, reconfiguring into teams, and involving technical support groups. Briefly describe the five stages of the transition to teams (see Chapter 1 and Chapters 4 through 8). Don't minimize the challenges of the transition.

New Roles and Responsibilities. Outline how team members, supervisors, and managers will function under self-direction. If you know that you will absolutely have to phase out certain positions, explain the career options available for those peo-ple. If you may or may not have to phase out positions, don't raise the issue at this time.

Team Member Selection. The employee awareness session is a good opportunity to ask for volunteers. Explain the selection process—job application, questionnaire, interview, essay, per-sonality inventory, or other procedure—and review the team member selection criteria.

Compensation. Explain that compensation procedures may evolve to reinforce the behaviors that contribute to the suc-cess of self-directed teams.

Hiring. Will it be a human resource function? Will the teams eventually do it? What's the supervisor's role? Lay out your best thinking so far and ask for employees' reactions.

Job Security. You will need to address this issue directly. If a com-pany can't come out and say that every satisfactory performer who wants a job will have a job somewhere in the organization, chances for success decline drastically. Often a company eases apprehensions by saying, "We'll guarantee a job for the first year and a half." If you can do more than that, say so. But don't prom-ise what you can't deliver.

MORE MATTER AND LESS ART

Cascading awareness usually means that immediate managers conduct the sessions for their employees, often with help from members of the design team and/or steering committee. This is not to say that you shouldn't bring in an outside person. If you do, however, be careful. Plants in one big manufacturing outfit routinely used a favored consultant to conduct their awareness training—a charismatic speaker who communicated his views with rhetorical flourish. Some employee groups found him in-spirational, but others responded poorly. "Why is this guy work-ing so hard to persuade us," they would ask, "instead of *educating* us?" Since there's no buy-in without trust, the princi-ple here is that your awareness training must do nothing to un-dermine that trust.

SELECT INITIAL WORK-TEAM MEMBERS

Lore has it in successful companies that about 80 percent of employees are strong candidates for self-directed teams, 10 percent are marginal, and 10 percent (for a variety of reasons) are unsuitable. It's critical to choose initial teams from the top 80 percent, so that you establish a solid foundation for later teams. One common approach for identifying strong candidates begins with the employee awareness session. Interested people then sign up for interviews, fill out a questionnaire, or write a brief essay on "Why I would like to be a member of a self-directed work team."

The central question about any prospective team member is, "How will this person perform under the conditions imposed by self-directed teams?" The best candidates are people who want to expand beyond a specialized role, who like to contribute their ideas, who listen to others, and who demonstrate positive initiative in the absence of direct supervision. However, if your environment has not reinforced the behaviors that reflect those traits, these people may be difficult to spot.

For each work-team candidate, the design team will need to settle a number of important issues:

- Skills and experience.
- Expectations about participation in a team.
- Ability to handle protracted change.
- Eagerness for personal and professional growth.
- Ability to handle new responsibilities.
- Ability to reach compromise in group decision making.
- Responsiveness to the needs of co-workers and customers.
- Ability to contribute practical ideas.
- Ability to learn and apply new skills.
- Level of literacy (sufficient to handle administrative tasks).

Not every strong candidate will be a Rhodes scholar, and for that matter, not every Rhodes scholar will be a strong candidate.

But to promote the success of the first teams, you'll want to find the most qualified people available. As you group these people into teams, you should strive for a cross section of skills, experience, ages, and personalities within each team. That way, team members can learn from one another and more easily achieve the operational flexibility that lies at the heart of self-direction.

If you must work with pre-existing conventional teams, make doubly sure that the team members understand why they're moving to self-direction, and that you have strong facilitators to assist them every step of the way.

Most companies have plenty of qualified work-team candidates, but since work-team assignments are likely to be seen as plum jobs, you may run into selection problems if senior employees have first right of refusal. Seniority simply does not guarantee that someone is "promising material" for a self-directed team. So, if bumping rights prevail in your company, explore the possibility of an exception in this case. You may be able to negotiate a trade-off, perhaps by giving training to marginally qualified senior people so that they're ready to join the next wave of teams.

SPECIFY TEAM BOUNDARIES

Everyone involved in the transition needs to understand from the outset that self-directed teams are not *unmanaged* teams; they are *differently* managed teams. Over time, teams earn the right to exercise increasing authority over their own activities, but even fully empowered teams operate within firm boundaries. Early in the transition, the teams usually assume responsibility for managing job boundaries within the team; supervisors retain responsibility for boundaries between teams; and managers oversee boundaries between departments and between the organization and the outside world. As the work teams mature, they gradually take on more responsibility for interteam and interdepartmental boundaries, although managers continue to hold the teams accountable for achieving mutually established performance goals. The overall purpose of team boundaries is to make sure that information flow and accountability are managed to promote true productivity and sustain high-quality work life.

THE BEAUTY OF BOUNDARIES

The need for team boundaries should surprise no one. Every member of a well-run organization, from the CEO on down, functions within a framework that both requires and prohibits certain actions. Self-direction, therefore, does not mean that teams are free to do as they please. Work teams operate within a clear structure, a charter, if you will, whose purpose is fourfold: (1) to give each team a clear sense of its own separate identity, (2) to harmonize team efforts with corporatewide objectives, (3) to ensure the accountability of the teams, and (4) to make sure that teams conform to fiscal, legal, and other critical guidelines. The parameters outlined earlier by the steering committee (see page 53) established the framework for the entire transition to teams. Now, the design team, working with affected managers and/or supervisors, must establish a framework within which the teams will assume increasing levels of freedom.

In deference to the STS principle that "you can't legislate productivity" (see page 71), successful organizations usually define boundaries in terms of a few key requirements and limitations that ensure accountable action in line with corporate and legal guidelines, such as:

• The scope of job redesign (usually covering content and daily duties).
• Initial quality and production standards.
• Necessary recordkeeping, reporting, and procurement functions.
• Notification in case of procedural changes and/or safety violations.
• The metrics required to meet the production requirements.
• The requirements for communication, customer satisfaction, and safety as outlined by the steering committee.

- Adherence to Equal Employment Opportunity guidelines, and other applicable laws, and HR policies.

EVERY BOUNDARY HAS TWO SIDES

While boundaries limit the actions of teams in ways that benefit the company, they also benefit teams and their managers. Boundaries provide a reassuring link between the new teams and existing systems, and between the past, present, and future of the organization. In this way, boundaries serve as an operational and psychological anchor for teams and managers during the ambiguities of transition. Without boundaries, anxious team members—feeling like untethered astronauts drifting in space—may fail to coordinate their activities; equally anxious managers may fail to delegate responsibilities that they fear the teams may mismanage. Further, by channeling teamwork toward well-defined goals, boundaries help shape the social norms and technical innovations of the teams. Although you can't legislate productivity, firm boundaries actually promote the productive efforts of teams and their managers. An Olympic hurdler achieves greatness in part because she must run precisely 100 meters while leaping over barriers precisely 3 feet, 6 inches high. In the same way, team boundaries can encourage both discipline and productivity by resisting the fits and starts associated with unfettered freedom.

Finally, team boundaries help managers and supervisors retain appropriate control of operations for which, in Stage 1, they are still largely accountable. Both during and after the gradual hand-off of operational control to the teams, firm boundaries give managers the framework they need to continue managing successfully.

REVISE THE PRELIMINARY PLAN

Members of the design team now meet with the newly selected work-team members, team leaders, facilitators, and participating line managers to conduct a workplace analysis and revise the preliminary plan. For employees, this is a first opportunity to contribute their ideas. For the design team, it's a first opportunity to build commitment to the resulting plan.

Workplace Analysis

Analyzing what's actually going on in participants' work areas normally brings a deluge of comments and suggestions. A critical tool during this part of the session is a large diagram of the building layout, which gives people a tangible reference point for talking about what they do. Participants begin by physically locating their department and workstations, and then drawing in traffic and work flow patterns. A group of trainers in a southern vocational-technical consortium looked at a state map, as well as a blueprint of their immediate facilities, to assess how the clustering of clients (other self-directed teams) affected their work.

Once participants fill in details on the diagram, they discuss what happens now and what they believe should happen, listing their ideas and suggestions under the following headings:

- Existing and perceived standards.
- Common deviations from those standards.
- Causes and effects of common deviations.
- Potential solutions to work flow problems.
- Strengths to be maintained.

Finally, the group evaluates their ideas and agrees on amendments and additions to the technical aspects of the developing plan. This kind of analysis is a detailed process usually requiring the help of an experienced internal or external consultant. (For further explanation and an example, see "Workplace Analysis," pages 291–296.)

Polishing the Plan

Some of the energy generated during the workplace analysis usually carries over to the discussion of other sections of the preliminary plan: roles and responsibilities, training, systems, and schedule. The group process here is similar (participants discuss the plan, make suggestions, and agree on revisions)—although at this point you can expect less animated discussion because of limited employee experience in these areas. Later, as the teams gain experience and confidence, they'll have plenty of suggestions.

Whoever leads this session (usually one or more design team members) will have to encourage employee participation by guarding against ridicule of any naive or infeasible ideas. This is where things start getting dicey for supervisors and managers in attendance, who until now have made most of the operational decisions. But even if a new team member makes an obviously rash or self-serving proposal, the practical wisdom of the group normally prevails. From the session leader's point of view, the key objective now is to let the teams know that they do and will have a genuine opportunity to improve procedures for achieving team performance goals.

BEGIN TRAINING FOR TEAM MEMBERS

At this point, training begins in the technical, administrative, and interpersonal skills that help team members participate responsibly in the long-term transition to teams. Self-directed teams will fail if team members do not receive the training they need at start-up, throughout the transition, and during the long period of mature self-direction. Therefore, a comprehensive long-term training plan is a must. (For more information, see "Team Member Training," pages 297–302.)

TECHNICAL SKILLS

Necessary technical skills depend entirely on the finished product or service the team as a whole will turn out. The activities comprising each job in the various teams (machine operator, accountant, secretary, etc.) must be defined clearly so that team members can easily learn the basics. Then the most accomplished team member in each skill (or an outside expert, if necessary) conducts cross-training, either one-to-one or in a group, for the entire team.

In addition to on-the-job training, many companies take advantage of training programs available through state or local agencies. In the early 1970s, several Sun Belt states began offering technical training as a way to attract industry, and the practice is now spreading to other regions. Georgia and South Carolina, for example, have "quick-start" programs, which screen potential employees for a specific company and train them using a mock-up of the actual work setting, complete with equipment. The company can either hire these trainees or not, as it sees fit. States with such programs are attracting many of the companies moving to self-directed teams.

ADMINISTRATIVE SKILLS

The administrative skills include not only items about processing key documents and procedures to run the business, but also information about the business. Often included in this section is information about the competitive marketplace, the organizational direction, and the rationale for policies and procedures. This information provides the context for the policies and guidelines that the teams are now expected to assume.

Training in administrative procedures may be conducted by a supervisor (who, after start-up, will no longer be the sole practitioner) or an outside person. Not only will teams need to process the day-to-day paperwork, they eventually will have to understand the role of costs in order to make intelligent trade-offs with other operational realities. And they will also need to understand the business environment and marketplace conditions. Ideally, every team recruits or develops a team member who can interpret financial data and teach other members to do so for themselves. To begin, the new teams should learn the current procedures for such basics as timecard processing, procurement, interacting with other groups, and budget analysis. The list grows as the teams assume wider responsibilities, and start-up procedures usually change later to support the evolving needs of the teams. For team members to perform their administrative tasks, basic literacy is important.

Interpersonal Skills

"Interpersonal skills" is a catch-all phrase for a variety of essential individual and group functions: listening, giving performance feedback, making your point in a team meeting, group problem solving, learning a new job, peer counseling, conducting team meetings, resolving conflicts, working collaboratively, and a host of others. Some people erroneously call these skills "soft" because they focus directly on improving human interactions. In contrast, anyone experienced in self-direction will tell you that interpersonal skills are as "hard" as they come. Using these skills, the teams create the social half of productivity, and for that reason interpersonal skills are every inch as critical as technical and administrative skills.

In 1989, when the American Institute of Research surveyed over 800 quality improvement and human resource managers across the country (many involved with self-directed teams), researchers discovered a solid consensus about the importance of interpersonal skills in a team environment. The survey, in fact, confirms what virtually every company involved in self-direction has learned through direct experience: Interpersonal skills aren't just nice to do; they're mandatory for the success of the teams. In this new environment, work-team members must learn to apply all of the interpersonal skills previously used mainly by the most accomplished supervisors and managers. Why do team members need these skills? "Even for simple little things," says Ron Smith, a product engineer with Square D in Columbia, Missouri. "You got two guys sharing the same press. One of them comes up with a good idea, but it involves rearranging some of the equipment. Now, under self-directed, he's got to check with his counterpart, certainly, and maybe with the entire team. Not that you take it into total democracy, but you at least have to communicate what you're going to do so you don't irritate your fellow team members. Otherwise, conflict will start to arise."

Critical as these skills may be for self-direction, they're often the most difficult to learn. Employees bring with them a lifetime of social habits, which often undercut the give-and-take of the truly self-directed team, so even a work team including people with strong interpersonal skills is well-advised to bring in a credible outside trainer (a respected senior employee, for example, or a human resources development professional). That way, no team member appears to be imposing his or her style on the others.

Group problem solving, with its large interpersonal component, is essential for self-directed teams, who must devise cooperative solutions to mutual problems. Team members will need training in a step-by-step process that clearly defines key concepts like *symptom, cause, solution,* and *action plan.* But since most people find it difficult to reflect on their own thinking patterns, it is again best to bring in a person from outside the team to demonstrate good problem-solving habits and teach everyone a simple method that isn't the property of one team member.

Later, teams will need to improve their skills in maintaining strong customer-supplier partnerships. No team is an island— the team depends on internal suppliers, and internal customers depend on the team—and team members must recognize and act on that fact of corporate survival. Training should help them communicate their needs to suppliers, ask customers for performance feedback, and negotiate mutually acceptable work standards.

Facilitators, roving advisers and leaders of team decision-making sessions, will need intensive training in a specialized group of interpersonal skills, including structuring of team meetings, maintaining the pace of group decision making, stimulating and building on the interplay of opinions, and helping the group adhere to a structured problem-solving process.

The most carefully researched and widely used way to learn all of these interpersonal skills is through a training method called "behavior modeling." Very different from "behavior modification" (which methodically rewards or punishes specific actions), behavior modeling is really quite simple: First the group discusses the need for and benefits of a particular skill, such as giving constructive feedback to a fellow team member. Next, participants learn to identify the three to seven specific behaviors that comprise that skill, for example: (1) State the constructive purpose of your feedback, (2) describe specifically what you have observed, and so on. The group then watches and analyzes a demonstration, or "model," of someone using the skill, normally on videotape. Finally, in small groups, team members practice the skill by using real-world examples and then give each other feedback on how they did.

After a series of practices, they plan and commit to each other how they will use their new skills in a team setting. The powerful benefits of behavior modeling are (1) team members learn behaviors, which are what really count on the job, rather than discussing theory, and (2) people gain confidence by mastering the skill in a practice setting, so team members are much more likely to use the skill back on the job. People *behaving* in new ways is what most markedly separates work teams from traditional work groups.

PREPARE THE MANAGERS

During start-up, the design team must prepare participating supervisors and managers for the incremental hand-off of their own decision-making power, and for the anxiety they inevitably feel when they do so (see Chapter 3).

MANAGER TRAINING SESSIONS

Like the fledgling teams, managers will need support, reassurance, and new skills to make a go of self-direction. That's why many companies institute regular manager training sessions to educate managers about the transition and provide a forum for ideas and experiences. A major focus of these sessions is helping managers to realize that giving up some of their long-time duties does have benefits, in particular the extra time they now have to take some important matters off the back burner. "The main payoff of our sessions is learning how to be more creative," says Paul Logue of Eaton Corporation. "Now we're taking care of a lot of the things we'd left lying—OSHA guidelines, quick die-change, bringing the public schools into the factory, and child care facilities for employees. We're realizing that autonomous teams give you more time to be a true manager, instead of mucking up what the employees should be doing." Transition sessions also teach managers how to build the trust of their teams by forsaking some of the symbols of rank, for instance, or simply by joining a team for an after-hours event.

Among the skills covered in these sessions, establishing performance expectations is probably the most effective in helping managers overcome their jitters about whether or not teams will turn out acceptable work. This kind of stress was the major issue for managers at the TRW Space Park facility in Redondo Beach, California. After working in small groups with special counselors to learn stress reduction techniques, managers reported success not only in reducing the *effects* of stress, but also the *causes* of stress. (For a detailed discussion of training topics, see "Manager and Supervisor Transition Training," pages 303–308.)

CREATING A HAND-OFF PLAN

Some managers and employees experience difficulties because of the ambiguity associated with a transition to self-directed teams: Who's supposed to do what, and when exactly do they start doing it? Some supervisors and managers don't feel bewilderment so much as anger and resentment about losing their control over daily operations. These people, especially, must be held to clear guidelines governing how and when to hand off decision-making authority.

You can minimize both confusion and resistance with a formal hand-off plan that clearly outlines the step-by-step transfer of responsibilities to the teams. To prepare a hand-off plan, supervisors, managers, and team members begin by listing all of the operational tasks performed by either group. Then they sort the tasks into categories based on the ultimate division of responsibilities when the teams are fully self-directed:

1. Should be done by any available team member.
2. Should be done by a team leader.
3. Should be done by a facilitator or manager.
4. Should be done using a procedure or policy.
5. Should not be done at all.

Having agreed on who will be doing what during the distant stage of full self-direction, the group sets performance standards for all tasks, specifies the training required to perform each task, devises a way to certify team members in each task, and sets target dates for handing off each task to the teams. Like the transition plan itself, a hand-off plan is often revised later to meet any needs unforeseen at start-up. Companies using hand-off plans find them a welcome rock to hang on to when all else seems to be in a constant state of flux. (For details and an example, see "The Hand-Off Plans for Supervisors and Support Group Tasks," pages 309–310.)

According to Bert Brown, machine shop superintendent at Centrilift in Claremore, Oklahoma, this is how a hand-off plan actually works: "Right now, for example, I'm responsible for the daily reporting of payroll. But shortly, we plan to transfer that responsibility to the teams." A major fear of managers during start-up is that responsibilities will get lost in some gray area, with no one clearly in control. "It's really very black-and-white with this hand-off design," said Brown. "At one point I have responsibility. The team and I negotiate the transfer, and when they meet the criteria, they take over. If it turns out a team isn't handling something—we're usually in agreement when that happens—we renegotiate. I take over for a while and send it back to them when they're ready."

Closely allied with the hand-off plan is the "role expansion plan" for individual team members. During Stage 1, the supervisor sits down with each team member and develops a unique plan outlining the technical, administrative, and interpersonal skills the employee needs to master in order to take on specific new duties. The plan also identifies necessary training and tentative dates for the training. Usually every six months, the supervisor (or later, the team leader or facilitator) and the team member revise the plan for the next period. Eventually the plan is incorporated into the performance review process. (For details, see "Team Member Role Expansion Plan," pages 321–324.)

ENCOURAGE RESPONSIBLE PARTICIPATION

Within two months of implementing work teams, a prominent midwestern glass company lay in shards, almost unable to function. Managers tiptoed around the teams for fear of trampling their fragile autonomy. And team members, in the mistaken belief they had to reach full consensus before they could act, stared at each other in wide-eyed paralysis. Then, with the shattered transition one step shy of the dustbin, somebody posted a handwritten note in the central meeting room. The blunt advice contained in that note was exactly what people needed to get it together:

Guidelines for Responsible Participation

1. If you're a stakeholder with relevant knowledge and skills—SPEAK UP!

2. When other knowledgeable stakeholders express their ideas—LISTEN UP!

3. In either case, work together to make the most of what everyone has to offer.

The lesson here is that before a transition can even get started, team members need the *skill*, the *will*, and the *opportunity* to participate responsibly. Several examples will serve to illustrate this point:

- In Georgia, Marlin-Rockwell sent work-team members, rather than managers, to interview equipment vendors and examine their wares. The team recommended a quarter-million-dollar purchase of needed production equipment. Managers accepted the well-thought-out recommendation, then promptly sent the team members back to learn how to set up and operate the new hardware.

- In Kansas, Lawrence Cable invested considerable time and money preparing selected team members to train recruits in all of the skills required to work successfully on a self-directed team.

- In Oklahoma, Centrilift established a multilevel team to review the formal appeals of terminated employees. President Joe Cox, the final arbiter, never needed to veto a disposition. (See "Peer Disciplinary Review Committee," pages 325–330.)

Stories like these illustrate one fundamental fact: Until executives, managers, supervisors and team members start making responsible participation a cultural priority, self-direction will never really take hold. That's why many companies find it necessary during start-up to abandon two of their most cherished traditions. Specifically, they (1) strip away the trappings of rank and (2) give the teams a prominent role in planning.

IS THERE LIFE AFTER PERKS?

What inspires responsible participation is the kind of multilevel trust that blossoms only when management proves that "we're all in this together." In some companies, however, status symbols (like reserved parking) and *un*-status symbols (like time clocks) provoke a "we–they" mind-set that chokes off responsible participation. Maybe managerial perks like off-limits washrooms with terrycloth handtowels serve a higher purpose than keeping employees in their place. If not, any company serious about the bottom-line benefits of self-direction is well advised to phase out, or extend to all, the traditional symbols of rank.

Losing perks is especially traumatic now because managers are not only losing the symbols of power, they're also losing some of the power itself. "At start-up," says Paul Logue of Eaton, "we felt that one of the main stumbling blocks would be the managers. So we brought in a professional, a consultant, who helped us understand our strengths and our blind spots." The Eaton managers began to realize that in the past they achieved status in the organization mainly by controlling peo-ple—an inappropriate mode when employees are learning to manage themselves. The consultant helped these managers un-derstand that as they lost the traditional *symbols* of rank, they were tightening their grip on the traditional *functions* of rank. Consequently, the managers were making it difficult for team members to take on new responsibilities. As Logue puts it, "No matter how much you say you want to pass on responsibility, it's very difficult for you as a manager to do it. You have this sense that—'that's my job! What good am I if I'm not doing those things?'"

Beginning now, during start-up, managers have to get used to the idea that instead of managing people, they'll be managing ideas, standards, systems, and technology. Area managers, for example, may be the first line of control for several self-directed teams. Part of their job is to keep watch on performance stan-dards, work with the teams on revising standards, and ensure the fit between team standards and the needs of other groups; but their job is not to tell the teams how to achieve those stan-dards. Other managers might take full responsibility for re-search and development in particular product areas; but they may exercise direct control over no one at all. Once managers begin taking on new, vitally important duties, and once they see that status doesn't necessarily depend on how many people they manage, the need for perks begins to fade.

THE PLAN IS COMMUNITY PROPERTY

In some minds, giving teams a bigger say in planning implies the elimination of one or more layers of mid-management—that is, the elimination of some of the people who traditionally engage in planning. This strategy can work if a targeted layer is blocking or duplicating a layer beneath it, but shearing out an entire layer is often a measure far too extreme for the circumstances. If a particular manager has only the power to say no to subordi-nates, it's usually enough to eliminate that one position, or allow the manager to say yes as well. In any case, before you rev up the chainsaw to cut out a layer or two, consider less radical ways to expand the work-team role in planning:

- *Establish an open-door policy.* Encourage managers to invite people and their ideas into the planning process, and make sure managers walk out their doors to interact with teams in the work setting.

- *Allow the teams direct access to the raw data that drives planning.* With today's management information systems, often all that's necessary is to provide the teams with computer terminals—and to relax password policies.

- *Make the perception match reality by changing non-team job titles to reflect a reduced role in planning.* As the work teams assume greater responsibility for operational planning, find new ways to describe the people who formerly handled these duties. "Quality control manager," for example, might become "quality services manager"; "production control clerk" might become "production resources clerk."

The Payoffs of Responsible Participation

With the transition well under way at Eaton's forge division, Paul Logue and the other managers are collecting the payoffs of their efforts to prime the pump. Before their support sessions, managers had planned to redesign a graphite spray system that keeps molten metal flowing into the dies. "But after the managers had a weekend training session in the country," says Logue, "we realized the only way the teams would succeed was for us to let go and get people involved. We asked a team of employees to work directly with the vendor and design a whole new spray system. What they came up with works 50 percent better, is easier to maneuver, saves us in product quality and volume of parts, and gives us better die life. Other plants are now coming in to see what *we've* done. If we hadn't gone on our weekend safari, as we call it, that wouldn't have happened. And the employees really did it all themselves."

No matter what measures you choose in order to amplify the responsible participation of work-team members, remember the cool advice of those STS researchers diligently measuring productivity in the depths of a British coal mine: "Make only the necessary rules to start with, and make constant redesign a cultural norm."

THE ASHES OF
CONVENTION

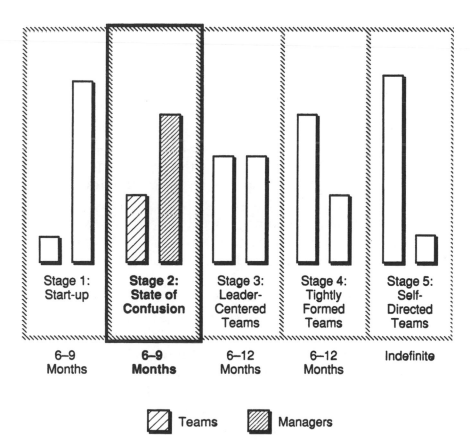

Stage 1: Start-up	Stage 2: State of Confusion	Stage 3: Leader- Centered Teams	Stage 4: Tightly Formed Teams	Stage 5: Self- Directed Teams
6–9 Months	6–9 Months	6–12 Months	6–12 Months	Indefinite

Teams   Managers

A Planning Framework (The Transfer Of Decision-Making Authority)

S tage 2, *State of Confusion,* is something like the rainy first night of a child's first camping trip, when the temperature drops, the wind howls, and the tent leaks. Regret, frustration, hostility, dread—one fierce emotion after another—chill the high spirits of team members and managers like an unexpected northern wind. Gone are the cheery faces. Gone is the crackling bonfire of past practices. And what looked like a crackerjack idea only last week now looks like a miscalculation of the first magnitude.

No matter how carefully you prepare, the disorder and early sorrow of Stage 2 are a necessary, natural, and (thank heavens) temporary part of every transition. How could it be otherwise? Only now do people begin to see what it means to abandon the habits and reframe the beliefs of a lifetime. Team members worry about job security as they struggle with new skills and learn how to act on their own good judgment; managers long for predictability and agonize over how and when to defer to the teams. The simple fact is that no one turns the world upside down without feeling some distress.

During the state of confusion, usually lasting from six to nine months, teams and managers confront the sobering truth of self-direction. Team members realize they must do more than simply learn a new role; they now see how their role, like Proteus, becomes a different beast every time they think they have it mastered. Managers and supervisors realize that for them the transition means more work and more *worry* than the stable cosmos they left behind. Not only must they learn a new job, they must perform their old job until the teams can manage themselves, and they must respond immediately whenever a new team runs into trouble.

Certainly you need to prepare people for Stage 2. One Cummins Engine plant, for instance, held multilevel "prediction workshops" to plan for the approaching storm. And while participants hoped to bypass Stage 2 entirely, session leaders who had heard about temporary confusion in every site they studied hoped at best to post only a few small-craft warnings. So intense is this state of confusion that some companies now employ certified grief counselors to help people (particularly supervisors) cope with their sense of loss.

In short, good preparation won't be enough. You will also have to take action during the state of confusion to ensure steady progress toward stability. With 20/20 hindsight, companies that weather Stage 2 often wish they had done even more to:

- Make managers visible.
- Clarify team roles and responsibilities.
- Reinforce positive behaviors.

MAKE MANAGERS VISIBLE

Despite the bravado of certain teams, managers must continue to make themselves available by conferring, clarifying, and coaching throughout Stage 2. Because it was a three-shift plant operation Greg Audette, director of operations at the GE plant in Burlington, Vermont, believed that "now was the time every manager should sleep on a cot in the office. There's just no way the teams can fend for themselves until they get a sense of their own identity." After much trial and error, Audette and many other managers followed four critical rules for coaching their teams through Stage 2:

Rule 1. Encourage the teams to reorganize for self-management. Attend initial team meetings and educate the teams about expectations and resources. Demonstrate and help team members learn solid interpersonal skills.

Rule 2. Monitor team performance against clear standards. Use simple, low-key methods the teams can use later to monitor themselves. Search out and reinforce anything the teams do right—or nearly right—so they'll know that the standards are real.

Rule 3. Hand off new responsibilities as soon as the teams are ready for them. Adhere to a negotiated hand-off plan and find opportunities for the teams to flex their new authority in appropriate ways.

Rule 4. Act as an intermediary among the teams and between each team and the larger organization. Get the teams and technical staff together to plan work-process changes. Ensure delivery of requested resources. Promote communication between teams. Protect the teams from anyone who might want them to fail.

LAISSEZ-FAIRE WON'T DO

Too little direct involvement was the major Stage 2 problem for about half the plant and office managers at Centrilift in Oklahoma. According to vice president of manufacturing Jerry Hastings, "It was up to me to demonstrate the behaviors I expected" from the many members of his management team. He soon realized, however, that his untempered support for employee involvement had given managers the impression they should never intervene to help a team in difficulty, a common mistake in companies striving to integrate new values. "Once I recognized my own part in the problem," he says, "I saw that those managers needed more than permission to intervene." They also needed the skills to do so without crushing the shaky self-confidence of the teams.

Hastings began by putting the managers through a commercially available training program in coaching skills and by making himself as available as he now advised managers to be with the teams. During frequent one-on-one coaching with managers, he would sometimes ask whether his own coaching method might help the manager to work with the teams. That strategy succeeded, says Hastings, "only if I truly accepted the manager's decision to reject or modify my method"—again, precisely how he wanted managers to interact with the teams. Then, on the theory that good coaching requires responsive team members who in turn coach their peers, Hastings put every work team through formal training in listening and feedback skills.

STRANGULATION BY CHAIN OF COMMAND

Even more troublesome during Stage 2 is the manager who won't let go of old-style controls. With such a manager, team members see no break with tradition and therefore no need to evolve. As a result, they may never develop a cohesive team identity. Take Bill, a mid-manager in a Chicago-area production facility, who couldn't shake the conviction that "managers should manage and workers should work." Teams under his command (a carefully chosen word) simply did not develop normally and, like deprived children, quickly fell behind their counterparts. Eventually, he had to be relieved of direct control to become a strictly technical consultant to other managers.

Stay alert for managers like Bill who, despite continued efforts to help them change, cannot or will not coach their teams toward self-management. This is not to say that some high-control managers can never change. Sometimes, after a team reaches stable self-direction, team members themselves can help a valued but resistant manager to adopt a more interactive style. But a work team that has been dominated for some time by a high-control manager is like a car that has been badly wrecked: Even with expert repairs, it may never run quite right.

Shoot Later and Ask Questions First

What the teams need during Stage 2 is managers who combine elements of the old directive style with elements of the new interactive style. Managers have to provide enough structure for the teams to feel secure; but when team members ask for help, a manager's first response should be, "What do *you* think?" Many managers, especially the unconverted, will be looking (and even hoping) for signs of imminent collapse. For these people, the widespread confusion, frustration, and anxiety will seem proof positive that the teams want and need to be told what to do. But the truth is, instead of jumping in immediately, managers have to let the teams struggle—not so much that they get totally discouraged, but enough to learn how to stand on their own. When managers feel the urge to step in and straighten out a problem, they must first ask questions of team members in ways that help members find solutions for themselves. As a rule, when managers provide either too little or too much structure for the teams, Stage 2 turns into a full-blown nightmare.

THE STRUCTURE OF AUTONOMY

The fate of a start-up electronics plant in the Midwest clearly illustrates that work teams do not live by autonomy alone. The company built the facility, hired the work force, opened the doors, and told the employees, in effect, "You are now self-directed." With no hand-off plan clearly assigning responsibilities, people had no way of telling which decisions were to be made by teams and which were to be made by managers. With no well-documented specifications, employees decided independently what was shippable and what was not. As a result, within three months of start-up the entire plant found itself in perpetual confusion, perpetual conflict, and perpetual meetings.

On the other hand, teams in an Ohio psychiatric hospital successfully weathered the state of confusion because managers worked with team members to establish a structure for their efforts to manage themselves. One patient care team (including psychiatric social workers, nurses, and aides) functioned in a high-pressure environment to begin with, so the process of redefining their own roles held the potential for 3-D chaos. As a first step, the team separated the situations that called for a team member from those that called for a physician. Then they identified the training and certification a team member needed to treat each major category of patient complaints. Last, they established standards for each kind of treatment and identified in each case the point at which a team member could do nothing more for a given patient. Within this structure, as calculating as it might seem, the team achieved an unprecedented level of satisfaction among patients and patients' families.

Structure of this kind can substantially break the impact of Stage 2. Where teams shoot for well-defined goals and follow a clear, flexible hand-off plan, they usually emerge from Stage 2 with minimal trauma. Where they lack that structure, they may not emerge at all. (For details on developing hand-off plans, see "Hand-off Plans for Supervisory and Support Group Tasks," pages 309–320.)

CLARIFY TEAM ROLES AND RESPONSIBILITIES

Team members probably suffer more than anyone else during the state of confusion. Not only must they learn new skills, take on new responsibilities, and attain new goals, they must do so before a gallery of skeptics, nervous Nellies, and outright saboteurs. Supporters, therefore, need to clarify again and again exactly where and how the teams should focus their limited energy and resources. To achieve a firm group identity, the teams have to learn a variety of new behaviors; and like a drowsy overnight guest who walks into the closet instead of the bathroom, team members may sometimes forget where they are. Developing new reflexes to fit their new environment means that the teams have to stay focused on the fundamentals of their new role:

- Planning the overall work of the team.
- Setting priorities for achieving performance goals.
- Coordinating with teammates and support groups.
- Solving technical, administrative, and interpersonal problems.
- Scheduling and assigning work.
- Cross-training teammates and learning from teammates.

At first, team members must learn to be competent employees. Before they can manage themselves, however, every team member must learn most of the duties of a competent supervisor.

A SPECIAL KIND OF HERO

A common misconception of new teams is that team members individually exercise powers once held by managers. The truth is that executives, managers, supervisors, and first-line employees all delegate some of their power to a new entity of their own design—the team itself.

Consider the cultural backdrop for this confusion. Besides the obvious, what do Henry Ford, Henry Aaron, Henry Winkler, and Henry David Thoreau have in common? Like a thousand other beacons in the popular mind, they all personify the American hunger for heroic individual achievement. But against that need in the American psyche is an ancient need to contribute to a common effort. When, aboard the *Arabella* in 1630, Puritan John Winthrop said, "We must knit together as one," he wasn't talking about new sweaters for the New England winter. "We must delight in each other," he went on, "make others' conditions our own, rejoice together, mourn together, labor and suffer together." The point is that while a team effort is the sum of individual, sometimes heroic, contributions, a self-directed work team is no place for individuals to claim their promised 15 minutes of fame.

The intense need for individual recognition explains in part why some employees have extreme difficulty acting on the opportunities offered by self-direction. A respected employee in a transitioning Texas foundry, for example, decided to give self-direction a try even though he had serious misgivings. This fellow worked hard every day, had good ideas during team meetings, and stepped forward for a number of tough assignments; he volunteered, in fact, to be the first of several rotating team leaders. Yet he couldn't adjust to the work-team environment, as he said himself, because he missed the one-on-one contact (which he had enjoyed in his previous position) with the director of operations and other executives. Now that executives directed their recognition more to the team as a whole, it galled him not to get their special mention for what he considered his exceptional contributions to the team. Luckily, other, conventional parts of the organization wanted his services, so he was able to transfer out.

A good way to drive home the value of teamwork is to give the teams a formal role in recognizing the individual efforts of their own members. At the TRW turbine blade facility in Crooksville, Ohio, managers single out entire teams during regular recognition ceremonies. Then the teams recognize the special contributions of their individual members. Whether through public recognition or through one-on-one coaching, some team members will need considerable help before they understand and accept their new role in the total team effort. Individuals can thrive in a self-directed work team, but only if their pride in extraordinary team performance outweighs their need to be singled out for frequent praise. (For more ideas on recognizing work teams, see "Recognition and Reward Techniques," pages 331–334.)

PUT UP A SAFETY NET

Another source of team confusion during Stage 2 is epidemic worry: Can we learn all these new duties? What are these new duties? Will we meet our numbers? What happens if we don't? Will we lose our jobs?

Before the transition began, supervisors and managers took most of the heat when things went wrong, and even during hard times, the familiar hierarchy and well-thumbed rulebook gave first-line employees some sense of security. Now, with their increased visibility, new team members may feel exposed, and their anxiety can retard both their acceptance and their execution of new responsibilities. If team members clutch the old ways like a child with a tattered blanket, they can mire the whole transition in long-term confusion.

To overcome their own fears, the teams need a safety net beneath their initial attempts to manage themselves. Sometimes supervisors remain in a fairly traditional role until the teams master predetermined skills. Sometimes a new kind of manager (often called an "area manager" or "superintendent") supports three or four teams while they find their bearings. In many of the best transitions, the facilitator plays the key interim role. Xerox, for example, supports new teams with a small army of facilitators, non-team members with strong interpersonal skills who attend early team meetings, teach people how to manage themselves, and move on to work with other new teams. Each facilitator, often a former supervisor seen by the teams as "one of us," guides six or so teams at a time through the dark chasm separating the old from the new.

Facilitators also play a key role during Stage 2 at Solar Turbines in San Diego, California. Lisa Askew, manager of teaming development, recruits and coordinates members of Solar's "Teaming Council." This cross-functional and multi-level group is made up of selected volunteers who help teams during their early development. After six months of training, they facilitate meetings while training team members to take over; conduct training in basic tools for decision making, process improvement, and meeting effectiveness; and help teams to develop group dynamics understandings and skills. This early assistance has proved to be critical to the success of teams—critical to the avoidance of a permanent "state of confusion."

A MOVEABLE THINK-TANK

In most companies, technical support groups—again, usually one group for every six or so work teams—assist the teams during and long after Stage 2. Usually made up of former line managers and supervisors as well as technical experts, these groups provide the know-how acquired through long-term specialized training and/or experience. In manufacturing, for instance, a preventive maintenance team might include people from engineering, human resources, employee relations, and (if the company uses just-in-time methods) inventory control. In a service company, a client support team might include people from information services, accounting, human resources, and marketing. Every technical support group has at least two basic responsibilities:

1. *To circulate among the teams* and to let them know, especially during the state of confusion, that someone is available with advice and information they may find useful.

2. *To confer among themselves,* that is, to spend time away from the teams generating ideas and developing strategies that aid the efforts of the teams.

While they are circulating, usually about 30 percent of the time, support group members do their best to pick up on current issues affecting the work teams. Then they return to a shared meeting area and as a group bring their differing perspectives to bear on the issues. Their goal is not to impose solutions *on* the teams, but to expand the technical expertise *within* the teams— teaching the work teams, so far as possible, to do what the support teams do. As they work together away from the teams, they are always asking themselves, "How could team members tackle this problem in a way that will help them tackle similar problems on their own?" In this way, successful support people gradually hand off some portion of their specialties, say, 20 percent of the least technical duties of an engineer.

It's critical that support groups do their conferring away from the shop floor, for if they're constantly circulating, the teams begin to see them as meddlers or spies. But if the teams know that the support group has a job of its own (generating ideas and developing strategies), they are less likely to feel threatened and more likely to call for assistance. At least one TRW work-team site specifically recognizes the support group members called on most frequently by the teams, and not necessarily those with the highest profile or most impeccable credentials.

Everyone who supports the early efforts of the teams— supervisors, managers, facilitators, and technical support people—must take care to stretch the teams toward self-management without hyperextending the teams' new skills. If regular coaching fails to build their self-confidence, team members often need additional training. More seriously, if some team members decide self-direction is definitely not for them, they should drop out, if possible, or get special coaching. If certain people seem suited to self-direction but resist sharing their expertise, examine whether your system of rewards and recognition continues to reinforce the Lone Ranger approach. Even early in the transition, rewards should reinforce whatever you want to happen, typically through a pay system that recognizes both breadth and depth of skills.

REINFORCE POSITIVE BEHAVIORS

During Stage 2, managers, facilitators, and even team members must continually reinforce any correct or nearly correct team behaviors. Specific positive behaviors differ from company to company, but most fall under these now-familiar headings:

- Learning and using skills formerly used only by supervisors.
- Taking initiative to improve team productivity and quality.
- Focusing on results, not on job functions.
- Teaching skills to peers and learning skills from peers.
- Making cooperative decisions in light of team goals.
- Demonstrating pride in team accomplishments.
- Encouraging teammates to make individual contributions.

Team members can never get enough reassurance during Stage 2 that they're on the right track. When you recognize any behavior that remotely resembles self-direction—even with a simple "atta boy"—you encourage the best you can hope for at this point: a gradual approximation of genuine self-management. Positive reinforcement motivates further effort, dispels confusion, eases anxieties, and reduces both the length and severity of Stage 2. In contrast, the codified fault-finding known as "management by exception" has precisely the opposite effect.

CREATING THE RIGHT ENVIRONMENT

To build an environment that reinforces positive behaviors, make sure you have positive answers to the following critical questions:

1. *Is everyone clear about quality, cost, and delivery standards?* Clear standards reduce the ambiguity of Stage 2 by giving team members a well-defined target and by giving managers an additional tool for recognizing positive behaviors.

2. *Are there procedures for modifying performance standards?* It is far better to revise standards down or up than to overwhelm a struggling team or fail to challenge a brilliant one. In either case, be sure to negotiate all changes with the teams.

3. *Do the teams have ready access to feedback on their progress?* The teams shouldn't have to beg for hard data on their performance, data that is vital to both their developing "team-ness" and their ability to manage themselves.

4. *Do policies and procedures support self-direction?* Self-directed teams are, by definition, an exception to many of the conventional rules devised for conventional workers. Policies and procedures must therefore permit the teams to improve results through unconventional means.

5. *Are technical support groups responsive to the teams?* Recalcitrant support groups compound the frustration of Stage 2. Until they begin to realize the benefits of actively supporting the transition, they will need coaching and recognition as much as the teams do.

6. *Do the teams have the freedom to experiment?* To define its own identity, a team must try out methods of its own design. But unless you allow and reinforce these efforts—all of which imply some chance of failure—a team can hover indefinitely in the twilight zone of Stage 2.

7. *Do the teams have ready access to training and consultation?* Teams often request training or expert advice not mentioned in the transition plan. The organization must respond quickly to these usually well-founded requests.

8. *Is there a clear road map of the transition?* To guide their efforts, the teams need a formal map showing specific milestones, no matter how distant or how conditional. A good hand-off plan normally serves that purpose.

9. *Can the teams communicate internally and with other teams?* Reinforcement need not come from managers alone. For example, with a telephone, an on-line computer, or a centrally located white-board, team members can recognize—and *adver-*

tise—their own efforts. Daily recognition among peers helps turn mere teamwork into true self-management.

THINK POSITIVE

For the mid-managers at Centrilift, the phrase that came up again and again during the state of confusion was this: "Catch people doing something right, or approximately right, instead of something wrong."[1] That approach, both a philosophy and a skill, is the key to getting your teams through Stage 2. Its absence is a common cause of protracted turmoil.

Imagine the effect it will have on team members when they take initiative to improve productivity, maybe for the first time in their working lives, and get shot down for their trouble. One technical adviser recently described that experience for a team at the hands of a manager who answered requests for greater team autonomy with comments like, "I'm not gonna let the foxes in the henhouse." According to this technical adviser, "A team was having trouble with a certain solder paste, and they overheard some engineers saying the paste should be kept in a refrigerator. So they jumped in a pick-up and bought one on sale with $130 of their own money. For two weeks they waited to be reimbursed, and meanwhile they found out they didn't have all the information. The paste shouldn't be refrigerated. That manager criticized those people, saying, 'Uh-huh, all you're gonna do is put your lunches in there.'"

This manager missed an opportunity—an incredible bargain, really, at $130—to recognize the initiative of work-team members and to reinforce a valuable lesson in responsible participation. As it was, he probably reinforced another lesson entirely: Don't stick your neck out for the company, no matter what. "Fortunately," said the technical adviser, "we've got a new person now who knows when people are trying to do the right thing. And, I can't believe it, but more has been accomplished in three weeks than we have in the past year. It's like a dream beginning to unfold and come true."

TALK POSITIVE

Yet even when managers believe it's important to "catch people doing something right, or approximately right," they sometimes have difficulty putting that belief into action. For one thing, many managers are not used to recognizing positive employee behaviors. They may have managed by exception for so long, focusing mainly on deficiencies, that they feel uncomfortable praising employees for minor gains (much less for failed attempts). But positive recognition is not only a belief, it's also a set of observable behaviors that can be analyzed, demonstrated, and practiced like any other interpersonal skill. Now is the time to make doubly sure that managers value and apply this skill. If they do not, their manager support sessions are an excellent venue for focused training in this critical skill—including in-class practice in simulated work situations. One further point: Make sure that you lead by your example of recognizing their efforts to recognize the teams.

AT LAST, THE EMBRYONIC TEAMS

"At times you want to throw in the towel," confides Gary Wojdyla, director of operations at NCR in Ithaca, New York. "But I say to myself, the coming years are going to be tough, and we can't give up on our ability to be a future competitor. Five years from now, if we're going to be successful, I'm convinced that we have to have it. Once the work teams stick, their ability to manage, produce, and control production will be tremendous."

As Wojdyla has discovered, the anguish of Stage 2 is the anguish of being neither here nor there. Think of the life transitions between school and work, between one job and another, between work and retirement. In each case, you have to abandon one kind of structure before you adopt another, and that period between worlds can be filled with self-doubt. "Don't expect it to be easy," says Wojdyla. "There's a lot of rocks, a lot of hard spots, as you go to these work teams. And you're going to fall down. Several times."

But for most organizations, Stage 2 is no exercise in futility. Out of chaos comes order. Out of confusion comes confidence.

Out of trauma comes triumph. What's more, the experience of every successful team is precisely the same: It has to endure the confusion long enough to leave the old structure behind, but not so long that it gives up searching for the new. As Wojdyla points out, "You're changing a big culture. You're changing a very classical work environment into a new one."

Like most shared suffering, the passing torment of Stage 2 leaves a deep bond among team members, which in turn steels their resolve to make self-direction stick. Work-team veterans sometimes compare Stage 2 to the loss of a parent: Before employees, supervisors, and managers can fully embrace a new life, they must grieve the loss of the old. Surprisingly though, all this upheaval only occasionally brings a drop in productivity. For the most part, people accurately assess the challenge and, if anything, overcompensate for the difficulties of transition. Strong emotion is no stranger to the teams now, but neither are fortitude, collective effort, and pride of ownership. Finally, with regular coaching and recognition, each team experiences hard proof of its own emerging identity: the outline of physical and psychological boundaries, a plan for honing its own operational efficiency, and—most surprising—a new craving to play a strategic role in the company.

NOTE

1. This clever phrasing of the behavior needed to reinforce and encourage positive results is from Kenneth Blanchard, Ph.D., and Spencer Johnson, *The One Minute Manager* (La Jolla, Calif.: Blanchard-Johnson Publishers, 1981), 40.

CHAPTER SIX

WHO'S IN CHARGE HERE?

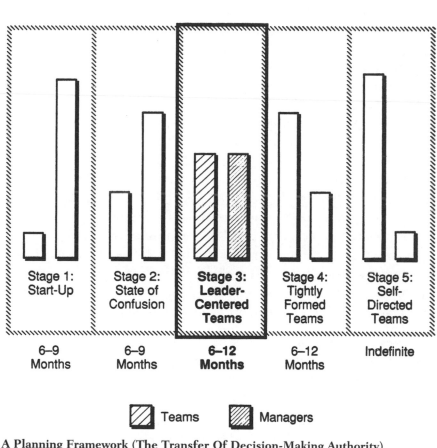

Stage 1: Start-Up	Stage 2: State of Confusion	Stage 3: Leader- Centered Teams	Stage 4: Tightly Formed Teams	Stage 5: Self- Directed Teams
6–9 Months	6–9 Months	**6–12 Months**	6–12 Months	Indefinite

◢ Teams   ◢ Managers

A Planning Framework (The Transfer Of Decision-Making Authority)

A fully self-directed work team is a miniature society in which every citizen has the skills, the experience, the opportunity, and in most cases the desire to lead the group toward ambitious performance goals. But before a new team can achieve that ideal, it must pass through Stage 3, *Leader-Centered Teams,* a phase that prolongs the same basic social arrangement—one leader and many followers—that team members have known all their lives.

Part of the conflict of adolescence is that teenagers, even when they resist authority, actually crave the structure provided by their parents and teachers. In a similar way, some working adults have a deep ambivalence toward their supervisors and managers, who grant security and predictability at the sacrifice of personal autonomy. It's therefore no surprise that most team members, eager to escape the chaos of Stage 2 but not yet ready for mature self-management, want a leader they respect to guide their collective progress.

Although it may seem like backsliding for a team to want an authoritative leader, the team is actually moving forward by attempting to find its center, its separate identity. Since conventional social units center around a clear leader, and since that structure is what employees are most familiar with, that's how they want to organize themselves now. By Stage 5, *Self-Directed Teams,* every team member will be capable of exercising leadership functions as necessary. Right now, however, most teams want one person *of their own choosing* to carry the flag.

As the teams develop a sense of identity under the guidance of a respected team leader, other key changes also occur:

- Team members begin thinking of themselves as technical generalists and take an increased interest in the quality of their final product or service.
- The influence of outside authorities wanes as team members learn basic supervisory functions, show increased willingness to get involved, and begin to challenge their managers.
- Team-generated routines evolve for team meetings, work assignments, and contact with the larger organization.

• Managers further withdraw from daily operations to concentrate on standards, regulations, systems, and resource deficiencies that inhibit team performance.

For managers, Stage 3 in certain ways comes down to figuring out what not to do. "The toughest thing for me was to hold my tongue when I sat in on team meetings," says Stephanie Spencer, production manager at the GE nuclear fuels plant in Wilmington, North Carolina. "I can't tell you how many times I knew the answer they were looking for. I also knew if they didn't sort it out on their own, we might as well bring back the old days." If managers don't tell you during Stage 3 that they feel like they're sitting on their hands, they're probably doing too much.

The paradoxical challenge of guiding the teams through Stage 3 is to support the chosen team leader and, at the same time, to diffuse leadership skills to all team members. In this way, team members can begin to break the pattern of reliance on a single team leader. To help them in that effort, planners and managers should make sure they:

• Encourage the rise of strong team leaders.
• Infuse the teams with a sense of their own identity.

ENCOURAGE THE RISE OF STRONG TEAM LEADERS

The desire for a strong leader is more than just an internal team phenomenon. Even if the teams have shown they can meet performance goals, and even if the intense anxiety of Stage 2 has subsided, non-team members (executives, managers, technical support people) also long for a single authoritative person in each team. Different companies deal with this widespread desire in different ways.

COMPANY-APPOINTED LEADERS

In order to reduce top-level worry over loss of control, many companies appoint team leaders at start-up: supervisors, facilitators, or team members with whom the managers feel comfortable. Company-appointed leaders can certainly reduce the turmoil of Stage 2 and help the teams achieve their performance goals. To be truly leader-centered, however, a work team must respect its leader and accept that person's authority; for unless the team accepts the company's choice as its own, that person is no leader at all.

Team acceptance is an especially touchy issue when these appointed leaders are former supervisors, people who often need substantial retraining and clear guidelines before they become willing to release operational control to the teams. "Most of our team leaders are former supervisors," says a maintenance technical adviser with a major telecommunication company. "They're getting leadership training—facilitation training—and our managers definitely expect them to be leaders, not supervisors. But even with focused training, old-line supervisors can easily slip back into the top sergeant mode. In a meeting recently, one supervisor happened to say, 'If a team wants something I don't agree with, I can just veto their vote.' His new manager said, 'Right. And I'll veto your veto if you veto a team vote.' So the message is getting out to the supervisors: 'You are now a leader. You are not a boss.'"

TEAM-APPOINTED LEADERS

When a team does accept the company-appointed leader (a common event), Stage 3 proceeds on schedule. However, an ineffective leader—someone the team perceives as technically incompetent, say, or power-hungry—can arrest the progress of the team before it achieves the relatively stable, leader-centered structure that characterizes Stage 3. In these cases, a team often rejects the company-appointed leader and either formally or tacitly chooses someone else. Even where the appointed leader remains in place, the de facto leader wields the major influence.

In order to keep the transition on schedule, managers must formally acknowledge each team's choice, even if a choice seems ill-advised. The company that refuses to accept team-appointed leaders in fact perpetuates the top-down rule it's ostensibly leaving behind. As a result, it crushes the still frail aspirations of team members to manage their own affairs.

Teams usually show good judgment by selecting leaders who encourage involvement and demonstrate superior technical, interpersonal, or organizational abilities. When they do not—when, for example, a leader pockets the increased pay, but ducks the increased responsibilities—managers should remind themselves that it's usually the team that suffers most, and it's usually the team that takes the necessary action. Team members know almost immediately if they're being had: "We never thought he'd be that bossy," they might say, or "Managers just don't respect him," or "She doesn't know half as much as we thought she knew." In an Atlanta plant, for example, a team discovered after a few months that their elected leader was unable to manage group decision making, and they spontaneously turned to a more qualified team member for help. Once they realized what had happened, they approached management, renegotiated the established length of a leader's term, and formally elected the de facto leader.

What kind of leaders do the teams choose? Charlie, a line worker at a plant in Vermont, is not atypical. Before self-direction, Charlie was a below-average worker; as a work-team leader, he was dazzling. "I never use to give it what I really had," he says. "There was no point. You weren't supposed to use your brain. Just crank that bolt and cash your paycheck." For Charlie, self-direction was a tank of pure oxygen. He campaigned for team leader and, once elected, made himself the nucleus of one of the most productive teams on the floor. What's the best part of his new role? "Team meetings. Now I've got a captive audience for my jokes." And the worst? "I didn't use to care if these people had problems. Now I guess I feel their pain as much as they do."

In another case, managers at the Marlin-Rockwell Gainesville plant objected to a leader candidate because he was an ex-convict. After considerable back-and-forth, this fellow convinced them that his habit of speaking his mind, which had rankled managers in other jobs he had had, would be an asset in the team leader role. He turned out to be the most active and positive team leader in the company.

The point is that by Stage 3, team members want more than anything to prove themselves capable of meeting their performance goals. Managers should remain vigilant, yes; they should also fight the urge to take charge, and they should relax in the knowledge that most teams deal with any ineffective leader in the same way: They withdraw their support and find someone else.

SELECTING A LEADER

A good way to ensure solid leadership is to work with the teams to establish selection criteria and a selection process. Whether the teams are choosing initial leaders at start-up or replacing leaders at some later time, selection criteria usually include the following:

- Maintains good relationships with teammates and managers.
- Can perform a number of the jobs performed by the team.
- Has strong interpersonal skills.
- Can organize and lead team problem-solving sessions.
- Shows strong commitment to the idea of self-directed teams.

The teams will also need to set up guidelines for a formal selection process, which should resolve basic procedural questions, such as:

- Should people nominate themselves?
- Do we want ballots or a show of hands?
- Do you need a majority to win, or just a plurality?
- When and how do we remove an ineffective leader?

Team leadership, whether elective or appointive, usually takes one of two forms during Stage 3: ongoing leadership or rotating leadership. (Neither type is permanent because every team member will eventually be capable of functional leadership, i.e., of performing any leadership function as required.)

ONGOING TEAM LEADERS

An ongoing leader can guide a team to the very brink of self-direction. The ongoing leader, who sometimes remains in place through Stage 4, *Tightly Formed Teams,* provides a single contact point for the organization as well as a steady source of advice and information for the team. However, since team members tend to rely on an ongoing leader as they once did on a supervisor, they may fail to cultivate the leadership skills and increased ownership essential to self-direction. A motor-winding team at Centrilift, for example, had an excellent ongoing leader who had been the lead operator in the days of conventional work groups. Eventually she realized that team members still expected her to settle their technical issues, so after conferring with the area manager, she decided to resign the leader position and function as an ordinary team member.

ROTATING TEAM LEADERS

A rotating leader is a team member who, at the discretion of the team, holds power for a specified term (often a month or a quarter, with no more than two consecutive terms). In some teams, everyone takes a turn; in others, a few members volunteer for a term. Rotating leadership fosters professional growth in those who serve, just as it reduces the danger of entrenched egomania. At the same time, it muddies the waters for both team members and outside people who must get used to a new leader from time to time. In an Indianapolis facility, for example, one star performer was elected and served out his term as rotating leader. But he did such an outstanding job that the manager kept going to him when issues came up, instead of dealing with the new leader, who hadn't yet had a chance to prove himself. A number of companies have overcome this kind of problem by establishing a specific work location for the rotating leader and then instructing outsiders to deal only with the person occupying that spot. Another common pitfall of rotating leadership became an issue at a plant in North Carolina. After four or five team members had taken their turns, later rounds of leaders included people with weak technical and interpersonal skills. Managers recognized the Catch 22—since one of their aims was to develop leadership skills in every team member—and they accepted the fact that these leaders would need extra help from facilitators and technical support people.

LEADER FOR A DAY

Paul Logue, human resources manager with Eaton Corporation in South Bend, Indiana, reported an unusual and, in this case, highly effective approach to rotating leadership: "We wanted to avoid the pseudo-supervisor role, so we devised a method where, right from start-up, each team member rotates into the leader job for one day at a time. Now it's routine. Each person takes on the responsibilities—material flow, SPC [statistical process control], log book, production records, preventive maintenance, all of it. This way, we find that the teams don't get too attached to one person." But didn't the teams resist the arrangement? "At first, some people didn't want any part of it. That fear of responsibility, of potential failure, of being hung out there—that was an obstacle. So the management team spent a lot of time right down on the floor, helping them out when they had questions. They had to learn what it means to be a leader. Once they got over the fear, they very quickly took to it."

PERMISSION TO CHOOSE

The continuing task for executives and managers, of course, is to preside over the gradual transfer of decision-making power to the teams. But even if that task translates in part as a nontask—allowing each team to choose its own leader—managers still need to explain up front that a team has the authority to choose its own leader and the obligation to accept responsibility for that choice. If they don't make that option clear at the outset, team members may fume under ineffective leadership, and productivity may suffer. Any company that appoints team leaders should portray them as recommendations and make it clear that as soon as the leaders have had a chance to show their stuff, the teams are free to accept or reject them.

In the short run, team-appointed leaders will probably make naive mistakes, miss obvious opportunities, or prolong the confusion of Stage 2; they certainly will fan the anxieties of executives and managers. Still, managers and teams have many options besides impeachment for addressing leadership problems. First, the team members themselves, as they take ownership of team results, will take steps to correct the mistakes of an unseasoned leader. Second, facilitators are available to counsel team leaders and members on interpersonal matters, managers on administrative matters, and support groups on technical matters. Finally, facilitators can help team members to redefine both their role and that of the leader so that everyone works together more efficiently. The practical truth is that the self-confidence teams gain in choosing their leaders and solving related problems pays off in rapid progress toward responsible self-direction.

INFUSE THE TEAMS WITH A SENSE OF THEIR OWN IDENTITY

The other critical task for managers during Stage 3 is helping team members see themselves as more than a collection of people performing isolated activities in a shared physical location. Where this notion persists, team members have not yet moved beyond the conventional view of themselves as specialized cogs in the apparatus of production. Equally dangerous is the ingenuous belief that teams should be totally self-managing—an unrealistic expectation for Stage 3, though not for the transition as a whole. The truth of Stage 3, like the teams themselves, lies somewhere between those extremes.

Helping teams find a middle path through this middle stage of development will take something other than paternalistic advice and detailed procedures. Executives, managers, facilitators, and eventually team members themselves must do everything they can to fortify the teams' emerging identity, which—like a teenager—is both separate from and dependent upon the parent organization.

PEER ROLE MODELS

Before team members can see themselves as something over and above a collection of individuals, they have to see what they are trying to become—if possible, by observing and interacting with teams that have reached or moved past Stage 3. This approach, essentially a form of peer counseling, usually has a profound effect on "adolescent" teams because at this stage peers exert far more influence than do conventional authority figures. TRW and Centrilift, among other companies, have conducted workshops (often videotaped for later study) that bring together mature teams and evolving teams. (For guidelines on these workshops, see "Mature Team-New Team Coaching Session," pages 335–338.) Sometimes new teams also sit in on regular meetings of mature teams.

If off-site visits are out of the question for a first wave of teams, facilitators and team leaders will have to bear most of the burden of demonstrating the interpersonal skills the teams need to master. But since leaders and facilitators often lack direct experience with mature self-directed teams, they'll need in-depth training and coaching in order to become credible models. To further clarify what the teams are striving to be, many companies also develop or purchase video-based skills training that contrasts effective and ineffective behaviors in team meetings and day-to-day interactions.

Developing strong internal role models is a primary reason many companies start their teams in a few sites, rather than going companywide right away. In selecting your initial sites, remember that other sites and other team members will eventually look to them for inspiration. For example, one primarily blue-collar facility made the mistake of selecting a laboratory as an initial location. For many months, planners heard the same refrain from second-wave sites: "Those teams are nothing like us. They're all engineers and professors. They all wear white coats!"

PASSING OUT THE PRIZES

In many conventional organizations, management recognizes the accomplishments of work groups and individual employees with formal awards (for example, a banner to be hung in a work area denoting 100 percent accuracy on delivery, or an "employee of the month" certificate with a write-up in the company newsletter). In the same way, companies moving to self-direction use these techniques, especially during Stage 3, to reinforce the emerging identity of their self-directed teams. Binney and Smith (famous for its Crayola crayons) publishes stories of outstanding team performance in an in-house newspaper devoted to the positive effects of self-direction.

Another effective approach to public reinforcement is to turn the tables and put the power of recognition in the hands of the teams. Historically, deciding who gets the formal awards is a powerful perk because it magnifies managers' sense of their own positive role to the company. By giving this power to the teams, you have precisely the same effect on them, for bestowing recognition contributes almost as much to a team's sense of itself as receiving recognition. A major component of any work team's identity is its pride in successfully taking on what used to be management functions, which usually carry the risk of high-profile failure. Giving out awards, on the other hand, is a management function with virtually no down side. Stage 3 is an excellent time to look at your policies for awards and recognition ceremonies and ask, "How can we revise these procedures so that the teams can do the recognizing?" To the extent that you transfer this power to the teams, you amplify both their positive sense of themselves and their positive effects on other teams. (For other ideas on recognizing performance, see "Recognition and Reward Techniques," pages 331–334.)

CONSTRUCTIVE DISENGAGEMENT

Many team members, as yet unsure of their abilities and charter, still seek daily advice and permission from their managers. And while managers should continue their Stage 2 functions—staying visible, clarifying roles and responsibilities, and reinforcing positive behaviors—they should also encourage the teams to seek leadership within the team and solve problems as a team. The fact is, Stage 3 is high time for the company to begin reaping the chief benefits of increased team autonomy: increased productivity and job satisfaction through the personal and professional growth of team members. Managers must invite and coach all team members to test their abilities to assist teammates in finding solutions to daily problems.

The principal challenge for managers during Stage 3 is to withdraw from daily operations and, by encouraging leadership behaviors in all team members, prevent the teams from relying too much on the nominal leader. A special danger at this point is assuming that strong team leaders will somehow impart their skills to other team members. Everyone needs training in leadership and problem-solving skills, preferably as an intact team. Indeed, very few transitions succeed without intensive, continuing training of this kind. "I've made a commitment to my personnel director," says a director of operations. "I'm willing to train every production person two hours every other week, bare minimum. And I didn't tell him when it stops."

During Stage 3, both coaching and formal training should concentrate on dispersing leadership and problem-solving skills to all team members.

CLOSE THE DOOR, GRAB A CHAIR, AND START WALKING

One company boasts of three highly successful techniques for building team leadership skills and promoting multilevel trust. In the first program, two or three work-team members sit in on regularly scheduled management meetings. Another program called "Sit a Week in my Chair," encourages work-team members to fill in for managers on vacation. A selected team member actually occupies the manager's office, handles paperwork, makes the rounds on the shop floor, attends meetings, participates in decision making, and deals with any issues that come up in the manager's absence. Both of these programs promote team decision making in the context of companywide goals and give employees direct experience with leadership skills that they can apply within their teams. In a third program, called "Walk a Mile in My Shoes," managers spend a day, twice a year, as a regular working member of a self-directed team. This technique, according to Jessup, has helped Newark Quartz dismantle many of the traditional barriers between blue-collar and white-collar workers—at the same time giving managers hands-on knowledge of the challenges their teams have to face.

Many innovative managers take a less formal approach to building leadership skills by simply inviting team members to management staff meetings and responding to their questions about the proceedings. In addition, such leaders often spend time on the shop floor modeling the kind of interactive leadership skills they want the teams to adopt. Some companies use a technique they call "seeding," in which team members spend time as adjunct members of other, highly successful teams. They observe effective leadership and, with time, integrate those behaviors into their own teams.

PUTTING ON THE PADS

A powerful, often overlooked source of identity for the teams during Stage 3 is their emerging ability to solve problems as a group. Not unlike a high school football team, the adolescent work teams have opponents, too—not other teams, but production problems. And, as in football, nothing acts more quickly to fuse a shared identity than the shared effort that leads to shared victory. By overcoming problems, work teams grow productive. By growing productive, teams achieve recognition. By achieving recognition, teams gain the pride and self-confidence they need to strive toward maturity.

WHERE THE RUBBER MEETS THE CROSSROADS

Problem solving is the crossroads for everything that team members learn through training and experience. It's the point at which technical know-how, administrative savvy, and interpersonal effectiveness come together in the one skill without which no self-directed team can ever really succeed. Much of what team members do in their regular meetings amounts to group problem solving. Impromptu problem solving in subgroups and with managers, facilitators, and technical support people is a daily part of work-team life. In addition, team representatives must be fluent problem solvers in order to deal with sticky cross-team issues. That's why the shared skills, tools, and vocabulary of a coherent problem-solving method contribute more perhaps than any other single influence to the unified effort and to the unifying identity of every self-directed team.

Ideally, of course, self-directed work teams don't have problems, only "opportunities for improvement." And, in fact, mature teams are so attuned to their work that they resolve many issues long before the crisis stage. Realistically, though, every team has problems it must solve by working as a group, especially during Stage 3, when team members are so concerned about proving themselves to the larger organization. Since the rush of work can mask emerging problems, many needed changes appear as bombshells (customer complaints, a sudden drop in productivity, rework), not as distant blips on the radar screen. To assess the symptoms, explore their causes, generate solutions, and carry out appropriate action, team members have to call on all of their skills. That's a tall order, especially when the pressure is on and they must use those skills in cooperation with others.

PROBLEM-SOLVING TRAINING

Because problem solving draws on everything team members learn in training and on the job, people are informally honing their skills from the first day of start-up. Training in group problem solving per se is usually well underway by Stage 3, once people learn the basics and come through their early confusion. Although training often starts earlier than indicated below, a typical sequence of training topics leading to and beyond group problem solving looks something like this:

Stage 1 *Start-Up*: Administrative and technical overviews acquaint team members with the team activities in which problems are most likely to arise. Training in basic interpersonal skills lays the groundwork for the give-and-take of group problem solving.

Stage 2 *State of Confusion*: Teams learn to do things together through their training in communicating expectations, setting job standards, and seeking help, among other skills. Technical cross-training prepares people to participate more knowledgeably in group problem solving.

Stage 3 *Leader-Centered Teams:* Training begins in four component skills of group problem solving: the basic problem-solving process, problem-solving tools and techniques, participating in and leading problem-solving sessions.

Stage 4 *Tightly Formed Teams* and Stage 5 *Self-Directed Teams:* As the teams learn to maintain cross-team relationships and, later, to manage their internal customer partnerships, they expand both their abilities and opportunities to engage in group problem solving.

How do self-directed teams find out what they're really capable of? In one sense, they simply solve problems. But make no mistake: Preparing your teams to tackle their own problems is no tailgate party. So vital is this skill to the identity and productivity of every team, and so common is the mistaken belief that team members will somehow figure it out for themselves, that anyone contemplating self-direction is well advised to give problem solving training some very careful thought. (For details on group problem solving, see "A Group Problem-Solving Process," pages 339–344.)

ICONS AND RITUALS

As Stage 3 unfolds, the teams develop a healthy sense of who they are and how they're different from everyone else. The team leader is getting comfortable with conducting meetings and interfacing with the organization. Team members begin to enjoy both the variety of their daily activities and the give-and-take of group problem solving. Everyone, managers included, revels in the good press the teams are getting for the tangible results of their efforts.

A sure sign that leader-centered teams have arrived is the paraphernalia and social activities each team brews up to proclaim its sense of itself: team names, team logos, and team slogans emblazoned on banners, T-shirts, caps, and coffee mugs;

team bulletin boards proclaiming this week's results and next week's goals; regular team lunches and after-hours events. Much later, these icons and rituals will fade—like the letter-sweaters and pep rallies of adolescence—as team members see that their ability to learn new skills allows them to move freely from team to team. But for now, this outward expression of commitment and stability is welcome proof that while the teams still have miles to go, they indeed have come through the most treacherous phase of their journey.

A CONFLICT OF
LOYALTIES

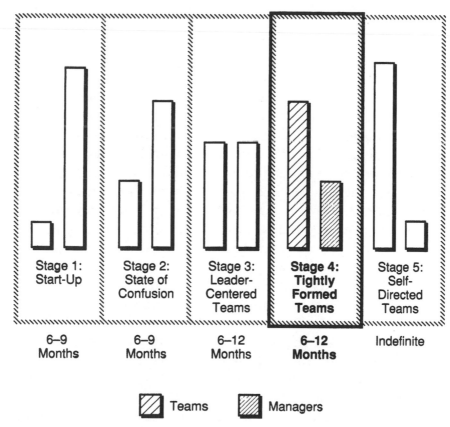

Stage 1: Start-Up	Stage 2: State of Confusion	Stage 3: Leader- Centered Teams	**Stage 4: Tightly Formed Teams**	Stage 5: Self- Directed Teams
6–9 Months	6–9 Months	6–12 Months	**6–12 Months**	Indefinite

◩ Teams   ▨ Managers

A Planning Framework (The Transfer Of Decision-Making Authority)

How can you argue with loyalty? From their earliest youth, Americans learn that loyalty animates every conceivable social structure—nations and marriages, football teams and corporations—and throughout life they cherish the least sign of loyalty in their families, co-workers, friends, and pets. How can you argue with the Pledge of Allegiance? How can you argue with the *Boy Scout Oath?*

Yet loyalty can have a down side, too.

It was a year and a half into the transition to work teams in a northeastern circuit board factory, and the self-confident teams were setting new standards for quality and productivity. No longer were they struggling to learn their new roles; and since almost everyone had taken a turn as rotating team leader, they had mastered the basics of self-management. They had reached the plateau, in fact, where some companies decide they have "team enough" and go no further. But one chronic issue, in itself not serious enough to offset the many genuine gains, continued to gnaw at a number of perceptive managers: If these were mature teams, why were they squabbling so much?

Several teams, for example, shared a certain chemical vat, in which they dipped hand-blown glass tubes, and an adjacent oven for drying the freshly coated parts. In the old days, anyone using these facilities would routinely shut down the oven, perform minor preventive maintenance, refire the oven, and refill the vat for the next user. It was simply the final phase of that particular task. Now, apparently because maintenance time was nonproductive time and because all the teams were vying to be the most productive in the plant, each team would monopolize the equipment, fail to perform the required maintenance, and blame the other teams for doing the same.

Problems like this, common during Stage 4, *Tightly Formed Teams,* are more than isolated glitches in an otherwise flawless transition; they are the outward signs of the primary remaining obstacle to responsible self-direction. The same narrow loyalty that raised leader-centered teams from the agony of Stage 2 now threatens to consume them in Stage 4. So self-absorbed are the teams that they often act only in their own behalf, mindless of the welfare of other teams and the company as a whole. A consultant with a telecommunications company describes the missing ingredient in Stage 4: "What I would call a mature team is much more able to truly hear the other team's point of view. There seems to be a greater empathy, if you will, and a greater ability to actually listen clearly and hear the other person out. More of a sense of 'we' and less 'me.'"

To the outside observer, the teams often appear to be doing just fine during Stage 4, and in many ways they are:

- They exhibit deep confidence in their ability to meet challenging goals with limited resources.
- They manage their own production schedule.
- They regularly communicate their resource needs to appropriate staff.
- They take steps to resolve conflicts within the team.

But don't let these signs convince you that the teams are home free. Notice also the subtler signs of unseemly self-interest, discontent, and in some cases outright dysfunction:

- Communication about internal technical and personnel problems—which once flowed so freely from the teams—starts to dry up.
- The teams begin to shield chronically nonperforming members from possible disciplinary action by outsiders.
- Rivalry among the teams, once healthy and good-natured, now takes on a serious, even sinister cast.

At *Start-Up* (Stage 1), managers began a massive transfer of decision-making power according to a plan and idealistic mission statement substantially developed by executives. During the *State of Confusion* (Stage 2), the teams tested but continued to rely on their managers, who helped them achieve a new identity and new levels of productivity as *Leader-Centered Teams* (Stage 3). Now, with the appearance of *Tightly Formed Teams* (Stage 4), team members take charge of their lives with a vengeance. During Stage 4, managers must help the teams take the final step, to responsible self-direction, by addressing the deep needs behind their symptomatic isolation and conflict. Some managers at this point break out the shears and start trimming wings—a step that can crash-land the entire transition. Other managers, for fear of resurrecting the state of confusion, simply accept the isolationism of the teams. However, to guide the teams toward full maturity, managers must take measured steps—shrewdly balancing action and inaction—that turn narrow team loyalties outward to embrace other teams and the company as a whole. Specifically, managers need to:

• Build and maintain two-way information-sharing.
• Make sure the teams get ongoing performance feedback.
• Hand off responsibilities according to plan.

BUILD AND MAINTAIN TWO-WAY INFORMATION-SHARING

Most teams by this point know enough to ask for technical help when they need it, but they often ignore and even resent unsought advice from well-meaning interlopers. Like the young woman whose parents show up at her new apartment and start rearranging the furniture, the teams have an overwhelming need to control their own environment. At the same time, they need regular contact with the larger world in order to achieve well-balanced maturity. Executives and managers must therefore show considerable openness in providing information to the teams and considerable tact in soliciting information from the teams.

INFORMATION-HOARDING

In a conventional company, three organizational layers often consolidate power by hoarding three different kinds of information: Executives lay claim to strategic information (about goals), middle managers to operational information (about results), and first-line supervisors to tactical information (about methods). As a conventional company moves toward self-direction, however, the will to power must give way to the will to productivity; in other words, information-hoarding must give way to information-sharing. If the work teams are to manage themselves responsibly (and in Stage 4 they're nearly capable of doing so) they need access to all three kinds of information. Just as important, when tightly formed teams start getting new information from formerly secretive sources, they tend to open up and share what they know—including what they may see as potentially damaging information about their own internal problems.

Most managers and executives find it hard to break the tradition of keeping "vital" information from first-line people, a view often rationalized with the argument that a leak could damage the company. But no one should expect the teams to work toward company-wide goals if the company won't trust the teams with the information they need to achieve those goals. When Al Webb, former vice president of finance at Centrilift, ignored the norms and got teams of nonexecutives deeply involved in strategic planning, he inspired better decisions and greater involvement in implementing those decisions. These teams worked with data on market research, on long-range goals, on competitive strengths and weaknesses, and on costs associated with all aspects of operation. Webb explains: "Sure, they were flattered to get confidential material. But that isn't why there hasn't been a single leak that I'm aware of. I knew from the start that once people knew the data was confidential, it would stay that way. Once they understood the consequences, they saw leaks the same way we do. On top of that, the fact that we did give them the information created the kind of trust you just can't buy."

"THE LAST HONEST PIZZA"

An incident in one New England factory illustrates how neglecting to share information, even when it involves less than top-secret matters, can harden the isolation of the teams during Stage 4. A major customer of this plant, pleased with recent strides in quality and on-time delivery, decided to sponsor trips to Disneyworld for three employees and their families. Managers, in all innocence, chose three team members they felt had earned special recognition, but the announcement of their names provoked a near revolt on the factory floor. "You have no idea who deserves to go," said one team member. "We can make anybody look like they're doing a good job and hide anybody who isn't." Managers decided the situation was too volatile to let the teams decide now and as a peace offering proposed a plant-wide pizza party for the following Friday. Still irate, employees boycotted the party and made their sentiments known in a hand-lettered sign posted on the central bulletin board: "Who chooses the people that deserve to eat pizza? You or us?" In retrospect, managers now see that it took them many months to rebuild the fragile trust they had worked so hard to establish.

VARIETIES OF ISOLATION

Whether or not it's aggravated by poor communication, the largely self-imposed isolation of the teams during Stage 4 tends to express itself in three symptoms: *protectionism, exclusivity,* and *rigid demands.* Not all teams exhibit all symptoms, but most exhibit at least one.

Protectionism.   Teams that protect poor-performing members are common during Stage 4. In one consumer electronics company, for instance, an engineering support team was well aware of a member who, in spite of repeated training, continued having trouble with several pieces of complex reprographic equipment. But simply because he was an accepted teammate, the team refused to divulge his incompetence by sending him for still more training. So vigorous was their support for this person that they allowed productivity to fall off whenever a second team member had to help him out.

Exclusivity.   This most frequent sign of isolation during Stage 4 is evident even in the most successful implementations. A large midwestern manufacturer, for example, proudly welcomes visitors (at a substantial per-person fee) to tour their self-directed sites and chat with managers and team members. There's no question the company has enthusiastic and productive teams, but managers there sometimes talk about a difficulty that belies deeper problems: The teams are extremely resistant to integrating new members. Normally, cliquishness like this implies that narrow team loyalty is an overriding concern in team decision making. Mature teams, on the other hand, readily accept and acculturate new members because their main concern is achieving objectives shared by everyone in the organization.

Rigid Demands.   Stage 4 sometimes marks the rise of strident team demands irrespective of company objectives or the needs of other teams. For example, a team in an Oakland, California, company wanted some expensive equipment that several team members were uniquely qualified to operate. Even though managers explained that other teams had to be able to operate the equipment in order to make it cost effective, the team protested and then grew sullen. Similar problems crop up whenever a team asserts its identity in a way that undermines cooperation with other teams. If an MIS technical adviser wants to set up an inter-team computer network, for example, one team might insist on an incompatible make of computer because one team member already knows how to use it. In most of these cases, the teams aren't rebelling for the sake of rebellion. But they're so internally directed, so intent on proving their worth as a team, that they feel subverted if they think they're not getting what they need to do their best work.

IS IT SAFE?

Before you can induce tightly formed teams to integrate their efforts with those of the larger organization, you'll have to make it safe for them to do so. By this point, every team recognizes that its efforts to achieve strategic goals almost always support the productivity of other teams. If the teams see one another as adversaries, however, no team is likely to make that overt effort. The solution here is to take steps that downplay competition, promote open communication, and highlight the benefits of teams' working toward shared goals:

- Set up a council of rotating team representatives who meet regularly to consider common issues and look for ways to build cooperation.
- Hold weekly plant review meetings in which reps from each team report on progress and performance issues. At Solar Turbines' San Diego facility, a team coordinator council (TCC) for all the maintenance teams meets weekly and has become a significant leadership force. As one member stated, "We're both honest and effective in this group, and we're becoming good business people."
- Rather than bringing entire teams together, establish a "link team" (with one member from each team), which convenes as needed to reduce competition or resolve other inter-team issues.
- At start-up, configure employees into teams that do not have to share equipment; if they must share, establish firm ground rules.
- Make sure your reward and performance appraisal systems reinforce inter-team cooperation.
- Begin technical cross-training between potentially adversarial teams.
- Develop training that helps the teams confront issues of inter-team cooperation.

Listen Carefully and Bury the Big Stick

Even with measures like these, willful work-team isolation will persist if managers take swift corrective action whenever a team reveals its problems. More fundamentally, trigger-happy managers reflect a failure to understand the underlying purpose of self-direction. Managers must see, and help the teams to see, internal team problems as opportunities for improvement, and they must encourage openness by coaching, not punishing, those who reveal that they may be having difficulties. Otherwise, the teams will continue to mask their problems in hard-eyed silence.

A related danger is the manager who takes well-meaning but unwelcome corrective action, like the senior manager who decided to act on his own after a team revealed its concerns about pay levels and discipline. With no further discussion, he bypassed the pay progression system and promoted one member of every team to the highest pay level. (In the teams' view, he'd messed up a good system, which they had helped to design.) Then he told a facilitator to take over team discipline because the teams were having problems. (Fortunately, the facilitator was sharp enough to talk to the teams instead of taking charge.) As a result, it was a good six months before the teams would freely express their concerns to this manager or anyone reporting directly to him.

NEW SKILLS AND NEW HORIZONS

Formal training during Stage 4 should emphasize the practical skills of building and maintaining strong partnerships with internal customers and suppliers, both within and outside the team. Many team members find it difficult, for example, to ask their internal customers for feedback on performance: Are we meeting your needs? What can we do to make you more productive and help you turn out better quality work? Questions like these can stick in the throat of people who have spent most of their working lives looking out for number one. That's why team members need focused training on the value of internal partnerships, clear demonstrations of the required skills, and structured practice in a safe setting before they use their new skills on the job.

Not only does such training contribute to productivity and quality improvement, it also chips away at the inter-team barriers that block the arrival of responsible self-management. To reinforce the training, some companies encourage teams that do not yet maintain strong internal partnerships to observe those that do. For example, the TRW corporate legal support team—clerks, paralegals, and research assistants—was a confident group, used to speaking out. The team held quarterly forums with its internal customers and internal suppliers to elicit feedback and clarify its own needs. Representatives from less active teams sat in on these sessions and adapted the format for their own use.

Find ways to motivate team members to use their new skills for developing inter-team partnerships, for advertising their discoveries, and for verbalizing their needs and problems to managers and other teams. Measures as simple as a traveling "supplier of the week" trophy can remind teams to continue using their partnership skills. Many companies print special forms—bright certificates or die-cut cardboard in the shape of a handshake or a champagne bottle—that team members can fill out and send to a helpful person or group. The unvarnished truth is that virtually any form of recognition, when genuine, will encourage risk-taking and magnify the positive effects of open communication.

"TAKE ME TO YOUR LEADER"

When outsiders need to communicate with a team, they may tend to bypass the team leader (especially rotating leaders) and deal with the team member they know best, a habit that can undermine a team's sense of separate identity. Gary Wojdyla of the NCR Ithaca plant describes one common approach to the problem: "If you were to walk out on our floor, you'd see a board, and it would tell you who is the current active team representative. A purchasing agent, or whoever, if he or she has an issue, simply looks at the board and walks over and communicates with that person."

Several teams in the TRW Gainesville plant felt the need for an even more emphatic solution, so they developed a nonstandard procedure that met their dual needs for separateness and for close cooperation with outsiders. Wearing special leader's caps with distinguishing team colors, the rotating leaders spent time each day at a small desk in their respective work areas. Both outsiders and team members routed all communications through the person at the desk (who also handled a full load of technical work) instead of going directly to team members. With a facilitator helping each new leader to understand the need for orderly communication, this six-month exercise gave the teams a strong sense of their own boundaries—a must for coping with the flexible boundaries and wide-open communication of full-blown self-direction.

MAKE SURE THE TEAMS GET ONGOING PERFORMANCE FEEDBACK

During Stage 4, it's important to refine the self-assessment procedures that help the teams follow their own progress and pinpoint areas where they need to improve.

If you've done a good job in setting performance goals, it's fairly easy for team members to identify both positive and negative influences on productivity. If you've set standards for individual skill development and for improving the physical and psychological environment, the teams can also track their own efforts to improve the social half of the socio-technical equation (see pages 70–73). Still, you will need to make sure that appropriate feedback procedures become an integral part of the way the teams do business.

Multimedia Feedback for Tightly Formed Teams

In the late 1970s at most of the TRW work-team sites, each team prominently posted a record of its progress on large, multicolored charts, which inspired daily discussion about problems and gains. Nowadays, computer terminals allow quick access to the latest information, but the small display tends to further isolate the already insular teams. Particularly at this stage, every team can benefit from the open discourse prompted by a "communication wall" with a prominent display of their recent efforts (computer printouts, hand-lettered signs, etc.). A conspicuous display of team results not only encourages innovative thinking within the team, it also gives the team a public identity and invites dialogue with outsiders, who in turn open up the tightly formed teams to fresh ideas.

Virtually any form of communication can increase the quantity and improve the timeliness of feedback on team performance. An Ohio plant, for example, has installed telephone lines so that the external customer (another plant within the same company) can contact the teams directly. In many plants, teams invite passers-by to comment on immediate team problems and questions written out on a prominent easel. This practice encourages openness and because the teams are asking for the feedback, it's usually well received. Any company with an MRP (manufacturing resources planning) system can install terminals right on the shop floor and give the teams open access to up-to-the-minute production data.

THE CLUSTER MEETING AND ITS COUSINS

Another way to highlight progress and keep the team in contact with the larger organization is the cluster meeting, which some companies introduce as early as Stage 1 to mitigate the isolation of Stage 4. A team meets with a manager in the production area for an informal, stand-up review of progress (typically twice a week for 15 minutes). Key factors for the success of cluster meetings are the attitude and behaviors of the manager. Specifically, the manager must make it clear that the team is the primary author of both past successes and creative solutions to current problems. For its part, the team must accept the manager's role in monitoring the way the team conducts business, as well as in securing needed resources for the team. (For more information, see "Cluster Meeting," pages 345–348.)

A more formal alternative to the cluster group is the round-table meeting, in which teams and managers conduct a regular operational review or, in a special session, recognize an achievement or consider an issue. In any case, discussion should focus on the teams and their role in achieving corporate objectives. Although the round-table meeting is an opportunity for multilevel input rather than a rigorous problem-solving session, the group often entertains ideas that come up as possible solutions to previously well-defined problems.

The pre-shift meeting, both a feedback tool and a communication tool, is another, almost universal event among self-directed teams. Each day, with no manager present, the full team gathers around a production board, reviews results for the previous day, and brainstorms any special action needed to meet the goal for that day. Every couple of hours throughout the day, a team member notes on the board how close the team is to the goal; if there's a problem, the team meets briefly to plan corrective action. To find out what's going on with a particular team, managers simply review the board.

ONE-ON-ONE FEEDBACK

The most potentially damaging kind of performance feedback at this stage is one-on-one feedback from manager to team member. Because that relationship carries so much emotional baggage and because team members by Stage 4 see the team as the primary source of discipline and support, it's important to find alternatives to manager-to-employee feedback wherever possible.

At a Blue Cross headquarters in the Midwest, at a state vocational training center in the Southwest, and at many other sites around the country, managers and team members have made a collective decision to defer to the teams on individual performance issues. When line managers or staff professionals learn of either productive or counterproductive activities within a team, they couch their feedback in terms of team performance and send their comments through the team leader to the person or people concerned. In other words, managers reinforce or correct the team as a whole, and the team reinforces or corrects the actions of individual members. As mentioned earlier, this approach is extremely effective in positive public ceremonies where managers recognize team results and team members recognize the individual contributions of other members. Some companies funnel performance feedback through the team as a whole by using bulletin boards or newsletters to spotlight accomplishments, offer solutions to widespread problems, and disseminate innovative ideas developed by the various teams. Binney and Smith, for example, assigns a facilitator to double as a kind of roving reporter, publishing and reinforcing creative efforts and transplanting good ideas from team to team.

Channeling individual feedback through the team is a theoretically sound practice that also promotes the bottom-line benefits of reinforcing team identity and accelerating the transition to full self-direction.

THE ULTIMATE IN FEEDBACK

At least three TRW work-team sites—Gainesville, Georgia; Crooksville, Ohio; and Falconer, New York—found Stage 4 an ideal time to introduce the ultimate in self-directed feedback: peer performance appraisal. Although an earlier attempt to introduce peer appraisal had proved premature, by Stage 4 the TRW teams were fairly clear about their roles and fiercely protective of their well-earned right to review themselves. It was during their first attempt, however, that the Gainesville facility (a first-generation TRW work-team site) learned a most critical lesson: The entire peer appraisal process will founder if team members haven't mastered the skills required to plan and conduct an appraisal session.

On the first go-round, team members insisted on doing what came naturally, and as a result the Gainesville plant nearly abandoned the whole idea of peer appraisal. Among the first volunteers to be reviewed was someone we'll call George, an outgoing man who had made the team primarily because of his physical strength. George provided a valuable service, but the women on the team found his behavior offensive at times, and everyone was tired of working around his dislike for administrative tasks. The team hoped to shape him up through a formal review.

Predictably, George refused to accept the judgment of the appraisal committee, and after a month of fruitless wrangling, no one could figure out how to deal with the anger and hostility the whole team was feeling. Finally, the team leader called in an internal consultant, and since management considered peer appraisal a critical issue, the consultant recommended special training. During two separate weekends, the team participated in two related workshops—one devoted to the concepts and vocabulary for analyzing performance and planning an appraisal session, the other to intensive skill-building in win-win negotiating. These new skills improved results back on the job. In a follow-up appraisal session, George grudgingly accepted that his behavior was damaging team performance, and he agreed to tone down his lame jokes and work on his administrative skills. What's more, the win-win negotiating skills helped the whole team to improve their interactions with internal customers and suppliers. These workshops in modified form became a regular Stage 4 event for most other TRW teams. (For an in-depth discussion of these matters, see "Peer Performance Appraisal," pages 349–356.)

HAND OFF RESPONSIBILITIES ACCORDING TO PLAN

During Stage 4, many companies continue to follow two separate but related plans to effect the orderly distribution of responsibilities to the teams:

1. A formal hand-off plan, initiated at start-up, governs the transfer of responsibilities from the managers and the broader organization to the teams. It outlines the administrative and other duties to be handed off to team members when, through specified experience or training, they achieve a minimum level of expertise. (See "Hand-Off Plans for Supervisory and Support Group Tasks," pages 309–320.)

2. A less formal role expansion plan, also developed during start-up, outlines the training and experience each team member needs in order to perform new technical jobs within the team and to function as a back-up for other teams. These multiple skills, both within and outside the primary team, give self-directed teams their characteristic flexibility. (See "Team Member Role Expansion Plan," pages 321–324.)

   In this way, distribution of responsibilities to the teams follows the hand-off plan; distribution within the teams follows the role expansion plan. The hand-off plan promotes continuing interaction between managers and teams, and the role expansion plan promotes continuing interaction within and among the teams—in both cases exactly what they need to combat the endemic isolation of Stage 4. Together, the two plans promote a healthy mix of autonomy and accountability: The teams have the plans to manage, and the managers make sure the teams implement the plans or get approval for exceptions. In this way, the company uses structure—the jointly developed plans—to encourage and protect the freedom at the heart of self-direction.

As teams or any kind of work groups evolved, support functions were established to take on tasks requiring some special expertise. Production control became the group to schedule what gets done when; quality services took responsibility for specifications conformance of products and services; human resources now directs things like interviewing, hiring, and training team members; maintenance has been given responsibility for equipment service and repairs—large and small; safety monitors safe practices like glasses and shoes and safe conditions like frayed electric cords. The list goes on.

Determining what teams can and should do to be more effective needs to consider all these opportunities for improvement, not just what the supervisory support function should hand back to the teams. At Solar Turbines, Ken Sweat has taken the lead to help teams and support groups to define appropriate hand-off tasks, describe what acceptable performance will look like, identify present owners of the tasks to become mentors for the teams, and establish an intranet-based assessment, scheduling, and reporting process.

E PLURIBUS UNUM

The principal task of Stage 4 is to expand the loyalties of team members beyond the narrow interests of the team, a task that requires open communication, carefully structured performance feedback, and continuing transfer of responsibility. When you succeed, you neutralize pointless isolation and conflict without destroying the teams' sense of themselves as distinct, self-managing units. Tom Stich, who has been the internal OD consultant for three corporate teaming initiatives over the past 15 years (United Technologies, Solar Turbines, and Hexcel), speaks of some lessons learned regarding a balance between team continuity and team member crossover. "Although it is important to give teams control of their membership, we encourage teams to be considerate of the resource needs of others and to interchange members. An unplanned benefit of such exchange programs is that a new set of eyes is really helpful in finding previously unseen improvement opportunities. And, after all, process improvement is a major payoff of teaming."

We've outlined some measures in this chapter to help teams transition through Stage 4 and on to the inter-team collaboration of Stage 5. Dave Lehmann, vice president of manufacturing for Solar Turbines (and the acknowledged champion of a comprehensive teaming initiative), summarizes a major transition concern. "We have seen that success can build egos to the point that good teams can become *too* self-centered. They need to win at the expense of others. Pride in achievement needs to be encouraged, but not at the expense of others." Dave recommends an open, intentional focus at this point on a concept needed to bridge the gap. *That concept is an emphasis on community, rather than on rights.* Our competitive world teaches us that we win "bragging rights." Our collaborative world emphasizes "community needs." This difference will be important if the organization as a whole is to be served. Rights and ego keep us at Stage 4. A sense of community is needed to go to Stage 5.

CITIZEN TEAM

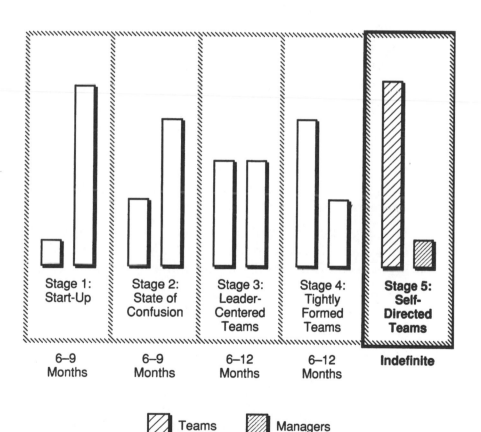

Stage 1: Start-Up	Stage 2: State of Confusion	Stage 3: Leader-Centered Teams	Stage 4: Tightly Formed Teams	**Stage 5: Self-Directed Teams**
6–9 Months	6–9 Months	6–12 Months	6–12 Months	**Indefinite**

Teams   Managers

A Planning Framework (The Transfer of Decision-Making Authority)

It's now two years or more into the transition, and, while no one has hoisted an official banner, hardly anyone mistakes the signs that self-directed work teams are a practical reality. Supervisors (if any are still in place) and managers have withdrawn from daily operations. Individual team members can and do perform any team-related leadership functions as required. Support systems respond quickly, and managers act on advice from the teams for improving those that don't. Lately, in fact, managers have picked up a whole new lingo to describe the quiet efficiency of their teams:

flexible (flek' - sə - bəl) *adj*: able to conform to changing conditions [the teams are ~ because every team member can perform any task in the primary team and many of the tasks of other teams]

fluid (flü' - ed) *adj*: available for different uses [the teams are ~ because they're able to replace current members with new members, re-tool to perform new functions, and farm out functions as required]

lean (lēn) *adj*: containing little or no fat [the teams are ~ because they actually look for ways to eliminate waste within and between all of their activities]

responsive (ri - spän(t)' - siv) *adj*: quick to react appropriately [the teams are ~ because they seek out, meet, and exceed the shifting expectations of both internal and external customers]

proactive (prō - ak' - tiv) *adj*: exercising foresight to prevent crises [the teams are ~ because they plan innovations to meet anticipated needs and continually streamline for increased productivity]

Buzzwords aside, hardly anything pleases executives and managers more than the many team members who now see themselves as coequal stakeholders in the long-term success of the company. One excellent example occurred in an offshore gas and oil production platform off the Louisiana coast, where Vastar Resources has a very successful self-directed work-team site. Dan Trull, area facilitator for the production complex, tells of the result of a successful effort to make the teams "bilingual"—to get them to speak in the language of management (money results) as well as the language of the teams (production and team development results). In their meeting area, the teams had developed a display board showing team objectives and accomplishments. With a little coaching, it was easy to add a column to the display which added for each item the immediate and projected dollar impact for the organization. It has now become part of the language used within and among teams, and when the executives from Houston came for a visit, they were duly impressed with the business teams on the platform.

An example of a different but equally important comprehension of being tuned into the needs of the larger organization is cited by Michael Walton, from when he was the internal project manager for the teaming initiative at the TRW Information Systems credit phone center outside Dallas, Texas. Michael recalls:

> There were dozens of times that one team had extra depth in
> people resources, and they readily agreed to member transfers.
> On one occasion, a team had to seek out someone with experi-
> ence in dealing with "irate" callers. On many occasions, a re-
> gional team needed someone to speak a foreign language com-
> mon to their regional customer base. Sometimes the need was
> for a member transfer, sometimes for a temporary loan. We de-
> veloped a team-based culture that was a benchmark site for
> other call centers, and I'm sure that the willingness to optimize
> for the organization instead of maximizing for any one team was
> an important key to our success.

Inter-team cooperation like this, quite common during Stage 5, *Self-Directed Teams,* is a far cry from the ethocentric rivalry of Stage 4. Now team members do whatever it takes to meet strategic objectives (not simply team objectives), even if that effort spells the literal break-up of the teams.

Other marks of maturity appear during Stage 5, which, like baseball, has no outside time limit. Now, for example, the teams make productive use of detailed information on strategic goals, contracts, competitors, and external customer standards; they implement innovative technical ideas to meet rising standards for quality and productivity; they evaluate and select new members and absorb people from other teams experiencing a temporary lack of work. Many team members even learn to see their piece of the business in a national or global perspective. The company, if it has kept pace, now provides training at the request of the teams, rewards the teams for superior performance, provides resources for the teams to reward individuals, and has gain-sharing or a pay-for-knowledge reward system. In some ways, though, a company that reaches Stage 5 is often notable for what it lacks:

- Time clocks.
- High-status work attire, office decor, and titles.
- Reserved parking and separate lunchrooms.
- A set schedule for breaks, lunch periods, and working hours.

AVOIDING THE ALGERNON SYNDROME

If Thomas Jefferson were to come back as a work-team consultant, he might well tell us, "The price of self-direction is eternal vigilance." He, of all people, would recognize that many companies reach Stage 5, only to start backsliding almost immediately. And when that happens, the effects can be worse than the blackest days of Stage 2.

Any team that has to watch the slow erosion of its power and freedom will experience something called "the Algernon syndrome," after the science fiction story "Flowers for Algernon" by Daniel Keyes. In the story, a severely retarded man is the subject of an experiment that slowly elevates his intelligence and creativity to celestial heights. He becomes John Donne, Wolfgang Mozart, and Stephen Hawking rolled into one. Then, just as slowly, his mind fails. Day by day, he watches his powers ebb, and every day he asks a faithful visitor to "bring flowers for Algernon," the lab mouse that precedes him in the experiment by a few weeks.

Like this unfortunate man, mature teams will regress—feeling betrayed, frustrated, and hostile—if management fails to meet their needs out of neglect or because of some unadvertised motive for implementing teams (to reduce headcount, say, or to excise managers, cut costs, or create "happier employees"). By the time the teams are approaching the gates of Stage 5, any ulterior management motives or lack of tangible support usually surfaces and often precipitates a steep decline in team productivity.

Besides minding your own motives, you can avoid the Algernon syndrome by striking a balance between, on one hand, making self-direction the matter-of-fact basis of daily operation and, on the other, perpetuating the growth and excitement of Stages 1 through 4. The trick is to sustain the activities that make self-direction a living, evolving part of the corporate body:

- Keep on training.
- Tailor systems to support the teams' productivity.
- Improve internal customer-supplier partnerships.
- Act out self-direction daily.

KEEP ON TRAINING

During Stage 5, productivity in some companies begins to slide because they allow themselves to take their teams for granted. These companies may fail to prepare their teams for tomorrow's technology, for new administrative duties, and especially for the interpersonal demands of their expanding role in operations. But companies that reap continuing reward through their teams—Procter & Gamble, Corning, TRW—recognize and act on one of the most fundamental facts of self-direction: Training and reinforcement, like food and oxygen, are forever required by teams and their managers.

Members of self-directed teams, as they take on new responsibilities, perform more and more of the tasks traditionally performed by managers. Consequently, almost anything you now consider a training topic for managers becomes a potential training topic for a mature team. During the earlier stages of transition, teams grow accustomed to regular training and regular recognition for their increasing competence; indeed, they come to regard training as part of the territory.

More to the point, training keeps the teams motivated by sustaining both the perception and the reality that "we are growing, taking on new challenges, making new and more valuable contributions to the corporate effort." Over and over, stalled transitions prove that when you stop training self-directed teams, they starve to death.

SAVE YOUR AMMO

Marginally successful companies tend to empty their cannons in a barrage of early training, then assume all is well for the next several years. Highly successful companies see training as a permanent process, not an event, and they pay close, continuing attention to several sets of training needs and several populations. New team members need everything from acculturation through the full range of basic skills. Old hands need training, retraining, and continual reinforcement to deal with new products, new processes, and new standards, or to file the rust off old skills for a new assignment within or outside their primary team.

As Stage 5 takes hold, full-scale training of new team members is the area most likely to get short shrift. But a covey of careworn transitions makes one point perfectly clear: The education and training essential at start-up are also essential for anyone who joins the transition at a later time. Companies like Solar Turbines—which has an educational development plan (EDP) that prepares every new team member in all necessary interpersonal, administrative, and technical skills—know that it's a time bomb to try to make do with technical training alone for new hires. For similar reasons, all new executives and managers need early and continuing training in order to master the daily interpersonal skills that give life to a mere belief in employee involvement. Many innovative companies periodically bring together new and long-time executives, managers, and team members for a special training event intended to revitalize commitment and update essential skills. (For details, see "Repotting Workshop," pages 357–360).

You Never Outgrow Your Need for Skill

Mature teams and their long-time managers will likewise need new knowledge and skills during Stage 5. Even the highly successful and widely imitated General Foods pet food plant in Topeka decided that front-line managers needed to polish up their interpersonal skills. Elsewhere, mature teams often find they need training in more advanced supervisory skills, advanced meeting leadership skills, say, or project management. At Corning, Director of Education and Training Ed O'Brien recommends that mature self-directed teams spend 20 percent of their time in classroom training. Procter & Gamble averages 40 hours of training per year per employee, and virtually every company that succeeds with teams has some sort of mechanism for identifying new training needs. Many organizations assign one team member the responsibility to assess learning and development needs for the team: This might including assigning each team to a specific trainer who regularly analyzes team needs and arranges for appropriate classroom and on-the-job sessions.

Several organizations (Hexcel Salt Lake City, Vastar Resources, and Solar Turbines, for example) have taken steps to establish a team member development function to make sure that someone is attending to the training and development needs of team members, and not just in terms of the production output skills. In the early stages of teaming, this is usually a coordinating job someone is assigned. At a later stage, this function is built into the team itself. In places where skill-based pay is part of the plan, team trainer becomes one of the skill sets to be considered.

Jacks and Jills of at Least Two Trades

Any company with a pay-for-knowledge compensation system has a powerful motivator for cross-training between teams, one of the primary ways to heighten the flexibility of mature teams. Under such a system, pay for team members has two caps: one for learning skills within the team and a second for learning skills primarily used by other teams.

At Centrilift, inter-team cross-training made it possible for an office person to fill in for a week in the shop, and for a shop person to fill in for a cost accounting clerk on extended leave. The plant general manager at Lawrence Cable was able to roll up his sleeves and help out in a production emergency because he had been certified in the requisite skills. Under these conditions, with ongoing training across team boundaries, people get a breath of air outside of their circumscribed roles, and the entire company benefits from "flexible, fluid, lean, responsive, and proactive" employees at all levels. No one learns every function carried out by another team, but every team should have at least two outside ringers to help out in a pinch.

MANAGEMENT BY STUMBLING AROUND

Stage 5 marks the rise of a widespread need for teams to coordinate projects involving managers, other teams, and other parts of the organization. Just how confusing these projects can be is illustrated by recent events in a company that builds CD scanning systems. A team found itself behind schedule on a major order, so the production manager unilaterally decided to order Japanese circuits boards to replace the domestic boards the team was having trouble with. The Japanese boards didn't work either, unfortunately, and had to be scrapped. So the team failed to make the deadline, blamed the manager for ordering parts without their approval, and ended up taking the heat anyway since it was their responsibility to meet the deadline. Snafus like this stem from ambiguities inherent in projects involving distinct parts of the organization—teams coordinating with managers, other teams, or technical support groups. Who owns the project? Who provides input? Sometimes the teams have final authority, sometimes they don't, but in each case roles and responsibilities need to be mapped out in advance.

Since the teams during Stage 5 are essentially groups of co-equal self-managers, every team member will need special skills—management skills—for coordinating people, activities, and resources not directly under team control. Focused training should therefore give the teams a coherent approach to setting objectives, securing approvals, planning action steps, budgeting, scheduling, making assignments, and monitoring the progress of cross-team projects.

As new people come aboard and as the teams take on new activities and strive for loftier goals, ongoing and energetic training is an absolute must.

TAILOR SYSTEMS TO SUPPORT
THE TEAMS' PRODUCTIVITY

By Stage 5, it's time that planning and control systems do more than merely coexist with self-directed teams. "My vision is you've got to provide extraordinary service, and to do that you've got to reorganize the entire workplace," says Al Ilg, former town manager of Windsor, Connecticut, and the powerhouse behind one of the few public sector agencies to implement teams. "It isn't just in one little shop," he continues. "I'm convinced now that the whole administrative structure has to be realigned to take full advantage of these self-directed teams."

Assuming that your entire operating unit (company, division, plant, or office) is moving toward self-direction, a concerted effort to match all systems to the teams pays off now in several important ways:

- The major drag on team productivity in Stage 5 is usually external—archaic systems jury-rigged to support (or at least tolerate) self-direction. With compatible systems, however, productivity can grow like a well-watered houseplant.

- The way the teams conduct their business has settled into relatively stable patterns. You can therefore make substantial changes now without fear of having to revamp the same systems in the near future.

- And finally, since later generations of teams are usually better off following the trail hacked out by the first teams, hospitable systems clearly mark the route and encourage new teams to stay out of treacherous territory.

A major systems overhaul has at least three aims: creating team awareness of strategic planning, creating executive awareness of operational planning, and creating team-friendly systems and procedures.

YOU SHOW ME YOUR PLANS, AND I'LL SHOW YOU MINE

Without reaching the "codetermination" mandated in some European companies (see page 30), many American companies do give their mature teams access to information bearing on strategic planning—particularly data on customer needs and expectations. When executives in an industrial equipment plant wanted to manufacture a pump customers could "use to death" and throw away, they immediately informed the teams of their decision in order to prevent the possible perception among workers of a decline in desired product quality. Once team members understood that the new pump was aimed at a specific market need, they came up with several innovative ideas on designing and building a disposable product.

By Stage 5, when the teams are getting intimately involved in operational planning, executives must make a special effort to stay on top of what and how the teams are doing. In a midwestern textile operation, for example, team representatives and managers meet weekly to plan operations. At the executive end, the manufacturing vice president, who understands the value of operational data in strategic planning, has established an executive review board—at whose monthly, day-long meetings key mid-managers report on team activities, objectives, and outcomes. It's common in many organizations to see team members and executives updating and briefing each other directly.

One high-profile indicator of the growing popularity of this reciprocal awareness of strategic and operational planning can be seen in the annual reports of some leading-edge companies. These glossy brochures (a window on the importance companies ascribe to current objectives and activities) now commonly include paragraphs on mission statements and the effects of employee involvement on strategic and operational planning.

TEAM-FRIENDLY SYSTEMS

Many systems and procedures in a conventional company not only fail to support self-direction, they actively block it. Over the years, departments evolve in order to manage the various systems (information, inventory, accounting, compensation, staffing, etc.) and for many reasons these departments set up safeguards to prevent access by anyone except their own experts. An information systems group retains exclusive rights over computer hardware, software, and passwords; an accounting group controls allocations and reporting, which in turn profoundly affect scheduling. The point is that many systems exist to make life easier for the experts, not to make frontline people more productive. Unless these conditions change, work-team productivity can fall victim to narrow, self-perpetuating systems that no longer make sense in a team environment.

Where is the balance between prudent control and easy access? How much should you depend on experts and how much on the do-it-yourself projects of the teams? These are the hard questions you must ask, and ask frequently, to cut yourself free of outdated systems that can weigh down the productivity of the teams.

Headed by Vice President Harlan Oelklaus, the Centrilift human resources team set about pruning one of the thornier systems in any organization, compensation and promotion—in this case, as it affected teams of field service technicians. Like most places, Centrilift's outlying service centers set pay and made promotions based on length of service and supervisor recommendations. But supervisors used vague and inconsistent criteria, and sometimes there was no discernible relationship between rewards and the employee behaviors the company wanted to encourage.

Oelklaus and his group began their analysis by identifying the team member behaviors that did or could promote responsible self-management. Then they defined the skills and knowledge that would make these behaviors more likely. Since members of these teams needed flexible, positive relationships with customers and peers, Oelklaus mapped out criteria for success in four categories:

1. Technical skills.
2. Work habits.
3. Interpersonal skills (as used with customers and with peers).
4. Project management (including project completion).

The human resource team then developed a set of objectives and testable and/or observable behaviors for each criterion and tied them to four levels of expertise—trainee, technician, specialist, and technical adviser. The resulting pay and promotion system visibly and rationally supported the purposes of self-direction.

During Stage 5, the organization needs to rethink every management system as Oelklaus rethought compensation and promotion: by establishing objectives and standards compatible with self-direction, by devising ways to verify conformance, by giving the teams ample authority and resources to correct deviations, and by building in reinforcement and rewards to sustain success.

RESETTING YOUR DEFAULTS

A training specialist in a New England plant had an awkward moment recently while teaching a group of teams how to use a new feature in the computer system. As she attempted to call up the current production schedule forecast, she got only the curt message: "Access Blocked." Later, when she inquired about this new kink, she found out that the corporate mainframe at a remote location required a password made available only to managers. Teams had not been allowed access to the password because they had no responsibilities that the MIS group officially recognized.

Similar events occur every day in other companies lke this one well into Stage 5 of the transition to teams. The problem? Teams run across something in one of the formal systems that blocks their progress. Most teams find ways around these glitches, but, even so, productivity is hampered, and the teams are reminded that they're still "experimental."

As self-direction spreads throughout an organization, managers and planners must make it as natural as possible for the teams to do some things differently. In a word, they must "institutionalize" changes that promote the effectiveness of the teams (e.g., giving teams access to essential production data). To institutionalize simply means to make the new ways the predictable action that will occur by default, as it were, if no other action is specifically requested. Otherwise, as self-direction spreads, so also will mismatches and frustration. The teams will be fighting the system and wasting time and resources better spent on producing quality goods and services. (For further details, see "Diffusion Strategies," pages 361–363).

IMPROVE INTERNAL CUSTOMER/ SUPPLIER PARTNERSHIPS

Before Stage 5—even with continued training—most companies achieve no more than efficient, civil dealings between internal customers and internal suppliers. But now that the teams understand their mutual dependence in attaining mutual goals, managers can achieve significant gains by handing off total responsibility to the teams for managing their own customer/supplier partnerships.

THE POWER OF CROSS-TEAM PARTNERSHIPS

Figure 8-1 illustrates how self-directed teams depend on each other to achieve the most fundamental of strategic objectives: meeting the needs and exceeding the expectations of external customers.

The large box represents the company as a whole—any company that receives materials or services from an external supplier and creates final products or services for an external customer. Inside the box, each figure represents one team, which is both an internal customer and an internal supplier to other teams. The light arrows show the flow of information about needs and expectations from customers to suppliers. The dark arrows show the flow of products and services from suppliers to customers.

For the company as a whole to meet the needs of external customers, each team has to meet the needs of its own internal

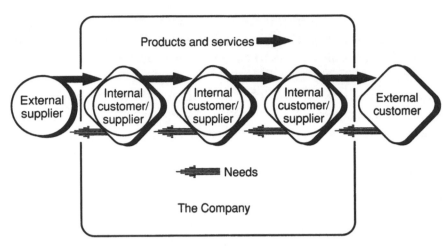

FIGURE 8-1. Team partnerships

customers, that is, other teams. Teams can never be truly self-directed until they take charge of these matters, for until they do take charge, outsiders must intervene to settle any serious cross-team issues.

The Principles of Partnership

Earlier, team members established strong ties within their teams. Now they must maintain those key relationships and develop new relationships with their internal customers' and suppliers' teams, through clarification of mutual expectations, and sometimes through exchanges of personnel. Regardless of the context, all of these interactions yield better results when they adhere to several important principles of interpersonal behavior:

Focus on the Work Process, Issue, or Behavior, Not on the Person.   When something goes wrong, it's easy to blame the person who appears at fault. Team members who concentrate on the work itself—processes, issues, or observable behaviors—tend to avoid the personal attacks that can destroy any chance for mutual gain.

Maintain the Self-Confidence and Self-Esteem of Others. People who treat each other as if they have little to contribute usually contribute very little. Even when the situation is rugged, team customers and suppliers must emerge feeling good about how they were handled. The habit of giving praise where it is due encourages a continued positive effort and smooths the interactions within and among the teams.

Maintain Strong Partnerships with Internal and External Customers and Suppliers. To grasp their role in the overall corporate effort, team members must understand that the quality of their internal partnerships is directly proportional to the quality of products and services delivered to the external customer.

Take Initiative to Improve Work Processes and Partnerships. The point of view expressed in the old saw "If it ain't broke, don't fix it" normally fades during the transition to full self-direction. People come to see that everything has room for improvement—even if it *ain't* broke. Behaviors reflecting this principle are the foundation for continuous improvement through cooperative effort, proactive problem solving, and technical innovation.

Lead by Example. By Stage 5, every team member is a leader, and every leader must make the actions match the theory of responsible self-direction. By their own example of cultivating strong working partnerships, individual team members can redouble the efforts of their counterparts.

INFORMATION, GIVER OF LIFE

Technology has made it possible to provide information quickly. This enables the teams to make effective business decisions. At

Marlin-Rockwell in Gainesville, Georgia, the director of manufacturing achieved outstanding success by giving people the technical data they needed to solve technical problems. On a prominent wall, each of the seven teams posted individualized results by the month, week, day, and shift, with a special section devoted to cross-team effects. The teams might ask managers for further information, but the teams themselves ironed out any mismatch between customer needs and supplier capabilities. In this way, information and a studied effort to focus on the work, not the person, prevented autonomy from turning into anarchy, customer-supplier issues from turning into customer-supplier conflict. This process remained vital through the years because the teams got factual, relevant, concise data, not preaching, hidden messages, and stacks of printouts to be sifted for the two lines that mattered. The process worked so well, in fact, that when computer access made it less critical to update the communication walls every shift, the teams still chose to keep them active.

In contrast, it was lack of information during Stage 5 that wrecked the transitions in a midwestern electronics facility. Support functions like accounting and production control, by holding on to old attitudes, remained outside watch dogs on the teams, made no effort to expand their traditional role, and continued hoarding information the teams needed to solve their own customer-supplier problems. Putting the right data in the right hands is the main challenge in handing off customer-supplier issues to the teams. But until a company learns that everyone profits from open communication, the teams will need trusting friends at the top to keep information useful, honest, and free-flowing.

KNOW THY CUSTOMER

Tim Miller, formerly of Suburu-Isuzu in Lafayette, Indiana, neatly summarized the ultimate purpose of strong customer-supplier ties. "My vision for this company," he says, "was that associates [team members] responded to you not in terms of title, but in terms of customer-supplier relationships. The only way to wean their customers away was to meet or exceed expectations in every way—both inside and outside of the plant." Do team members need direct contact with external customers? "Certainly!" says Miller. "I saw that in time part of an associate's life was that maybe every two years you spent a week in a dealership, with people who are looking to buy cars and bringing in their cars to be serviced. This is my whole point about the customer. You cannot allow something to go out the door that is junk. You cannot afford to let things go down the line that end up having to be reworked. So for people to think in those terms—and to see their team in those terms—I think that is the core of whether or not we were going to succeed."

ACT OUT SELF-DIRECTION DAILY

The key to prosperity through self-direction is managers who give teams what they need to make and implement decisions within their range of expertise. In that respect, no one is more critical than the "area managers" or "superintendents" (see pages 98 and 196), who link the teams to the larger organization for purposes of performance review, compensation, feedback, and final approvals. Together, these people are indispensable to the long-term survival of self-direction. They sponsor the teams, champion their ideas, secure needed resources, and in turn look good or bad depending on the teams' performance. Unless they deeply believe in self-direction and act out their beliefs every day, no transition can long endure.

What can these people do to support the teams? Corporate TRW explored this question with a poll of 22 teams well into Stage 5—a poll that produced the following list of key management behaviors wanted by the teams:

1. "Spend more time with us."
2. "Don't try to make our decisions."
3. "Get our input on management decisions."
4. "Give us credit when we deserve it, hell when we mess up on standards, and training when we need it."
5. "Improve our pay as we improve our profits."

These and other comments indicated that the teams thrived on the very responsibilities that managers often seemed reluctant to hand over—although the teams made it clear they neither wanted nor expected to function without management.

A parallel poll in the same company revealed that mid-managers wanted their bosses above all to delegate duties to fill the void left when the teams assumed control of daily operations. In response to the polls, executives acknowledged their own need to let go and authorized a hand-off plan, similar to the plan for supervisors and teams, to govern the transfer of responsibilities among all levels of management. This plan addressed the major concern of the teams (mid-managers unwilling to delegate) by addressing the major concern of mid-managers (executives unwilling to delegate).

The lesson here is that self-direction endures only when all participants clearly perceive direct benefits to themselves. And, from the executive perspective, the best way to motivate behaviors that support self-direction is to delegate the powers that mid-managers need to play a constructive, active, and valued role in the overall effort.

"FLOWERS FOR ALGERNON"

Given the right leaders, the right managers, the right teams, and the right systems, how long can Stage 5 last? Nobody really knows. Since 1973, self-directed teams have invigorated quality, productivity, and sales at Cummins Engine; since 1963 they've done the same at Procter & Gamble. But no matter how carefully you manicure your system, no matter how thoroughly you train and reinforce your managers and teams, no one is immune to cataclysm. One small plant, for years a model of enlightened self-direction, is a case in point.

During a decline in market demand for the goods produced by this operation, its parent company merged with another company, and the new parent promptly assumed primary control of the plant. When the long-time local manager got the axe about six months later, self-direction in the plant sustained a mortal blow. New management looked around and said, "Yes, you've been one of the most profitable operations we have, but once you're straightened out, you'll be a gold mine." New hard-wall offices appeared, along with new middle managers to sit in them, and much of the work force got their walking papers. Despondent survivors, caught in the throes of the Algernon syndrome, still managed an occasional wry laugh. "Don't forget," they would say in passing, "meetings cost us 88 cents per minute per person."

What's the moral here? Earthquakes hit, airplanes collide, markets dry up, and mergers sometimes crush visionary operations. Anyone who wants to build a monument to self-direction had best take out some earthquake insurance; when it comes to innovation, there's no such thing as terra firma. But even in the stark light of that sobering truth, if conditions are right and if you're willing and able to stick out the five stages of transition, odds are good that you can make self-direction pay off in your organization. And if you're just a little bit lucky, it could pay off in spades.

NEW HORIZONS FOR WORK TEAMS

All over the country, executives and managers involved in self-direction are telling a remarkably similar story. They speak of new levels of productivity, new commitment among workers, and new optimism about meeting the challenges of global competition. There is also surprising agreement about the major *internal* challenges of moving to self-direction:

- Overcoming the tradition of recognition and reward based primarily on individual as opposed to team effort.
- Easing the fears of executives and managers about what will happen when they seemingly "lose control" of day-to-day operations.
- Reducing mistrust between management and employees and building employee commitment to corporate objectives.
- Making sure the teams get the information they need in order to manage their own affairs.
- Keeping everyone focused on the objectives, rather than on the teams themselves.

Despite these similar challenges in every organization moving to teams, executives and managers agree on one other point as well. "There's no magic solution, no recipe, no map," says a human resources manager with Northern Telecom, "except for the very basics of your values: pride in ownership, quality in a product, and continually asking the question, 'Why do we do something the way we do it?'"

If you've read this far, chances are you're still thinking about the advisability of self-directed teams in your organization, and that's good, since no book in itself is basis enough for that decision. According to those who've done it, a critical step in making your decision is observing self-direction for yourself. "Visit a number of organizations that are doing it," says Ed O'Brien, Director of Human Resources, Corning International. "Take people with you—union representatives, cynics as well as supporters, people from all levels of the organization. Don't make it just a top management type of thing. Go, be open-minded, listen, and observe." Further, as former Northern Telecom Vice President of Human Resources John Hofmeister pointed out, anyone starting or thinking about starting teams "ought to read continuously about the experiences of others, about what's working and what's not. I don't mean superficial magazine articles," he said, "but well-researched academic articles that get into serious analysis of human behavior. Whoever undertakes [self-directed teams] had better understand that they just bought themselves an incredible new library. And if they don't read what's in it, they're going to have problems."

But before you schedule a site visit or begin reviewing the literature (see "Bibliography," pages 365–375), you may find it enlightening to hear the observations and advice of a number of executives and managers who have already decided to move forward with teams.

HERE TODAY, HERE TOMORROW

Virtually everyone successfully involved with self-directed teams will tell you point blank, and repeatedly: "This is not a fad." Certainly you've heard this line before; people say the same thing about whatever the current push happens to be. But in this case there may be more substantive reasons to believe them. "I attended a session last week with the Association for Quality and Participation," says Jerry Laubenstein, former vice president of insurance services with Aid Association for Lutherans (AAL), a fraternal benefit society and one of the most unique and successful insurance operations in the country. "There were something like 400 folks there who are involved in teams—companies of all sizes, from General Motors to AAL and others. Also, at the Work in America meetings I've attended, the companies involved in teams are very significant organizations—the Boeings, the Ford Motor companies, the Miller breweries, the General Electrics. They're all moving in that direction, and I don't see them moving that way because it's the latest management craze. It's too expensive and too much of a risk to move to self-managing teams lightly. You can experiment with quality circles and if you don't gain a lot, neither will you lose a lot. When you restructure, you're making quite a commitment."

Like Laubenstein, many other executives distinguish between a fad and a new approach they see as integral to their long-term competitive advantage. "You can never let your commitment wane," according to Bob Schmitt, the former director of operations for TRW's engines components group. "Otherwise, the teams fall apart, just like your quality circles, and you're right back where you started—what's the next acronym, what's the next brochure."

Even companies only recently involved in teams see self-direction as a permanent change in their basic mode of operation. "Since we're at the very early stages, relatively speaking," says Ed O'Brien of Corning, "I see 20 years of continuous challenge. The global marketplace and global competition and global expectations are changing at such a rapid rate that we will have to continue pushing. So I just don't see any end to changes and new challenges coming up."

CHANGING THE CORPORATE CULTURE

They read about it and saw it before they began; they experienced it directly within a few months of start-up; and when you talk to them down the line, these executives will tell you that the biggest challenge of implementing teams is making the profound changes necessary for self-direction to succeed.

"First of all, you're trying to change structure," says Laubenstein of AAL, "and that's a significant change for employees who have worked in a functional hierarchy for years and years. That's a difficult transition for many. The other thing is you're changing a culture from recognizing and rewarding the individual to recognizing and rewarding team output. That, too, was a difficult transition. We've been operating since 1902, and when we made the move to self-managing teams in 1987, we made major changes in the way we do business. The cultural change—that's the big impact on people."

Ed O'Brien of Corning tells a similar story: "For us, work teams have been a revolutionary new concept. It means we change the entire structure, a structure that has not fundamentally changed within Corning since 1945. Now we see a radically new way of doing things, which eliminates layer after layer in the old chain of command. The ultimate that we've seen is our new plant in Blacksburg, West Virginia. It was a greenfield operation, so we started it the way we wanted to, and in essence they have only three layers of people in that entire plant: the plant manager, the operating committee, and almost everyone else. When we have to retrofit, it's a much slower, more tedious process. But we're making good progress."

It may be some consolation to know that the problems and principal steps in changing a corporate culture seem to be the same all over the world. "Virtually every one of our operations has work teams in one form or another," says Bob Schmitt of TRW. "I could point you to operations in Brazil, Germany, France, the United States, England—all using the basic concept that leads them toward self-direction. In my mind, they are not significantly different, other than the language. We have operations in France that have taken off on their own under a good manager who brought them from a loss to a profit as a result of the basic concepts—work teams, just-in-time, improvement of quality. The manager was a leader, and understood. That was the key difference. The location is secondary."

In a staunchly traditional company, self-direction eventually requires nothing less than total role transformation for everyone except the "naturals," those who encouraged employee involvement even under the old regime. "My role hasn't changed that much," says Jerry Laubenstein, "but the first-line manager's role has changed significantly. In the current environment, first-line managers are no longer decision makers in day-to-day operational issues. They find themselves coaching, facilitating, and what we call 'boundary bashing'—opening the way for employees to do something different. The manager is still providing overall corporate direction to the teams, but the teams are now deciding how they're going to do their work and who is going to do it. They schedule their own time, the manager no longer does that. They schedule their own overtime, the manager no longer does that. They schedule their own vacations, the manager no longer does that. So I think the significant cultural change in management has been for the first-line manager."

FEAR OF FLYING

A principal reason many organizations choose not to implement teams is the fear, in certain cases justified, that first-line employees will fail to make and carry out effective decisions. Advocates of employee involvement may bluntly charge that management is simply unwilling to yield operational control. But most executives with wide experience in self-direction have come to grips with this much-feared loss of control. "In the final analysis, [executives] control very little now," according to John Hofmeister, the person responsible for implementing the first work teams at GE (in the 11 Motor Business plants). "Most control in a large organization is an illusion," he continues. "People basically follow habit, so control is an ebb and flow process. If the workers have respect for the people leading them, and the people leading them know how to use their influence skills to obtain correct behaviors, control is a non-issue. As a safeguard [when you go to work teams], you have to establish that there continues to be responsibility and accountability at various levels of the organization. [At Northern Telecom,] we're shifting those accountabilities and responsibilities, but in the final analysis we're not shifting them away from the chief executive on the site."

Bob Schmitt, formerly of TRW, concurs with that view and adds a further point:

> Managers who understand where they fit and where the teams fit never give up true responsibility or control. And in fact, when you give more responsibilities to individuals, you have more time to manage the business. You don't have to count pencils and calendar pads. You're out looking to increase the market share, to improve the products, to increase the probabilities of being competitive through teams. You're beginning to see what's happening with the workflows, the through-put times, the quality. You're seeing the profits increase as a result of the reduction of scrap and rework and the increased concentration of people. You deal with questions like "What's the next level of training?" and "Do I have to put in gain-sharing?" You're managing a business, not each individual operation, and you're going to direct the mission far better now than if you paid attention to all the details on the floor. If managers don't understand that process, they're going to have difficulty installing teams.

THE POWER OF THE VISION

Whether they're former skeptics or lifelong believers in what Corning calls "partnership in the workplace," most executives who have overseen organizational transformation through self-directed teams now marvel at the power of employee involvement.

"In a conventional system, the employee can be taken advantage of," says Al Ilg, former town manager of Windsor, Connecticut, and widely considered the top town manager in the country. "They're given work that is unfulfilling, that they're not proud of. The result is they spend eight hours and they consider it an interruption in their leisure time. I really believe the people on the shop floor and front line deserve better. They just deserve it. They deserve to be treated like adults, and they haven't been.

I think it's about time we stopped asking people to check their brain at the door."

For years, Ilg managed a traditional city government, and for years he wondered how he could motivate public sector employees to superior performance. "They just didn't have pride under the hierarchy," he continues. "There's very little concern for the customer in the typical bureaucracy. Self-managing teams gave us a way to respond to customer complaints, very quickly, because the person who is doing the job is the one who's going to respond. That was what drove it—what we call delighting the customer. The employee has the power to deal with that complaint immediately. The employee responds, and the employee is proud of what they accomplished because they get the feedback directly from the customer. And we get supervisors the hell out of the way of the transaction. We're moving management, one way or another, out of the way. Traditional management is the problem, rather than the solution, and for 28 years I always thought it was the solution. Now I find out it's not."

Ilg is a practical man, vitally concerned with bottom-line numbers and with satisfying both external customers (the citizens of the local community) and internal customers (elected officials and city employees). But if pressed, he will sometimes talk about the underpinnings of his approach. "There is a spiritual element to this whole thing, frankly. You've got to have a vision, and you've got to have a purpose. If you think about religious leaders, they had no real power except the vision. They convinced people to follow that vision with anecdotes and stories and metaphors and parables. Then they turned to those people and said, 'It's up to you.' They didn't tell them how to do it. There's very much of that in this—the overarching vision and then getting people charged up to go out and do it. The power in the person who has the vision is the vision itself."

THE FUTURE OF TEAMS

While self-direction is no fad, no shallow catch-phrase, neither is it an end in itself. From all accounts, self-directed work teams are one of the most effective tools now available, given the needs of contemporary workers and the current state of the world market, for tapping the unrealized potential of America's organizations. Even so, the distant future will undoubtedly bring something new. "All industries go through cycles," says Bob Schmitt, "so there may be a recombining [of our basic concepts—work teams, just-in-time, and quality improvement], I don't know. But our mission is to find out what works best, and that mission will be here forever."

John Hofmeister, who saw and helped GE to realize the potential of work teams long before their current popularity, makes that same point even more explicitly: "The issue is broader than work teams or [employee] participation. The issue is ultimately organizational capability. What are the mechanisms by which an organization achieves its optimum capability? What the excitement about work teams represents is a release of energy that comes from increased democratization and egalitarianism. If you release that energy, you have now obtained more capability. Your organization is now doing more things with the same input. That's a whole lot more than just an increase in morale; it's an actual increase in productivity."

But what's the next step beyond teams? Hofmeister continues:

> If you approach it from the standpoint of "How do we achieve optimal organizational capability," then in today's workplace, high levels of employee participation are an improvement. As time goes on, I think we'll move beyond the fascination with work teams—I'm talking 25 to 50 years from now—to the next plateau, which may well be more individualism as opposed to collectivism in the workplace. With new skills and new competencies, people will begin to achieve more and more as individuals. With more technology, and more emphasis on information, there will be less interest in teams and more concern in how the individual can achieve optimal capability. These individuals, with increased competence, can work in larger and larger teams. Eventually we may get to a point where in a 300-person plant, the only manager is the plant manager. It's going to take an incredible amount of organizational learning, and a whole new generation of people to achieve that kind of

end point. It's a fascinating process in global organization today, but the end point is not work teams. Work teams are one tool to achieve greater organizational capability.

What the future holds for the team concept or American industry no one can say for certain. What the present holds is growing more apparent every day: Self-directed work teams are helping more and more companies to liberate and focus the energy, the commitment, and the old-fashioned Yankee know-how that make the American people what they are.

SPECIAL WORK-TEAM ISSUES

THE PHILOSOPHY
OF TEAMS

L et us now turn our attention to another dimension of teams—the conceptual or philosophical framework that supports their creation, development, and maintenance. As the team concept catches on, managers are having to challenge long-held assumptions that no longer seem valid in light of the behavior and thinking of self-directed teams.

Managers are often willing to sign up for the opening chapter of a team initiative. But more often than not, they want to bring teams into a particular area without considering the teams' long-term implications—for the entire organization and over the long haul. However, it is important that organizations consider these long-term implications *before* they begin. Failure to do so will endanger the long-term sustainability of teams. When teams suffer losing battles in their efforts to get off the ground, it's due in part because managers are laboring under three common misperceptions regarding self-directed work teams:

- Employees (and team members) know their place, and "managers" are somehow in a position to define their place for them.

- Teams do not require a different way of looking at the work.

Note: This chapter is based on the writing and thinking of Seth McCutcheon, Managing Partner, Domicile, Raleigh, NC.

- Management alone is responsible for the well-being of the business and accountable for the results.

These assumptions must be challenged and defeated before a self-directed team environment can become fully functional and sustainable.

ASSUMPTION: EMPLOYEES KNOW THEIR PLACE BECAUSE MANAGERS DEFINE THEIR PLACE FOR THEM

As the world shifted from an agrarian-based economy to an industrially based economy in the early part of the century, workers flocked to the cities to find work in the burgeoning factories. As a general rule, these workers could neither read nor write. Numbers and measures were largely alien to them. Their focus never wandered outside their minuscule piece of the work process; in fact, the idea of a work *process* would have been totally meaningless and incomprehensible, since it was of no concern to any worker what occurred upstream before the work reached his machine or after it left it. Workers mechanically performed repetitive tasks in an environment alien to all they had known from their agrarian existence.

Under such conditions, no business would have even considered asking employees to make decisions on behalf of the business. It was far better that they perform a simple task and perform it the same way over and over for as long as possible without interruption. Any conversation with another worker was simply a distraction, and independent decisions were not allowed. This concept of the worker as a simple cog in the machinery lay at the foundation of the management theories advanced by Frederick Taylor, the father of scientific management.

The years from 1870 to 1920 were also a period that witnessed the emergence of the professional middle class. Managers represented the owners or the interests of capital, and because of their unquestioned allegiance, they inevitably forged an adversarial relationship between themselves and the workers. Barbara Enrenreich, author of *The Fear of Falling,* depicts this time as:

> a period of violent clashes between the working class and its traditional antagonist, the capitalist class. In strike after strike—from the coal fields of Tennessee to the mines of Colorado to the mills of Massachusetts—workers confronted the armed power of capital or its proxy, the National Guard. In the 1880s the Knights of Labor, with 700,000 members, declared that "the attitude of the Order to the existing industrial system is necessarily one of war." In the 1900s, the revolutionary Industrial Workers of the World attracted a million members; and the Socialist Party's Eugene V. Debs won 900,000 votes in the presidential election of 1912. Throughout this period, the knee-jerk capitalist response was repression: armed guards to break strikes, beatings, jailings, and lynchings to crush the militant leadership of the working class.[1]

The fact that workers were capable of thinking on their own *was* a negative. If they could think, then they might well think of insurrection. If they controlled the process of production, they were then in a position to slow or stop it. The logical answer, then, was to define the roles of manager and worker in a way that removed these liabilities.

WHAT WAS THE ROLE OF THE MANAGER IN THIS NEW ENVIRONMENT?

The role of the professional manager was to perform the mental work and to control those who performed the manual labor. Under scientific management the objective of managers was to reduce the work to simple, repetitive tasks that could be performed as rapidly and as many times as possible. Employees knew better than to argue or disagree with those who were paid to do all the thinking. They also quickly recognized the manager as someone who did not represent their best interests.

Not only was the thinking of the new professional manager shaped by this organizational philosophy; it was also shaped by the expectations of the business owners. The manager was typically under enormous pressure to produce as much as possible and as quickly as possible, and it was unequivocally clear that although managers produced nothing themselves, they were fully accountable for all that was turned out. Given this way of conceptualizing work, it was inevitable that managers would break work into the simplest tasks that could be mastered by the worker and then turn those fragmented tasks into jobs.

In addition, managers were responsible for all the other ancillary activities related to production, such as buying raw materials, making deals with suppliers, forging agreements with customers, building plant sites or additions, and purchasing capital equipment. Typically the manager's work took place in a stable business community where competition was limited or nonexistent, where markets could grow with little or no bounds, and where change occurred slowly and predictably.

Now let us spring forward to the 1990s. The nature of workers has changed dramatically. The average hourly employee does in fact read and write and has some if not considerable facility with numbers. He or she most likely manages a household budget, maintains and balances a checking account, decides where to send the children to school, negotiates car purchases and mortgage loans, and makes investments in securities. The sophistication and complexity of skill and thought of the industrial worker today is light-years ahead of what it was at the time the foundations of organizational thought were institutionalized.

The role of the service employee is an even more radical departure from the portrait of the worker created during the industrial revolution. Yet if you look at the modern service environment, you will see that many of the work and management practices of white-collar jobs are a holdover from another era. Though we hire skilled and educated people, we create "paper mills" using principles and work practices lifted right from heavy industry—a system predicated on uneducated workers who perform best if given simple, fragmented tasks.

Today's business world bears little resemblance to that of our grandfathers. Competitors appear and disappear overnight. Regional players become global giants. Markets become fickle and saturated. Change occurs at breakneck pace, leaving managers to wonder if long-range planning is even possible. Yet the changes that occurred in the role of management have been considerably smaller, and as a consequence, little is different in how the employee is defined. There is still a sharp division between those who think and those who do. Managers are still managers. Employees are still employees. And the boundaries remain firm and impregnable.

ASSUMPTION: TEAMS DO NOT REQUIRE A DIFFERENT WAY OF LOOKING AT THE WORK

The second assumption that controls current-day thinking is rooted in a patriarchal mentality. Assumption of power and control is seen as being the right of those who raised the capital, but it is predicated on a society in which the purchase of additional or newer capital equipment or the building of new or larger facilities is the surest means of prosperity and competitive advantage.

Such an assumption is no longer valid. Just as the rules of thought from an agrarian-based society held no sway in the industrial era, so do the rules of thought that served as a sound basis for business during the industrial era hold no sway in the information era. Peter Drucker said it well when he proclaimed that "we are entering the knowledge society in which the basic economic resource is no longer capital, but it is and will be knowledge."

In *Beyond Reengineering*, Michael Hammer suggests that the capabilities of high technology and robotics have removed from the labor force the necessity of performing repetitive tasks that can be performed more precisely and predictably by automation.[2] Therefore, more work shifts toward knowledge work; and the ability to share, tap, and profit from the collective knowledge of the organization has ultimately become the final arbiter of competitiveness. When you begin to conceive of employees as repositories of knowledge, rather than performers of tasks, then the notion of teams begins to take on a new meaning.

Teams represent the natural vehicle for the sharing and exchange of information supportive of successful task completion and customer fulfillment.

ONE CRAFTSMAN DID IT ALL

If we track back to the time before the industrial revolution, we would find that manufacturing was done by artisans and craftsmen working either alone or in small groups. Typically one person handled the entire work process. That is to say, if a group of craftsmen turned out chairs, then each person in the craft group made a full chair. One did not make legs, another the seats, another the backs, and so forth. It was likely that each person was personally acquainted with the customer for whom he was making the chair and had heard the customer's requirements firsthand. Furthermore, it was most likely that the craftsman who turned the chair over to the customer upon completion also received final feedback and received the money. There was no fragmentation of the job. The craftsman conducted the entire process—from the ordering and receiving of raw materials to the delivery and collection.

The industrial revolution changed all that. According to scientific management the job should now be broken into simple, repetitive tasks. One person working at a lathe would now turn legs all day. Another would sand, another polish, and another attach and glue the legs to the body of the chair. There was no need for anyone to talk to anyone else. If someone had a problem with the quality or quantity of work done by the person in the line before him, he addressed such matters to his supervisor, who "owned" the process. All decisions were made by the manager, and all communications were handled by him.

Is there any set of conditions that could conceivably be more unnatural? Could the worker possibly be more estranged? Of course, given the lengthy, complex processes necessary to create sophisticated outputs, whether it be building a telephone switching system or processing an insurance claim, it is unrealistic to assume that we can ever hope to return to a "natural" working environment where a single individual conducts the entire process.

But teams come close. Teams are the set of human linkages that makes it possible for a group of people, working in concert, to rejoin the fragments, own the product, handle the communication and decision making, and hold each other mutually accountable for satisfying the customer.

When you provide a group of people with a common goal that relies on their shared abilities and knowledge, employee involvement becomes a naturally occurring phenomenon. It is not an artificial structure imposed over the task. People naturally gravitate toward solving problems and finding solutions; and in a supportive environment, they are quick to share knowledge, information, opinions, and perspectives.

Yet in most organizations, even some of those that are implementing self-directed teams, old beliefs and attitudes prevail. These organizations create a work environment for employees where:

- No meaningful information about their individual performance or the performance of the business is readily available.

- Employees are hired by managers without ever meeting, being interviewed by, or even being introduced to their peers.

- People receive raises that are not tied to individual-, team-, or business-based performance.

- Groups of employees talking or sharing ideas is viewed as a waste of time.

- Questions and problems come from employees, and answers and solutions come from managers.

- Success is defined as promotion to management versus continued growth in depth and breadth of knowledge and skill.

Although many companies today espouse employee involvement, it is common for their internal business systems (communication, compensation, performance appraisal) and support systems (recognition, recruitment, private washrooms, and reserved parking spaces) to continue to echo century-old thinking.

ASSUMPTION: MANAGEMENT ALONE IS RESPONSIBLE FOR THE WELL-BEING OF THE BUSINESS AND ACCOUNTABLE FOR THE RESULTS

It is fair to say that if the manager is charged with carrying full responsibility and accountability for the results, then the employee is not. Yet ironically, though many managers do not wish to give up their traditional duties, which they view as badges of their professional status and professional-class distinction, they can be quick to lament the fact that their employees don't feel a sense of accountability and responsibility.

In a true self-directed team-based organization, managers are accountable, but not for the results. They are accountable for developing teams. This does not simply mean saying nice things about teams and calling for team meetings. It means helping to map out plans that will enable the teams to meet clear team goals that the managers help set. It means managers are accountable for defining specific measurable standards that will serve as guideposts for various levels of technical, administrative, and interpersonal skill development, and then holding themselves and the teams accountable for meeting those goals. It means managers are accountable for facilitating team process and for putting relevant information on the table and teaching teams how to read and analyze that information.

It also means managers must be accountable for providing timely and appropriate intervention in the event the team falters. Managers must learn to carefully gauge when to step in and when not to and how much direction to provide when they do step in. They must learn to model and demonstrate behaviors that encourage team members to become more capable and self-reliant. In such an environment, teams quickly learn that *they* are responsible and accountable for producing results, and they willingly call upon the manager to help them develop the skills and competencies they need to meet those goals.

RECREATING THE ROLE OF THE "COMPLETE" EMPLOYEE

Employees must be rejoined with what has been taken from them—the intellectual component of work, accountability and responsibility, and the right to a sense of ownership and pride in what they do. As long as we use the label "management" to signify that which has been removed from employees, we will never be able to create "whole" employees. If a "house divided against itself cannot stand," then an employee who has given up an essential part of self cannot function at high levels. Since the ability to self-manage is what makes the employee whole, the missing piece must be rejoined. In the new paradigm, every employee must also be part manager.

And what of the manager's role? It can be redefined to mean developer of teams and employees, coach, orchestrator of resources, runner of interference. It is not simply a gentler, kinder version of the old archetype. In *Leading Self-Directed Work Teams,* Kimball Fisher poses the question this way:

> Imagine you are an anthropologist 200 years in the future who comes upon the pay plan of a major current American company. What conclusions would you draw from the ancient artifact of a company of the twentieth century? Would you find it curious that the people who actually designed, built, or delivered the products and services of the corporation were among the lowest paid people in the operation? Would that be supportive of the written corporate statement you find that says the quality and customer focus are the primary goals of the operation? Would you wonder why such a corporation reserved its lowest rewards for the people who actually touched the product and worked with customers? Would you wonder what was really important in that operation? Is it really customers and quality they value, or is it control?[3]

Rethinking our definitions turns the pre-information age concepts of "manager" and "employee" upside down. But even if the role of manager is reabsorbed into the concept of employee or team, one critical component is still missing. This is the role of "leader," and it is indispensable in an environment of "whole" employees and teams.

The Role of Leaders

The role of leaders has been passionately discussed in academic circles and in organizations for the past ten years; yet we seem to have made little progress in understanding leadership or in creating leaders in organizations of "whole" employees. The task of leadership is to create organizational meaning. Employees are drawn to and motivated by meaningful work that calls forth the best in each person and challenges them to continually raise the bar.

Business produces three primary outputs—wealth for the shareholder, value for the customer, and opportunity and security for the employee. At the same time an organization is a social and cultural entity and must answer fundamental questions for all its members, such as why are we doing what we're doing? Who cares that we are doing this, and how do those who care benefit? Where are we going in the future? Where do I as an individual fit in? How do my efforts impact others?

A significant problem arises when everyone knows *how* and no one knows *why*. If Peter Drucker is correct in saying that the final reserve of competitiveness is the ability to tap the will and abilities of the individuals who compose the organization, then overmanaged and underled companies are in serious trouble.

What we are attempting to tap is the discretionary energy of the organization. Discretionary energy is that measure of ability, knowledge, will power, and sheer force of character that can never be demanded, but must be given freely. It is that reserve of pure passion that can never be extracted, but must flow from what one believes to be worthwhile and perhaps even noble. It is that special store of energy and desire that in volunteer organizations drives people to previously unimagined levels of performance and personal and group fulfillment. Discretionary energy flows, never because the business demands it, but because the context of organizational meaning allows it. Much like creativity or artistry, we cannot force it; we can only create an environment that gives rise to its expression.

It is critical that we not delude ourselves. As managers, the choice is not whether employees will have the proper outlets and context for volunteering their discretionary energy. They will find an outlet somewhere. They may find it in church, in civic organizations, or among groups of friends, but they will find it. As managers we only get to choose whether we will create an environment with rich enough meaning that employees will be motivated give their discretionary energy in their place of work.

SUMMARY

Management was born in the fevered pitch of violent labor unrest and mass illiteracy. It looked on employees as simple cogs in the machinery. By contrast, leadership is the creation of context for "whole" employees and teams in an environment where people rise to the challenge, an environment for which they feel personally responsible and accountable. Leadership is the creation of context that includes purpose and direction and defines what it means to be a part of the organization. Leadership gives space for employees to share in the struggles and rewards of management.

"Whole" employees have discretionary energy to give which far exceeds the minimum requirement to do the job. This discretionary energy can never be demanded. It can only be freely given in full measure, and such giving only occurs in the rich context of meaning provided by leadership.

Perhaps in the early days of implementing teams it was OK to introduce teams simply to create a more participative and satisfied work force without relinquishing managerial responsibilities. Perhaps it was OK to look at "going to teams" in a strictly practical and mechanistic way. But now that our understanding of teams has matured, it is time to turn the mirror back to management and ask, "What are our unspoken assumptions? What are we truly trying to create with self-directed work teams?" One thing is clear. Self-directed teams are not just vehicles used by management to perform work. They are vehicles for organizational growth and transformation.

NOTES

1. Barbara Enrenreich, *The Fear of Falling: The Inner Life of Middle Class* (New York: Pantheon Books, 1989).

2. Michael Hammer, *Beyond Reengineering: How the Process-Centered Organization Is Changing Our Work and Our Lives* (New York: Harper Business, 1996).

3. Kimball Fisher, *Leading Self-Directed Work Teams* (New York: McGraw-Hill, 1993).

C H A P T E R

E L E V E N

DEVELOPING THE ROLE OF SUPERVISORS AND MANAGERS

Interest in self-directed work teams grew quickly in the late eighties and early nineties, and one of the factors driving that interest was the focus on white-collar productivity. Organizations rightfully concluded that too much time and resources were devoted to monitoring and controlling the behavior of front-line workers. Companies usually began their cost-cutting efforts by thinning the number of support people—those with the technical skills necessary to keep the plants and systems running efficiently. But this could only go so far before equipment and systems began running on the ragged edge. In searching for other cost-cutting opportunities, organizations realized they couldn't make further cuts in technical staff without compromising performance, so they started looking instead at the supervisors, specifically, whether many of the supervisors could be eliminated by driving ownership and decision making to the lowest levels in the organization. Now, organizations are more aware of the increases in productivity, quality, and employee satisfaction.

Organizations were eliminating the very people with the knowledge needed to empower teams. Supervisors and manag-

Note: This chapter is based on the writing and thinking of Jerry Smolek, President, Smolek Associates, Indianapolis, IN.

ers were in the best position to know what information and knowledge were needed to help teams make informed decisions. They had been making many of those decisions for years. They knew the strengths and development needs of team members and were the ones best qualified to coach teams and individuals. In addition, through their years of experience, they understood how to work the hierarchy to get what they needed. They also knew what work-arounds to employ when things did not function properly. For example, the supervisor might know that if a piece of equipment bumped a pole that had a temperature gauge mounted on it, the gauge would give a false reading. So if the plant technician were checking for heat buildup, he'd know it was always a good idea to also lay a hand on the equipment and feel for temperature rise. This was typical of the hundreds of little things that made supervisors knowledgeable guides and coaches. It was also why eliminating them often deprived the teams of a valuable resource.

But it wasn't simply the elimination of supervisors that made life difficult for teams. It was often that the supervisors were quick to develop an adversarial relationship with the very people they were supposed to manage. This was generally due to management's lack of awareness of the supervisors' unease about teams and the lack of responsiveness in addressing those concerns.

WHY SUPERVISORS RESIST

When a move to teams is not skillfully handled, supervisors are likely to start dragging their feet; and in subtle ways, they will sabotage the effort to get teams up and running. This unsupportive behavior is driven by fear and by a lack of understanding of the team environment. Here are some of the most common concerns that supervisors have:

Job security. The supervisor feels that if the team takes over more duties, his or her own job will disappear—an extremely logical conclusion when organizations are implementing teams in order to eliminate supervisors. Although supervisors delegate more responsibility and tasks to lower levels, they often feel they are working themselves out of a job. Many in management believe it's their responsibility to eliminate work and become more efficient; however, few are inclined to eliminate their own jobs.

Loss of control. When work has been delegated to a team, supervisors may not be enough in the loop to always have their finger on the status of the work. That can give supervisors a strong sense that they have lost control of the team. There are also other ways that supervisors can feel a loss of control. Team members may come up with a way of determining how the work is to be done that differs from what the supervisor would have chosen. They may assign one person to a given task, whereas the supervisor would have picked another. Or they may decide to forgo overtime to get a job completed, whereas the supervisor believes that such overtime is warranted.

Loss of prestige. Everyone in the community knows what a supervisor is. A supervisor is a *boss.* Inherent in the position is a certain status. On the other hand, friends and family do not know what a "production coordinator" or a "first-line salaried support person" is; and in a team environment, it may be difficult for the supervisor to state what he or she does for a living. For the status-conscious, this can be a bitter pill.

Loss of power. The supervisor can experience a loss of power when the team takes over the job of deciding who does a particular task, who works overtime, who may take vacation and when, and whose problem has priority. When teams are instituted, it is *they* who take on the appraisal process and decide which team members have excelled and should be accorded special recognition. Supervisors who have surrendered such symbols of power may unexpectedly find themselves fighting to regain control.

Lack of knowledge. Supervisors are frequently at a loss to know how to support the teams, because they came up through the ranks or followed a technical track and never acquired a background in management and development. This leaves them with many unanswered questions, such as—What is required to support team members' growth and development? Do teams establish goals? Do self-directed teams need measurements? What kind of training do team members need? What should they do to support the teams? What is meant by boundary management? How much guidance should they provide? What decisions should they delegate? Having so many unanswered questions makes the transition to teams forbidding; and with so much to learn, supervisors can easily fall into resistance and drag their heels.

Lack of skills. Another way that supervisors feel helpless has to do with a lack of team-based skills. It is often unclear to the supervisor how he or she is supposed to work with the teams. Precisely what does a coach do, or a facilitator? How do you train people in problem solving or interpersonal skills? How do you go about helping teams set goals without actually setting the goals for them? How do you resolve conflict between team members or between teams? How do you diagnose dysfunctional teams? Although supervisors need the proper skills to counsel, train, coach, facilitate, build, and nurture teams, it is often unclear precisely how they are supposed to acquire these skills. They may also fear that they will be unable to develop the additional skills necessary to further their own career.

Lack of measurements. Will supervisors be measured on the output of teams or on the actions they take to develop the teams? Under the traditional hierarchy, supervisors are measured on the output of their area. If they meet or surpass projections, their bonus is forthcoming; if they don't, it isn't. Teams change the rules of the game. Effectiveness is now measured not only on how much the team produces but also on how effectively the supervisor develops and intervenes with the teams and helps them grow. In the new measurement paradigm, supervisors move from quantitative to qualitative metrics. Points are earned, not for turning out more product, but for such things as reducing the frequency and severity of team conflicts. Unfortunately, many managements fail to spell out the new ground rules. In fact, such measurements are often not even factored into the supervisor's work plans and goals.

Lack of rewards. How will the supervisors' work with teams affect their performance appraisal? How will it affect their promotability? Or their salary? The standard performance criteria are based on productivity and quality level, whereas in a team environment, the criteria are based on interpersonal competence and leadership.

REDEFINING THE SUPERVISOR'S ROLE

To gain the cooperation and support of supervisors during the transition to self-directed work teams, the supervisors need to be brought into the team building during the early planning stages of the redesign. Here are some of the ways in which supervisors can get up to speed and play a more active role.

Training plans. Training for team members will be required on a number of levels, and these needs will vary, depending on where the team is in its development. The process begins with a needs analysis to determine what education and skills are required by team members to take on new responsibilities. This must take place early in the planning stage, and all supervisors should actively participate in creating the empowerment plan. This plan outlines which decisions will be delegated to the teams, what the teams will need to know, and what training they'll require to make the proper decisions. During the implementation, the supervisors may themselves require additional skills training in how to create, structure, and coach teams. Later, as the teams require less of their supervisors' services, management may want to offer the supervisors skills training in other areas to help them become more marketable when it is time for them to move on to new assignments.

Position guides. The team needs to develop position guides that discuss and summarize the new roles. These guides should cover such subjects as team development, boundary management, and coaching.

Work plans. Managers and supervisors will want to jointly develop work plans that reflect the new roles and responsibilities. Included in these plans are a description of how the supervisors will coach the team during the transition. For example, what are the supervisor's plans to:

- Hand off decisions to teams?
  - Prepare teams and team members for the transition?
  - Provide teams and team members with feedback?
  - Deliver training to teams?
  - Prepare themselves for their new role?
- Prepare themselves for their future role?

Performance measurements. Supervisors should become involved in developing new performance measurements that reflect the team members' expanded roles and responsibilities. These measurements include such elements as the establishment of team measurements, the degree to which teams are prepared to make decisions, and the amount of self-development training already completed.

Rewards. Yet another way that supervisors can become involved is in tying rewards and recognition to how well team members support the new team concept. Promotions are logically granted to those who effectively lead the team implementation, with higher salary increases for those who do the best job in supporting the teams. Visibility within the organization as well as public recognition of their contributions can also be provided to those who are most effective in their roles.

The challenge of the design process is to develop clarity, understanding, and commitment within the supervisor-managerial staff. It is a big challenge. These groups tend to feel they have the most to lose and, in reality, *do have more personal behavioral changes to make and more new skills to develop* than any other group within the organization. Supervisors and managers need to lead the change while at the same time be willing to change the way they go about doing their own jobs.

When the design team completes the redesign and the new plan is ready for implementation, supervisors and managers should be able to clarify the direction in which the organization is moving, describe their role to anyone who inquires, and provide direction and coaching to teams and team members as necessary.

A PROCESS THAT WORKS

There are many roads to take in redesigning the organization, so it's important to keep some basic thoughts in mind when selecting a design process. First, the education of supervisors and managers needs to occur *during* the design process, not after. This runs counter to the traditional approach of first coming up with the design process and then announcing it.

Second, it is the extensive dialogue around individual issues and concerns that promotes commitment. This commitment occurs because people's concerns, fears, and objectives have an opportunity to surface and be resolved through open, constructive dialogue.

Third, it is important to remember that the process itself becomes a tool for selling the team initiative, because it models how the organization will work in the future. In an open design process, there is ample opportunity to demonstrate how to effectively resolve conflict and build consensus. Here are some of the questions that should be addressed as part of any effective design process.

- How can the organization be structured so that it relies on teams to function effectively?
- How can technical and team support resources be placed closer to the teams?
- What resources will manufacturing teams need to more effectively meet customer requirements?
- Which tasks add only marginal value and can be eliminated?
- What tasks currently being done by the members of the salaried support team can be reassigned to the teams?

- What new tasks are needed to support the team's development, and whom should they be assigned to?

Once these and other tasks have been addressed, the design then needs to move ahead by developing the following tasks:

- A *position guide* reflecting the new roles and responsibilities associated with the new tasks. (Developed by the salaried team support members and agreed to by the plant staff.)
- A *training plan* based upon the needs identified on the storyboard, i.e., the delegated tasks and new tasks. (Developed by the salaried team support members and the plant staff.)
- A *work plan* focusing on the behaviors needed to support and develop the teams. (Developed by the salaried team support members and approved by the plant staff.)
- A *compensation system* that rewards the appropriate behaviors.

In addition, it will be necessary to put into practice the training needed for the supervisors to fulfill their new roles and to evaluate how performance has stacked up against the work plan.

THE DESIGN TEAM

Every consultant seems to have his or her own preferred way of managing the transition to teams. Our proven approach calls for the formulation of steering committees and design teams. (See Part 3, "Tools and Techniques for Implementing Teams.")

The make-up of the design team should include a representation of supervisors. (There may be only one person on a small design team.) In addition, the design team must have frequent interaction with *all* the supervisors so they can contribute to a plan that describes how the work teams will be empowered. In the process, the supervisors will gain a clearer understanding of what needs to be accomplished, how the team initiative is going to be carried out, and how the teams fit into the new system.

The mechanics for including the supervisors can be handled through a design team subgroup, which makes specific recommendations to the total design team. This subgroup consists of supervisory members of the design team and their peers. The supervisory subgroup is charged with recommending training plans, position guides, work plans, and measurements. It is also responsible for coming up with suggestions on how to reward and recognize supervisors and mangers in their new roles. Its charter might also include identifying ways that individuals can go about engaging manager support for their newly defined role.

DEFINING THE SUPERVISOR'S ROLE

The redefined responsibilities of the supervisor can be drawn from at least five essential areas:

Retained responsibilities. It is naive to expect that teams will be able to perform all the tasks that are currently performed by supervisors. The more likely scenario is that the supervisors will retain at least some of their current responsibilities. Over a period of a few years, we've found that about 75–85 percent of tasks currently performed by supervisors are likely to be performed by the teams, while the remaining 25 percent are retained by the supervisor.

Team support. As decision-making tasks are delegated to the teams, supervisors will need to provide information and knowledge to enable the teams to effectively handle the new tasks. The teams will need help in structuring themselves as teams as they undertake such tasks as establishing a clear mission and defining goals, measurements, and group processes. When teams get stuck, which they will, they will need the supervisor's help in diagnosing and designing effective interventions to help them get unstuck. Over time the need for these support tasks will subside, though they will never disappear entirely.

Unmet challenges. Whenever we've asked a group of supervisors if they have time to accomplish all that needs to be done, they inevitably say no. They believe they spend an inordinate amount of time doing less value-added work and express frustration at being almost fully occupied with fire fighting. They feel they could contribute more to the success of the enterprise if they had more time. Freeing up the supervisor's day can allow them to take on additional challenges.

Delegated work. As a rule, managers believe the supervisors should delegate more responsibilities to the production and service workers. Yet, they, the managers, seldom see the need to delegate their own work any lower in the organization. It's as if all the decisions are being made at the right place in the organization except at the supervisory level. With a thoughtful work redesign and a continuing dialogue between supervisors, managers, and other organizational groups such as human resources, a significant number of tasks performed by managers could be handed over to the supervisors.

Aspirations. Some supervisors have other career goals. As time becomes available, they can be assigned special projects to develop their skills in other areas. This may include attending college courses and outside seminars to prepare them for the future.

While the role of the supervisor ought not be eliminated, it is imperative that it be changed. When the team design is carefully thought through, teams end up with greater responsibilities, supervisors end up with work that is more meaningful, managers find time to address higher-level issues, and the organization as a whole benefits by having everyone committed to its success.

THE MANAGER'S ROLE

And what of the manager? Like it or not, managers function as role models, and whatever attitudes they project will end up being reflected in the actions of their subordinates. Thus, managers have to be prepared to train, coach, and counsel supervisors in a manner consistent with how they would like the supervisors to support the teams. Managers have to be more interested in identifying and fixing problems than affixing blame. They have to encourage experimentation by accepting failure as natural among those who take risks. And they need to review their own decision-making process and be willing to delegate decision making to those who are qualified to act on the manager's behalf.

If it appears that a certain decision has to be made personally by the manager, he or she has to be especially careful not to inadvertently send a wrong message to the supervisor. Some decisions require an advanced degree or a higher level of expertise or more extensive experience than the supervisor can offer. Perhaps the information is restricted to a certain level or cannot be broken down below a certain level of detail. In these cases, the manager has to communicate to the supervisors that a failure to pass along specific responsibilities is not a command and control issue.

In cases where the decision can be pushed down to a lower level, the manager has to be certain that the necessary information is shifted down to the people who have to make the decisions.

WHAT ABOUT NONBELIEVERS?

What of the supervisors who do not believe in what the team initiative is designed to accomplish or in how the manager is going about it? The manager first has to listen to their concerns and address whatever issues he or she can. It is wise to assume that hesitation on the part of supervisors is for a legitimate reason. Ultimately, however, the supervisors must be counted upon to support the transition.

If the team environment doesn't match a supervisor's management style and beliefs, he or she won't be able to make the necessary decisions to further the objectives of the team operations. If the supervisor continues to resist or engage in overt or covert sabotage, the person has made the choice to leave. It is wise for the manager to handle the supervisor's departure compassionately with outplacement assistance. But it is necessary to handle it.

WHEN DOWNSIZING IS INEVITABLE

Finally, despite their best intentions, organizations sometimes do have to downsize. During those times, let common sense prevail. When possible, take advantage of attrition through such things as retirements and promotions. If it must be sooner versus later, consider offering early retirement packages to volunteers. Make it clear that it is OK for people to opt out of the process and volunteer to take jobs elsewhere in the organization. If after trying these alternatives additional reductions are still needed, then provide those being separated with as much outplacement support as possible.

While it is sometimes necessary to downsize in order to reduce costs, be aware that downsizing while implementing self-directed work teams is more likely to maximize the teams' chances for failure than for success.

SUMMARY

Assuming the organization has recognized a need to change to a high-commitment organization, the role of the first-line salaried support person is critical. Supervisors must own the vision of the future organization. They need to understand their redefined roles and what tasks are being delegated to whom, and why. They have to be given the necessary skills training. They should be measured on desired behavior. And they need to be recognized and rewarded for their successes.

Most important, supervisors need to be involved in the redesign process from the very beginning and not have the team environment completely worked out and presented to them as a fait accompli. Keeping them involved at every stage makes them willing partners and is the best assurance that the team initiative will be successful.

WHEN PROCESS IMPROVEMENT IS NECESSARY

One of the greatest strengths of empowered teams is their ability to look at the work, identify non-value-added steps, and improve overall productivity. Yet many self-directed work teams never get the chance to become involved with anything more challenging than task modification. The difference between process improvement and task modification is huge, and consequently, it is worth taking a moment to understand where these differences lie.

COMPARING TASKS AND PROCESSES

Let us start with an example that is easy to relate to: housekeeping. Whatever the job may be, the issue of organizing and maintaining the work space is always important because housekeeping directly affects appearance, effectiveness, safety, and compliance. In *task improvement*, the usual approach is to identify the specific tasks and assign individuals or groups to work those tasks. For example:

- The safety committee makes a monthly audit, identifies unsafe practices and/or unsafe conditions, and assigns a group to remedy and document those tasks.

- Individual members are assigned the daily task of sweeping up and returning tools to their proper place.

- An efficiency expert observes the work and defines where products and tools should be placed for maximum effectiveness.

In *process improvement*, it becomes important for those who perform the tasks to understand how any one task influences, or is influenced by, other tasks in the process, and how the *total* throughput of goods or services can be improved. In the course of redesigning the process, the team may have to undo old habits of thought related to segmented task improvement and focus instead on the flow of those linked tasks. This calls for defining all the steps in the process—beginning to end—in order to achieve the desired outcome. In the example cited above, it means that each person would become involved in establishing and maintaining an orderly, safe, and effective work space in which the *entire* team can operate.

Here's another example that may help to clarify the difference between continuous process improvement and the less comprehensive task improvement:

- *Assuring availability of critical supplies.* A heart surgery team was wrestling with the problem of the timely availability of critical supplies to be used in heart bypass operations. Months of piecemeal task accountability experiments had caused only moderate improvements. An unintended side effect was the bad feelings and finger-pointing that occurred across the separate disciplines whenever problems arose.

  To remedy the situation, surgeons, nurses, technicians, attendants, management, and materials procurement members of the team spent a half day with a consultant during which time they created a flow diagram of precisely what took place in the process of maintaining adequate supplies. The components in the process ranged from maintaining convenient and safe storage to assessing value and knowing what and when to reorder.

At the conclusion of the day, the consensus was that the process mapping and analysis had provided more than just solutions to effective storage and retrieval. It had provided a unique opportunity to understand the common dedication to patient care and professional development that existed across the team. The fact that some of the best process improvement ideas came, not from surgeons, but from technicians and attendants, helped to develop a more profound level of personal respect among team members. Creating a well-defined map of this one process ultimately led the whole team to improve its ability to think in terms of defining and improving other processes, one step at a time.

A commonly used approach in process improvement is to involve the whole team in a "5-S" workshop early in the life of the team. Some managers use this as the very first team-building event. "5-S" is named after five Japanese terms starting with S that are critical components in the establishment and maintenance of a workplace in which everything you need, and only what you need, is arranged in an orderly and efficient way. The process has built-in practices for embedding orderliness into the team culture. The advantage of 5-S is that the whole set of linked tasks and practices is owned by the team, and the process itself becomes a discipline.

What unleashes the team's passion and what focuses attention on the power of teams is the individual's respect for the value of professional interdependence and cross-functional thinking. It is the recognition that "I alone as the surgeon (or technician) do not have the answers, but rather it is our interdependence in the service of satisfying the customer that produces extraordinary results."

ROADBLOCKS

Unfortunately, many self-directed work teams are set up to fail because they are never asked to become involved with anything more challenging than task modification. In such cases, management tries to overlay teams on an unexamined process, but since the process itself has inherent weaknesses, few tangible improvements result.

Several other contributing factors can also interfere with a successful process improvement effort.

- Management may lose interest because process improvement is tedious and requires a significant investment in time to identify the non-value-added variances in the work.
- Even when variances are identified, operating procedures may have been imposed from above, and improvements may be impossible to make because those who have conducted the analysis do not have the authority to implement them.
- Certain kinds of critical knowledge can be lost when the team is first established. For example, the work-arounds that employees come up with over time often fall through the cracks when those tasks are distributed to the team.
- Managers may have an innate resistance to addressing process improvement because the exercise brings to light how much front-line workers know and how much management doesn't about the specifics of the work.

For all these reasons and more, process improvement may never get off the ground, and managers can end up blaming teams for a failure to perform when the real causes lie elsewhere.

HOW TO ENCOURAGE CONTINUOUS PROCESS IMPROVEMENT

Three conditions occur in organizations that successfully support continuous process improvement:

1. Teams and individuals have the know-how to make it happen.
2. Leadership provides the integrated framework in which process improvement can be sustained.

3. Those who contribute to the improved process are recognized because the outcome of the organization is impacted.

THE KNOW-HOW TO MAKE IT HAPPEN

Teams allow the organization to function with fewer levels of management, but for this to occur, each manager must be capable of overseeing an entire process rather than just a small piece of it. It also means that managers must accept that they can't know all the relevant information and must be willing to defer to the front-line employees who are doing the work. Employees, in turn, must be able to handle the expanded responsibilities. This requires the mastery of certain essential tools.

Flow diagrams/process maps. These are basic tools that allow someone to graphically portray which actions occur and in what sequence. Just as an electrician uses a circuit diagram to indicate energy flow and the components that make up the electrical circuit, so does a flow diagram or process map provide an easy-to-understand picture of the particular sequence in which a process unfolds. There are dozens of different symbols in standard protocol books, but about ten symbols have proved universally appropriate at the work-team level. (See the diagram, Building A Process Flow Chart, on page 204.)

Interviewing/active listening. Before any improvement effort is undertaken, teams need a snapshot of what is presently being done, rather than simply jumping in and changing the process pell-mell. Unfortunately, the people who can provide that information are often reluctant to speak out for fear of rocking the boat. Thus, to elicit meaningful data, management must create a safe environment where anyone who wants to add information to the mapping process feels that he or she can "say it like it is" without fear of being judged.

Data analysis tools. The same team tool kit should also include general problem-solving tools that will be needed as process improvement abilities develop. The basic set of tools can be found in "Tool 15—A Group Problem-Solving Process" (pages 339–344).

BUILDING A PROCESS FLOW CHART

STEP 1   Begin by selecting a task to chart. Start with something fairly simple, such as making a copy or ordering a part. Avoid the more lengthy and complex tasks, at first.

STEP 2   Start the questioning. The first question is "What is the first thing I would do?" (Avoid minor details such as "raise my right arm.")

Begin with the *start* circle, then choose the appropriate symbol to show that first step, and write the action within the symbol.

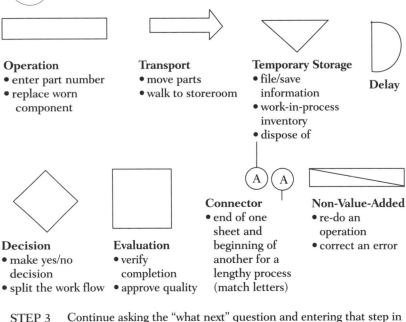

Operation
- enter part number
- replace worn component

Transport
- move parts
- walk to storeroom

Temporary Storage
- file/save information
- work-in-process inventory
- dispose of

Delay

Decision
- make yes/no decision
- split the work flow

Evaluation
- verify completion
- approve quality

Connector
- end of one sheet and beginning of another for a lengthy process (match letters)

Non-Value-Added
- re-do an operation
- correct an error

STEP 3   Continue asking the "what next" question and entering that step in the appropriate symbol until you have charted the complete process to a successful conclusion. Connect each step with a line (use a directional arrow on the lines).

STEP 4   Follow the "best case scenario" through all the way first. Then, return to the first *decision* symbol and trace the alternate routes. Make sure that all alternate paths have been completed.

STEP 5   Discuss the process you just mapped in terms of what you have learned about it, and how it could be improved. Later, prepare a summary analysis.

PROVIDING THE FRAMEWORK IN WHICH PROCESS IMPROVEMENT CAN BE SUSTAINED

For process improvement to take place, management has to highlight the interdependencies required by the various functions, and the groups must foster innovation through a ruthless examination of the hand-off points. They must also maintain a customer frame of reference that guides employee actions.

All this requires a ready supply of information from the manager as well as from support people—engineers, highly trained technicians, brokers, financial analysts, and the like. Support gaps occur when (1) the manager sabotages the team effort by holding back vital information because releasing it would jeopardize his or her image as a technical expert, (2) the team becomes overly dependent on subject-matter experts outside the group and makes little effort to acquire its own in-house expertise, and/or (3) teams members do not make the time available because of the demands of their day-to-day jobs.

Formal leaders can help close these support gaps by reaching out to other functions or groups for information and resources that are not available within the team. Generating information may call for formal supervisors to work together and for various workers outside the team to explain how they go about doing what they do so the teams are able to develop their own internal capabilities.

Teams that are helped to become self-supporting usually become good at continuous process improvement. Managerial support generally takes the form of help in improving the business processes, rather than production processes. When teams demonstrate they can run their operation in a business-like manner, it encourages the leadership to continue cascading the necessary knowledge and skills to team members.

RECOGNIZING AND REWARDING THE RIGHT BEHAVIOR

When one studies the folklore of organizations, those individuals who are most often elevated to folk hero are the firefighters—the people who attacked a big problem and saved the day. For example:

- An engineer gets the "silver dollar award" for a new patent, but not for improving the product reliability curve.
- A maintenance team earns a pizza party for working overtime to put a critical machine back into service, but the team's premier preventive maintenance record is taken for granted.
- A member of the security team is written up in the company paper for rescuing a squirrel from the storm sewer, but her greatest pride comes from making people feel welcome when they come through the gate.

Dramatic examples make great reading in the company newsletter, but for process improvements to truly take hold, there has to be a visible and significant effort to recognize teams and individuals for *incremental changes in a process.* Only in this way can process improvement become institutionalized as part of the culture.

Leadership must actively search out opportunities to provide public recognition to teams and individuals for their process improvement successes. Individuals who excel should enjoy a moment of notoriety, and their specific contributions should be spelled out. These are the individuals who become the role models for the team and who ultimately have a significant influence on the behavior of others. Creating public recognition also satisfies the team member's need to belong to a group that can make a difference, and to be acknowledged for his or her own efforts.

In short, when people receive recognition—not just internally but from customers and shareholders as well—productivity and quality increase and customers end up being delighted.

SUMMARY

Continuous process improvement can be one of the most significant contributions that teams can make to the organization.

But to realize substantial improvements, organizations have to (1) differentiate between task modification and continuous *process* improvement, (2) help teams develop the necessary know-how to achieve real process improvement, (3) direct managers to provide the necessary support to sustain the improvement, and finally (4) provide visible and significant recognition for any accomplishments made. Being able to identify and remove the dysfunctional elements in the system and tightly align the process to the customer brings out the best thinking of all the team members and makes it more likely that the process improvement effort will succeed. This systematic approach to process improvement is ultimately at the heart of what makes teams effective.

WORKING WITH UNIONS

Everyone agrees that organizations with unionized employees cannot make a successful shift to self-directed work teams without full cooperation of both management and the union(s). Yet the relationship between these two groups is often adversarial, and there are people who think it will—and should—remain that way. In fact, union leaders are split on the issue. Some, like the leaders of the United Auto Workers, believe in a nonadversarial approach and see teams as a way to move in that direction. Others see the team concept as primarily a means for suppressing worker dissent.[1]

How, then, to proceed? Management and unions have been adversaries for so long that it will take time—and the willingness of both sides to try out new ways of working together—for mutual trust to develop. Without this base of trust, progress will be slow and probably not very long lasting. Those who have been successful say that the key is to be prepared to move slowly and with patience.

GUIDELINES

Union attitudes toward work teams vary, depending on the particular industry, company, union, local, or official. The rest of this section of the book gives general guidelines, which may prove helpful to organizations that want to explore self-directed work teams in cooperation with their unions.

Include unions in discussions of work teams from the very start, regardless of the time and effort.   You need to make sure the union has the opportunity to listen and contribute from the beginning of your initial explorations so that you can plan together to take everyone's concerns into account. You need to begin what may be a long process of winning the union over. At all costs, you must avoid springing something on the union that was dreamed up in secret management sessions behind closed doors.

Be prepared for slow going at first. Don't give up simply to move ahead faster with your plans. If the unions aren't involved, your plans won't be worth much. Unhappy unions have gone to court to force organizations to give up teams.[2]

Put yourself in the shoes of the union—and union officials.   Initial union reaction to work teams can range from positive, to guarded skepticism, to out-and-out opposition. For some unions, the fact that the idea comes from management is reason enough to reject it. For others, the thought of giving up their adversarial stance with management is philosophically unacceptable and personally unthinkable.

Unions fear that no matter what management thinks or says, the long-term impact of work teams will be to cut back on jobs, force workers to give up hard-won concessions, and remove team members from the umbrella of further union protection.

Some unions suspect that organizations introduce the idea of work teams as a tactic to weaken or remove unions. Others say simply that work teams don't work, at least not with enough certainty to be worth the effort involved. In making this point, they may point to some recent examples, such as Rohm & Haas's Plexiglas-manufacturing facility in Knoxville, where the introduction of work teams could not prevent a plant from closing down two years later.

Union officials also have concerns about their own future in a world of work teams. Traditionally, union officials get elected on their ability to take a tough stand with management and win concessions for their membership. They fear that work teams, by blurring the distinction between management and labor, may eventually make this ability and, therefore, their jobs unnecessary.

In contrast, some officials feel strongly enough about work teams to take the lead with their membership in advocating the transition. But even if they personally favor work teams, many union officials feel that they can't afford to be seen considering them seriously without the risk of being voted out of office—unless everyone agrees that work teams are the only alternative to losing jobs and/or closing down a facility. As a corporate negotiator said, "Union officials can't risk going out on a limb. What happens to their credibility if management shifts its direction?"

Patch up old wounds first.   If the organization and the union(s) have unresolved issues, resolve them first. This will clear the air, demonstrate good faith, and help build the trust needed to move forward.

Start small and informally.   Instead of making a head-on assault, find a union or union official willing to work with the organization and start there. Don't insist on putting initial arrangements in writing or getting widespread approval for changes the organization wants to make. If self-direction is thought of as a pilot effort, everyone involved will have much more flexibility. People will be more willing to experiment with new approaches if they are not labeled "permanent" or "official."

It may also be beneficial to emphasize the employee involvement and teamwork aspects, rather than always talking about "work teams," which may be a loaded term for many unions. For example, in the early stages of working with an international building services company, the union representatives were more comfortable talking about "worker involvement networks," leaving "team" out altogether.

Given a choice, don't start in a facility with a long history of problems.   It's tempting to introduce work teams in troubled plants and offices, where desperation can motivate people to try anything. Keep in mind, however, that work teams may not necessarily solve the fundamental, probably ingrained union problems of those facilities. Efforts to make work teams grow won't pay off if the seeds are planted on rocks.

In one Connecticut production plant with a particularly adversarial union-management history, the two sides agreed to spend two years on increasing employee participation as far as Level 2—characterized by round-table meetings—and only at that point to raise the issue of work teams again (See "Employee Involvement: Alternatives to Self-Direction," pages 247–256.)

Stress initial benefits that unions can support.   Don't use the introduction of work teams as a strategy for cutting back jobs. Unions are in business to protect jobs and improve working conditions, so the organization needs to make its approach to job security clear from the beginning. If possible, guarantee that reductions in the work force will come only through attrition. Job classification is another key union issue that is better avoided at the beginning.

Explore possible trade-offs.   To overcome union reluctance to relax work rules, the management at the Armstrong World Industries plant in Pensacola, Florida, agreed to go ahead with a plan to manufacture a new line of tiles. This agreement increased the likelihood that the plant would provide employment for union members for a longer period of time, and allowed team members to restructure and assign work more flexibly.

Don't over-sell work teams.   Work teams are not cure-alls. If the organization is financially precarious, work teams cannot guarantee its survival. Market conditions and other factors beyond team or organization control can still force a facility with very successful work teams to close down.

Be prepared to go out of the way to prove sincerity.   To test just how sincere the organization is, union representatives may file more grievances than they did before, or push for relaxation of certain rules, like eliminating the use of time clocks at lunch. The organization's responses will be closely observed, so be sure everyone involved lives up to exactly what was agreed on; and remember that any extra distance traveled will help pave the way for further cooperation on the work-team issue.

(Negotiations should make the point, for example, that relaxing the time-clock rule indicates a willingness to trust employees, not a change in the length of the lunch hour.)

Hang in.   The advent of work teams changes the rhythm of interactions with the union. The old way was like warfare. As one union official put it, "You fought a pitched battle every time the contract came up for renewal. In between, you lobbed in grievances and put out fires." With work teams, the organization and the unions will start working together in a different way. The focus will shift from working strictly to the letter of the contract, to working out day-to-day issues. As a result, things may not always feel final or tacked down. There may be backsliding. Neither side will be able to retreat into militance. Both will be taking the more rewarding, and more difficult, path of daily cooperation.

Be prepared to deal with managers or supervisors who try to undermine arrangements with the union.   Until work teams are running smoothly, some managers and supervisors may try to undermine their growth by sabotaging special arrangements that may have been made with the union. For example, if the steering committee has encouraged teams to set their own overtime schedules, don't let managers and supervisors continue to decide these matters. Unions will see in this behavior a continuation of the old power game, not a shift to the broader empowerment promised by self-direction.

Make information and training about work teams available to union officials when appropriate.   Like every other job, the job of union official will change in a work-team setting. Although it is not appropriate to provide specific training to union representatives, the organization can make sure union officials know about a public seminar or training session that some employees may be attending. Also, consider including union leaders in awareness programs conducted by the organization. One approach *not* to take is to put on special training or awareness programs just for union officials. This approach separates groups instead of bringing them together, and can make unions suspect that they are not getting the complete picture.

If you need to improve overall union-management relations in your organization, consider seeking outside help.   One source, the Federal Mediation and Conciliation Service (FMCS), is a valuable neutral party that helps organizations make the transition to a mutually beneficial union-management relationship. FMCS has been very successful in helping both sides learn the skills of negotiation to mold an improved relationship.

Give thought to the role the union should play in the future.   Once work teams are up and running smoothly, what role will or should the union play? This is a tough question to answer; there aren't many existing models. Yet, in most cases it's clear that the unions won't—and shouldn't—disappear. One possibility is that the union will begin representing work teams against the threat of a new management team or corporate owner who might want to dismantle the teams.

NOTES

1. Eric Mann, "Work Teams Muffle Labor's Voice," *New York Times,* 11 June 1989, sec. 3, p. 2.
2. Richard Koenig, "Quality Circles Are Vulnerable to Union Tests," *The Wall Street Journal,* 28 March 1990, sec. B. pp. 1, 4.

CHAPTER

FOURTEEN

TEAMS AND MEASUREMENT

In the same way that a sailor can become lost at sea without a compass, teams need measures to tell them where they are weak, where they are strong, and where they are headed. Building a dashboard that keeps track of critical performance parameters is the most powerful way to ensure that a team is contributing to the overall business results.

Many teams shy away from measurement, saying "it's too hard to do" or "we'll do it later." Resistance also comes from other parts of the organization. For example, if information is seen as synonymous with power, those at the top may jealously guard any measurement data that comes along. Often, the internal mechanisms for providing performance data are faulty and inaccurate and are unable to provide the level of information needed by the team.

It has been repeatedly demonstrated that generating data on team performance on a regular basis is the only way to document and sustain the improvements resulting from team activities. What's more, those teams who regularly monitor their key processes are more likely to survive beyond the first six months. For this reason, each team should have a well-designed, well-balanced dashboard.

This chapter is based on the writing and thinking of Anne Marie Michaud, AchieveGlobal, Montreal, PQ, Canada.

This special-interest section will answer some common questions about teams and measurement for both start-up teams and mature teams. We'll look at the relationship between team decision making and measurement, as well as the roles the manager and team leader play in helping to generate the necessary metrics.

THREE TYPES OF MEASURES

Three different types of measures give a picture of how successfully teams are being implemented. Metrics can be used to determine:

- *The overall health of the business.* Ideally, organizations using teams as a management strategy will have pinpointed those performance indicators that are the most responsive to team interventions.

- *How well the teams are performing.* Is the team meeting its objectives? Are team members directing their energies in the most productive areas? What kind of performance gaps exist, and is the team directing its efforts to close those gaps? If the performance gap on a particular measure is clearly greater than in other areas, then that's where the team's problem-solving efforts should be directed.

- *How effectively the teams are being brought up to speed.* Measures are needed that keep track of such things as the number of team members who have gone through training, the transfer of decision-making authority, and so on.

USING MEASUREMENT TO FOCUS TEAM ACTIVITY

You are more likely to see an improvement in the overall business numbers when teams are focused on those activities that have the greatest impact on overall team performance. Team measures can be used to answer three key questions:

- *How should work be prioritized?* When teams monitor performance measures on a regular basis, it becomes obvious when certain activities are lagging behind. These are the areas that call for special emphasis. Activities should be planned to ensure that all team measures are trending in the desired direction.

- *What areas call for continuous improvement activities?* There will be some areas where performance falls outside of acceptable limits. Measures that track daily performance can identify those "hot spots" so that the team can focus additional time and energy on them through day-to-day, incremental improvements.

- *When should team processes be redesigned?* During the regular review of team performance measures, teams will note when a performance gap on a particular measure is too large to be addressed through incremental improvements. A performance gap of more than 5 or 10 percent usually suggests more radical measures such as redesigning the process that is being measured.

WHAT TEAM MEASURES SHOULD BE REGULARLY TRACKED?

The ideal set of measures gives the team a complete picture of its performance, reflecting many key facets of group performance. Typical categories of measurement are:

- Financials such as cost, ROI, and revenue.
- Throughput.
- Quality measures such as yield, complaints, and returns.
- Cycle time.
- Level of customer satisfaction.
- Measures relating to safety and environmental concerns.
- Level of team skills development.

These measures are derived from several sources. One obvious place is the *process map* that outlines the team's primary process. These measures tell the team how effectively the process is performing. They also help the team to know where the bottlenecks or slowdowns are located so the team can intervene in a timely manner.

The team's primary process map can also be used to generate data on *speed or cycle time*. The process map shows where the majority of process costs are being incurred. Operational measures (such as how often schedules are being met) can point to areas in which volume and throughput can be improved.

Customer feedback and quality data can be derived from customer complaints, compliments, and returns. Many organizations solicit formal, ongoing feedback from customers. This feedback can be translated into team action to resolve a complaint or to prevent the recurrence of similar complaints in the future.

Preventive activity for *safety and/or environmental reasons* can be self-recorded. Most organizations have to submit safety statistics, and these statistics can be used as a source of valuable performance data.

Data regarding *team development* can be gathered from the implementation of the team's development plan. Or data can be derived from the team's self-rating on how the team is progressing in team learning and skills development.

CHARACTERISTICS OF GOOD TEAM MEASURES

A set of team measures that effectively guides team decision making and action planning needs to be balanced. That is, it needs to broadly encompass all the key dimensions of team performance. The measures also need to clearly illustrate the performance gap between actual and desired performance over time.

The desired performance levels can be based on several criteria, such as internal improvement targets, external performance benchmarks, an average of past performance, or the best level of past performance. They also may be tied to a goal or target derived from the annual budget, forecast, or tactical plan. The aim is to use the gap between actual and desired performance to focus the team's thinking on how to improve its numbers.

It is important, therefore, that the gap between actual and desired performance does not seem overwhelming to team members. To make the objectives more achievable, a series of intermediate targets can be set up by the team. Once the team has reached and sustained an intermediate objective, it can raise the bar to the next level. The goal is to keep team performance steadily trending upward through problem solving, process improvements, skill enhancements, and the adoption of those best practices that have been identified through benchmarking.

Team measures will be most helpful when they are stated in units that are meaningful to the team. For example, if the team is one of several in a specific business unit, then that team should receive specific feedback regarding its unique contribution to the overall results of the business unit. Ideally there would be no overlap in metrics, so that if an indicator improves, it is clear which team was responsible for the improvement.

It is also important not to keep that information buried but, instead, to translate it into a compelling graphic such as a chart or graph that can be posted in a prominent place. For example, posting the chart or graph in the team meeting room allows members to be instantly up to date on their performance and be aware of any performance gaps.

Teams can also use the achievement of performance goals as an opportunity to give peers positive reinforcement for their contributions and assistance. For example, "Thank you, Purchasing, for a job well done" could be posted to acknowledge the purchasing department's contribution to a drop in operating costs.

HOW TO RESPOND WHEN A TEAM SAYS: "YOU CAN'T MEASURE WHAT WE DO."

When measuring an intangible—for example, when somebody provides a service of some sort—you might want to follow this sequence of steps that will allow you to come up with meaning-ful numbers:

1. Begin by finding out what the recipients of the service are saying about it? What do they like? What do they feel could be done to improve the quality of the service delivery?
2. Draw a macro map of the process that includes such subprocesses as gathering data, performing analyses, and recommending a follow-up.
3. Document on the process map precisely where positive and negative customer experiences occur.
4. Problem-solve the negative experiences and analyze what does seem to be working well.
5. Build an action plan.
6. Design measures to track the fulfillment of the action plan to prevent future client dissatisfaction.

Measures can consist of a self-recorded tally of positive and negative experiences, a self-assessment of skills and behaviors, or simply a record of activities. What is important is that you are measuring those actions or activities that will prevent further customer dissatisfaction by translating the intangible aspect of service delivery into tangible, actionable measures.

COMMUNICATING ABOUT MEASURES

Measurement data is the lifeblood of the organization and should be communicated throughout the organization on a reg-ular basis. In an ideal communication plan each team partici-pates in a monthly measurement review. At the monthly review, financial and nonfinancial results are discussed, with an em-phasis on clarifying the performance gaps. Team members are invited to participate in gap analysis and problem solving of any measures on their scorecard that are trending in the wrong di-rection.

A good place to start is to see how often the organization reviews its financial data. If a monthly financial report is issued, teams can coordinate the review of their own performance measures with the monthly corporate figures. This will make it easier to identify any cause-and-effect relationships.

SHARING PERFORMANCE DATA

Teams are sometimes concerned about sharing their scorecards with the rest of the organization for fear of being criticized or humiliated for poor performance. This is where the manager can play an active role. Low numbers may indicate to the manager a need for additional coaching or training. By taking the position that all information, good or bad, is simply useful data to be acted upon, the manager can take the sting out of weak numbers. If the manager maintains a positive, optimistic attitude, teams with low scores will be more inclined to see those numbers as opportunities for improvement, rather than as a cause of embarrassment and low self-esteem. Team scorecards are also an opportunity for everyone to celebrate and reinforce clear performance gains.

Similarly, posting graphs detailing the performance of *individual* team members indicates the team's current strengths and weaknesses with an eye to those areas that need special attention. Many organizations provide display boards in or near team meeting rooms for teams and team members to post their measures. This makes it easier to use these metrics during team decision making and problem solving. (By contrast, those charts and graphs won't be very useful if they are displayed in a building other than the one the team is meeting in.)

If teams meet in a semipublic place where the confidentiality of data is a concern, the team leader can distribute graphs and other supporting data as handouts to be collected after the meeting, instead of creating a permanent display. Corning, Inc., which strongly believes in the motivational value of graphically expressed performance data, has come up with another way to display the data that does not reveal privileged information. The company simply does not add unit values to the scale on the left-hand side of the graphs, making the graphs meaningless to outsiders.

ASKING FOR HELP

It is the role of the team leader to figure out how to remove the obstacles that prevent the team from getting its work done. Team members and leaders should keep in mind that they do not have to go it alone. Not only do they have the resources of their own team, but they also have the resources of other peer groups. For example, the team leader is usually a member of a team composed of other team leaders. Thus, if the team leader has questions about measures or other resources that cannot be solved within the leader's own group, he or she can draw upon the other team leaders for advice or support during a peer group meeting. Team members can also request subject-matter expert help directly from support groups. Different types of help will be needed by the teams at different times.

If the team's measures are on a downward trend, team members should be encouraged to rally organizational resources to help them, especially since if one team misses its target, it can put the entire organization at risk.

USING TEAM MEASURES TO MANAGE EFFECTIVELY

When measures are trending in the right direction, the manager can be confident that performance targets will be met. When indicators are trending downward, the manager can quickly jump in and provide coaching and help the teams problem-solve.

Managers are accountable for educating teams on how to interpret team data to make sound business decisions. Getting managers to do this, however, is easier said than done. Managers spend many years learning how to make effective decisions and are promoted because they demonstrate an ability to review and analyze business data and guide those who report to them. Not surprisingly, then, it often becomes difficult for these same managers to give up that role and empower the teams to take it over. To avoid problems, the senior team should make it very clear that the role of the managers is to empower team decision making wherever team activities can lead to increased customer satisfaction, improved quality, and reduced cycle time.

HELPING TEAMS TO FUNCTION INDEPENDENTLY

If business improvement depends on fast, effective decision making at all levels, front-line teams who lack understanding of how to make effective decisions are detrimental to business results. An empowered team is able to interpret the data relating to its part of the business process and knows how to translate the data into actions that enhance performance levels.

The most effective team leaders ensure that everyone on the team understands the numbers on the dashboard and how they can be improved through what the members of the team do. These team leaders make sure that boundary issues are resolved, that obstacles preventing team progress are removed, and that any necessary resources are provided. Where possible, they encourage the team to manage its own work behaviors and policies, such as those relating to attendance, scheduling, timeliness, and vacations.

If the team has been struggling to close a performance gap and has never fully succeeded, it may be time to introduce new capability to the team. Perhaps additional training or education will increase the ability of the team members to raise performance that extra notch. Team leaders should feel free to request such training as needed. Cross-training within the team also enhances team capacity. The more that people know how to do multiple jobs within a team, the more likely they are to be able to spot ways of enhancing performance.

If a specific technical skill is lacking in the team, the team leader might ask another function or department within the organization to lend the team a subject-matter expert to work with team members and coach them. Or perhaps a new hire should be considered to broaden the skill base of the team.

Performance can also be improved by soliciting feedback from team members. Many companies use 360-degree feedback to ensure that leaders receive performance evaluations from direct reports as well as from peers. Such feedback is also effective in helping to develop team leaders.

Linking the compensation system to performance improvements is an additional incentive to raise the bar another notch.

ALIGNING MEASURES ACROSS THE ORGANIZATION

As teams become self-directed and perform at increasingly higher levels, it becomes more critical to have their activities aligned with the corporate mission and vision. This can be a sticky problem. If an organization has 100 teams, and each team develops its own performance measures, sets its own targets, and problem-solves its own performance gaps, how can the organization be sure that the teams are all pulling in the same direction? There is a need for an alignment tool that allows key operational issues to receive the lion's share of attention from all teams across the organization.

THE MEASUREMENT ALIGNMENT GRID

One way to guarantee across-the-board alignment is by drawing up a measurement alignment grid. To do this, the management team at the site identifies between five and seven key performance indicators critical for executing corporate strategy and/or achieving performance objectives. These performance indicators are listed on the left-hand side of the alignment grid.

The grid is then distributed to every team within the organization. Each teams enters a performance measure of choice into the cells representing that team. For each organizational indicator, the team should answer the question: "What metric will tell us how well we are doing with our part of the operation?"

Once all teams have completed the grid, the senior team can see if the collective measures add up to the performance level required by the organization. If a team has chosen a measure that overlaps with that of another team, or if the measure seems inappropriate, there is an opportunity at this point to establish a dialogue about it between the team and the site's senior management.

Measurement Alignment Grid

KEY BUSINESS OBJECTIVES OR ORGANIZATIONAL PERFORMANCE INDICATORS	BUSINESS UNIT TEAM	FRONT-LINE TEAM	SUPPORT TEAM TRAINING
Volume of product	90,000 units	8,000 units	25 hours per employee per year
Cost of product	$20 per unit	$20 per unit	Not to exceed new budget
Quality of product	97% yield	97% acceptable	90% of course participants rate course satisfactory
Customer satisfaction	100% on-time delivery and no complaints	100% schedule efficiency	Supervisor reports improved on-the-job performance 45 days later
New-product development	100% new-product testing completed as scheduled	15 new ideas per month	Develop three new seminars by third month

KNOWING WHEN AND HOW TO INTERVENE

One of the major challenges team sponsors face is determining when and how to intervene, especially when dealing with a mature work team. Sponsors often fear that if they intervene too frequently, they could be accused of not trusting the work group, whereas if they do not intervene at all, the team may not reach its projected goals or problems that are looming may go unheeded.

The following is intended to help sponsors determine a starting point at which to intervene and offers a diagnostic process that makes use of existing organizational measures.

EVALUATING UNIT PERFORMANCE

Before intervening with work groups or teams, it is helpful for the sponsor to clarify the business metrics that will be most responsive to work-group activity. These metrics will be different for each organization. For example, in a mature organization where *cost efficiency* is key, teams should be focused on those cost factors that can be impacted by work groups, such as the costs associated with sales, service, manufacturing, and operations.

In an organization for which *innovation* is key, the appropriate team metrics may look at speed to market, percent of revenue from new products or services, number of patents, and growth of market share.

Team-sensitive metrics may change over time as the business continues to mature. The intent is to identify a subset of the organizational numbers used by line management to gauge the health of the business which will be sensitive to improved work-group performance. Expected improvement targets can be set for each measure.

As long as the team-sensitive numbers are trending in the desired direction, there will typically be little need for team sponsors within management to step into the team's business other than to share information and provide needed support.

DECIDING WHERE TO INTERVENE

When the organization is operating as desired, the activities of individuals and/or teams are aligned with (1) the interests of the business unit or enterprise and (2) the expectations of the customer.

One of the first checkpoints for the sponsor is to determine how clearly all these alignments are reflected in team behavior. If the team metrics are not up to standard, the sponsor may elect to intervene at several points:

- The sponsor can determine how clearly the individual and group actions reflect and support the organization's vision and values. How well have the *vision and values* been operationalized down through the ranks? Management sponsors must clearly promote their leadership philosophy and values and make sure the organization's systems are in alignment. Team leaders at all levels should be held accountable for maintaining the focus on team measures and results.

- The sponsor will want to examine how tightly the team and individual *strategies and goals* are linked to customer needs. He or she will want to ensure that underperforming groups fully understand the effect of their actions on the strategies and goals of the organization, and that work groups are receiving useful data about their performance. At the team and individual levels, the sponsor wants to determine whether teams have been chartered effectively, and whether they know how to deal with boundary management issues.

- Sponsors will want to review how *measures of effectiveness* are used within the organization: How effectively is the business meeting customer needs? Is the information received in a timely manner to allow work groups to react? Are leading indicators being tracked? Are performance gaps being resolved effectively? At the customer/stakeholder level, sponsors will need to know whether the teams truly understand how to identify high-leverage opportunities and whether the key stakeholders have been brought on board.

SUMMARY

Team measures are critical to any organization that intends to sustain a team installation. Measures tell you if the introduction of teams is leading to an improvement in business, if there is a rise in employee satisfaction, and if customer satisfaction is on the climb. Wherever possible, team measures should be derived from or appended to the measures that are currently being used to run the business. This prevents the creation of a whole new set of data-gathering mechanisms. As teams become more business-focused, team measures can then be used to keep everyone moving in the right direction.

COMPENSATION SYSTEMS THAT SUPPORT TEAMS

Compensation systems exert a big influence on an organization's ability to carry out its strategies. Once teams are up and functioning well, usually by Stage 5, *Self-Directed Teams* (see Chapter 8), an organization needs to start looking at its compensation system to decide whether or not the system supports work teams. Changing the basis on which employees are compensated is a serious undertaking. One of the reasons to wait until teams are functioning is so that the teams themselves can have some say in the matter.

Upon examination, some organizations may find that their compensation systems do not need a major overhaul. Others, though, discover features in their existing systems that reward people directly or indirectly for the following "anti-team" behaviors:

Concentrating primarily on individual achievement. If the organization's compensation plan rewards individual effort, employees will concentrate their energies on individual achievement rather than on helping the group do well. A good example of this is the piecework system, which pays workers according to how much each one produces. As the manager of a men's apparel plant

---

For many of the gain-sharing and pay-for-knowledge concepts in this section, the authors are grateful to Dr. Michael Schuster, Professor Emeritus at Syracuse University and Managing Partner, Competitive Human Resource Strategies, Narragansett, RI.

said, "For years we've paid operators according to how many pairs of pants they could tack belt loops on, or whatever, so that's all they were interested in doing. Now suddenly we're telling them to work together in teams and figure out ways to improve their jobs. If we want that to happen, we're going to have to change the way we pay them."

Striving to move up a hierarchical organization structure. Features that tie the ability to earn more money to a move up the organization structure don't work well in organizations with teams. Teams result in a flatter organization structure, with fewer opportunities for moving up. As one team member put it, "Going to work teams means we have removed a lot of rungs from the corporate ladder."

Building up and protecting seniority. One of the advantages of work teams is their ability to re-configure themselves in response to changing markets or work requirements. Tying pay increases to seniority can get in the way of this flexibility.

In other ways, an existing compensation system may not actively conflict with work teams, so much as fail to encourage needed growth in certain areas. Two critical areas are:

Skill development. When employees are rewarded for how well they perform a task, they are indirectly being rewarded for their level of skill. However, learning new skills is basic to team success and needs to be rewarded more directly. Team members have many new skills to learn: (1) each others' jobs, (2) team-related skills, (3) the administrative and management duties that enable them to be self-managing, and eventually (4) the tasks of other teams. Also, as teams grow and mature, team members need to enrich and deepen their performance and understanding of existing skills.

Employee involvement. Just as people take a greater interest in their houses when they own them instead of renting them, team members need to feel a greater sense of ownership of their work, their team, their department, and the entire organization, than do employees in conventional organizations.

The compensation system should reward people for this greater involvement.

There are two compensation systems that reward many of the behaviors and approaches employees need to adopt when they move to self-directed work teams: the gain-sharing system and the pay-for-skill (or pay-for-knowledge) system.

GAIN-SHARING

Gain-sharing is a system for sharing the improvements that stem from increasing productivity, reducing costs, enhancing quality, and/or improving the overall business performance of a plant or business unit. To measure these improvements, organizations establish a baseline of normal performance; anything over the line becomes an improvement and goes into a bonus pool according to whatever gain-sharing formula the organization has developed. Each team member/employee in the plan receives a share of this pool on a regular basis (usually each month or quarter) in the form of a check. Depending on the particular plan, the amount can be a share equal to everyone else's, or it can be based on some percentage of the employee's salary or on the number of hours worked.

A common way to establish a baseline, or standard, is to average performance over the past two or three years and use that as the starting point. If this is not possible, employees may have to agree to an "engineered" or estimated standard. Such standards are open to argument, however, and employees and managers need to trust each other before such standards can be adopted. Gain-sharing will not be possible unless agreement can be reached on this point.

Although not new (a gain-sharing system called the Scanlon Plan has been in existence for almost 60 years), gain-sharing has received considerable attention recently because it encourages employees to pursue many of the goals American organizations are trying to achieve: improved productivity, increased employee commitment, and organizational streamlining.

Since gain-sharing plans do not kick in until performance improves over the baseline standard, they motivate employees to work harder—and smarter. Still, without a vehicle to support and channel these increased efforts, an organization won't get the full benefits from gain-sharing. Therefore, many gain-sharing plans include committees and other employee-involvement vehicles. In the case of self-directed work teams, the teams themselves become opportunities for involvement.

Gain-sharing is sometimes confused with profit-sharing. The major difference is that profit-sharing is based on total business performance, which can include factors beyond employees' control, while gain-sharing is based on the efforts of individual units within a given organization.

For an organization with self-directed work teams, the critical gain-sharing factors and questions are as follows.[1]

CRITICAL FACTORS

Looking into the feasibility of gain-sharing is the responsibility of the design team. Selected work-team members contribute their ideas, and final approval comes from the steering committee. The issues and questions they need to consider are highlighted in the list below. The initial feasibility study (See "The Feasibility Study," page 265–272) may include specific answers to some of these questions, as well as baseline data that can be used to answer other questions.

Performance and financial measures. For gain-sharing to work, an organization needs a method for measuring potential gains that is reasonable, fair, and relatively easy to calculate.

Size of plant or facility. In general, facilities with up to 500 to 1,000 employees are best suited for gain-sharing: small enough so that team members can see the connection between their effort and their gain-sharing check, and large enough for a gain-sharing payment to be sizable. In facilities with over 3,000 employees, gain-sharing administrative costs tend to be higher, progress slower, communication more difficult, and considerable effort required to overcome the resistance to change.

Type of production. Baselines are easier to establish and gains are easier to measure in plants with a few unchanging product lines, more difficult when lines are diverse and/or change frequently.

Potential to absorb additional output. Since gain-sharing can result in substantial productivity increases, at least at first, the market must be able to handle this additional output—or else the organization must have a plan to deal with reducing or transferring its work force. (Information related to this issue is usually generated by the initial feasibility study of work teams.)

Impact of employee efforts. Heavily automated operations, especially continuous flow operations regulated by computerized production systems over which employees have little control, are not usually the best sites for either work teams or gain-sharing. Increased employee effort on a regular basis won't have much of an impact on improved performance. (However, even in these facilities, employees' ideas to improve equipment use can have a big one-time impact.)

Union-management relations. Although easier to install in a nonunion environment, gain-sharing is possible in unionized situations where both management and unions have a reasonably cooperative working relationship.

Planned capital investments. It is best to postpone gain-sharing until any substantial capital investment plans are carried out. Say, for example, you set up a gain-sharing formula based on a certain level of employee effort required to produce a certain output. If you then install automated equipment, you will have a hard time using that same formula to relate productivity gains to employee effort. This is especially true if the addition of new equipment will result in a sizeable reduction in the work force.

Local management. Gain-sharing is a complex process. The facility needs a good management team to manage it.

Top management continuity. Without the likelihood that top management will continue to be in charge, gain-sharing might not get the long-term support it needs to succeed.

DESIGN QUESTIONS

There is no single best gain-sharing plan for organizations with work teams; each organization must design a plan that fits its particular work-team structure. Such a plan should answer the following questions:

Which groups of employees should participate in the gain-sharing plan? Should gain-sharing be limited to production teams, or should support workers and support teams also participate? In general, the more an organization is using gain-sharing to foster organizational change and a broader commitment to organization-wide goals, the more inclusive it should be in deciding who participates.

How much employee involvement should there be, and how should it be structured? The approaches adopted for gain-sharing and self-directed work teams should reinforce each other. Gain-sharing flourishes in the same atmosphere of employee involvement that characterizes teams. Teams in turn can also use gain-sharing to learn about the economics of their organization and its markets. Establishing a gain-sharing administrative committee of team members helps underscore the organization's intent to get team members involved.

How should the bonus be determined? There are both financial and nonfinancial measures of productivity. Agreeing on a clear-cut, easy-to-understand approach to both types of measures is critical.

Financial measures include the relationship between the sales value of production and the costs of labor (Scanlon Plan) or between production value (sales value minus the cost of goods sold) and labor costs (Rucker Plan). These plans can be modified to fit special circumstances. Financial measures motivate team members to become familiar with the financial dynamics of the organization. They also require management to release financial data it might have once considered privileged.

Nonfinancial measures of productivity include output per hour, output per hour plus or minus a measure of quality, engineered time standards, absorption of indirect hours, and actual hours worked. In an organization with a good manufacturing resources planning (MRP) system, this information is already available.

How often should the gain-sharing be measured? Measuring gains and issuing bonuses more frequently means smaller bonuses, but these have a greater motivational impact because they are given closer to the time they were earned. The most commonly used time period is one month, although many firms operate on a quarterly basis, and some measure every six months.

When should gain-sharing begin? Although organizations may want to discuss gain-sharing earlier, they probably should not put it into action until after teams are functioning well, probably at Stage 5, and also when work activity is high enough to give team members a chance to earn a good bonus. Many organizations use the introduction of gain-sharing to reinvigorate Stage 5 teams, which may have become complacent and demotivated. A final word: Administration will be simpler if the gain-sharing year coincides with the organization's financial year.

PAY-FOR-SKILL (OR -KNOWLEDGE)

A pay-for-skill (or pay-for-knowledge) compensation system rewards employees not for what they do, but for what they know how to do. Under this system, jobs are defined not in terms of specific tasks, but in terms of the skills required to perform them. People increase their rate of pay by mastering new skills, not by building up seniority or moving to a higher-paying job.

A pay-for-skill compensation system supports many of the goals and strategies of self-directed work teams:

Employee flexibility. Employees with multiple skills can perform multiple tasks. This flexibility is key to the benefits that work teams can provide: reconfiguring quickly to meet changing market needs, responding to emergencies, and handling rapid changes in work flow.

Fewer, broader job categories. Traditionally, a job is organized around one or two skills. Both pay-for-skill systems and self-directed work teams have fewer job categories, although each category is broader and requires more skills.

Employee involvement. A pay-for-skill system can increase commitment and motivation no less than work teams can, by challenging employees to increase their abilities and expand their focus from their job to the larger organization. Lower absenteeism and turnover are among the immediate benefits of this expanded point of view. When an organization invests more of its resources in employees, the employees invest more of themselves in their work.

Leaner staffing. Organizations with pay-for-skill plans often find they can do more with less. With a multiskilled labor pool available, they do not need to hire as many new people. The fear that this gain might be offset by a need for more administrators of the plan has so far proved groundless.

HOW PAY-FOR-SKILL SYSTEMS WORK

Although there are many variations, a pay-for-skill system ties pay increases to the mastery of "skill units" related to the performance of an employee's job (or, in the case of a self-directed team, to team jobs). The program is typically administered by an organization's human resources department. Once the skills units are defined, and a system of tests and measurement criteria is set up, administering this new system may take no more time than it did to defend the inequities of the old one.

Team members can demonstrate mastery and receive certification in several ways:

- Passing a paper-and-pencil test prepared by the organization, a training institute, local college, or other recognized educational or training group or testing service.
- Performing the skill to the satisfaction of an expert (facilitator, supervisor, trainer).
- Performing the skill to the satisfaction of their peers (e.g., other team members).
- Performing a specific new skill on the job at a given performance level and/or a certain number of times.
- Successfully completing a designated training program or activity.

Upon successful demonstration and certification of the skill, the team member is then given an increase in pay. The system includes guidelines for whether or not skills must be learned in a specific sequence, whether or not recertification of old skills is required, how mastery will be demonstrated, how frequently a team member is eligible for an increase, and how frequently a team member must move to a new skill level.

In other words, there are both limits and requirements as to how fast an employee moves up. Some organizations add what are called *gates,* or points in the skills levels that require management approval to pass through. Gates put the brakes on upward employee movement and also give management the opportunity to see if its design of skills blocks and standards meets the needs of the teams.

THE CHALLENGE OF PAY-FOR-SKILL SYSTEMS

Pay-for-skill systems hold out a great deal of promise, and organizations with them say they like them.[2] At the same time, pay-for-skill systems represent a substantial commitment. Unlike gain-sharing, which is a bonus system, pay for skill is a base-pay compensation system and, once in place, is not easily altered or abandoned. That's why any organization considering a pay-for-skill compensation system should be aware of what it's getting into, especially in the following arenas:

Employee control. Under pay-for-skill, even with gates and other limitations, employees have more control than they did before over how far and how fast they move up the pay scale—especially when compared to performance-based compensation systems, in which employees must be hired or promoted into better-paying positions.

Planning. Setting up a pay-for-skill system requires massive amounts of planning and data, some of which will already have been generated in the process of changing to work teams.
- Each job may need to be redesigned to include a greater range of tasks so there are options for employees to broaden and deepen their skills.
- Jobs need to be described in terms of skills required, not tasks to be performed.
- Procedures for moving up the various skills levels need to be designed; these procedures should be fair and clearly understood, and they should clearly state what team members must do to increase their earnings.
- The likely present and future cost of the system needs to be carefully projected three to five years into the future, to make sure the organization can afford to stay with it.
- Training opportunities need to be developed and/or identified.
- Certification procedures need to be developed and/or identified.
- Elements for system evaluation and improvement need to be built in from the outset.

Type of skills. There are several types of team skills that pay-for-skill systems must include: technical, interpersonal, decision making/problem solving, administrative, and verbal and numerical literacy. Each needs its own process for training and certification.

Cost. Pay-for-skill will cost more in hourly wages, training, and administration than a standard compensation system. If, in the long run, the flexibility and other benefits won't more than offset these costs, a pay-for-skill system probably shouldn't be adopted.

GUIDELINES

The following do's and don'ts can focus the design team and steering committee on some critical issues. Ultimately, of course, pay-for-skill systems need to be set up within the context of the organization's own situation.

Make sure the management team at the facility is strong. Managing a pay-for-skill system is a big challenge; the management team responsible for it must be competent and confident enough to see that it is administered fairly.

Reevaluate your hiring and selection procedures. Because employees in a pay-for-skill system need to know "how to learn," it's important to look for this ability in job applicants. (Don't take school grades as an absolute indicator; poor school records can reflect boredom and lack of motivation as much as anything else.) Another point: Some organizations have found that a certain portion of their employees simply aren't motivated by pay-for-skill systems. Some may avoid training because they don't see themselves as competent learners; others may not think it's worth the effort.

Don't overlook the so-called soft skills. Work teams succeed or fail on their members' skills in problem solving, decision making, leading and participating in meetings, listening, giving feedback, and all the other communications skills that people need in the absence of "directive" leaders and a clear-cut chain of command. These skills are not always as easy to measure as the "harder," more technical skills associated with a specific task, but they're no less important, and the system that is set up should reflect this fact. In other words, this isn't "easy stuff" that can be casually evaluated against vague standards.

Plan for periodic review and updates. As technology changes, certain job skills may have to be redefined or recombined, and additional skill units may be required. Certification procedures may need fine-tuning.

Delay putting the system into place until work teams are up and running. Before installing a pay-for-skill system, it is necessary to redefine team jobs and develop appropriate skill training levels for each team. If the system is installed before the kinks in your work teams are ironed out, you may have to redesign large chunks of it.

Be rigorous. Pay-for-skill isn't about being nice to employees; it's about being fair and clear. Unless the organization adheres to standards, the program will lose employees' respect, and the organization could end up paying for half-learned skills of little real value to the team or the team members. In other words, don't be afraid to say no when someone hasn't met the requirements.

Beware of the downhill slide into ticket-punching. If employees sense that pay-for-skill means nothing more than putting in time in the training room or collecting completion certificates, the program will lose its freshness and ability to motivate people to higher performance levels. Avoid this trap by maintaining a balance between classroom certification and on-the-job skill demonstrations. Skill demonstrations can take more time and administrative support and be subject to more disagreements, but they create a liveliness in the system that cannot be achieved any other way.

Recertify to keep employees' skills sharp. Most organizations with pay-for-skill systems have procedures for periodically requiring employees to demonstrate that they (1) haven't forgotten a skill for which they received certification but haven't performed for some time, or (2) have mastered new aspects of a skill resulting from new technology and/or new safety regulations.

Avoid premature topping out. Most organizations provide restrictions on how often an employee can move to a new skill level. Typically, it takes a minimum of three to five years to reach the top of the scale, a much shorter time than in traditional compensation systems. Some organizations create the opportunity to earn more money beyond the top skill level by introducing gain-sharing at that point.

Cooperate with any unions involved. Although work teams are not based on seniority, preserving the value of seniority is an important issue for most unions. Some work teams compromise by discussing with the union which workers to retain during a layoff.

Be conservative. Once a new system is in place, change is difficult without creating uncertainty and concern. There's nothing wrong with keeping the old system until work teams are operating successfully. Even then it may need only minor adjustments.

NOTES

1. Michael Schuster, "Gainsharing: Do It Right the First Time," *Sloan Management Review* (Winter 1987): 17–25.
2. Nina Gupta, G. Douglas Jenkins, Jr., and William P. Curington, "Paying for Knowledge: Myths and Realities," *National Productivity Review* (Spring 1986): 107–123.

TOOLS AND TECHNIQUES FOR IMPLEMENTING TEAMS

INTRODUCTION

This section provides descriptions of some of the critical tools and techniques needed to manage the nuts-and-bolts of implementing self-directed work teams. The 19 tools and techniques described here have helped organizations navigate the process of exploring and establishing self-directed work teams—from early planning tactics, like conducting a feasibility study or training design team members, to later maintenance or expansion issues, like formally recognizing team efforts or spreading work teams to other locations.

The material in this section is a selection of seminar outlines, counseling how-to's, planning guides, charts, and step-by-step procedures. Some can be completed quickly by one person; others require several months and the involvement of many people. All of them, however, are based on the authors' experience with real organizations that needed practical help at certain critical junctures.

Specific tools and techniques included here are:

- Employee involvement: alternatives to self-direction.
- The steering committee.
- The feasibility study.
- Developing a mission statement.
- Design-team training.
- Designing and implementing awareness training.
- Workplace analysis.
- Team member training.
- Manager and supervisor transition training.
- Hand-off plans for supervisory and support group tasks.
- Team member role expansion plan.
- Peer disciplinary review committee.
- Recognition and reward techniques.
- Mature team-new team coaching session.
- A group problem-solving process.
- Cluster meeting.
- Peer performance appraisal.
- Repotting workshop.
- Diffusion strategies.

Each tool or technique is described in the following format:

WHAT—A brief description and explanation of its importance.

WHEN—Indicators and cues for when to use it.

WHO—Identification of the type of person who would be primarily responsible, and any others who need to get involved.

HOW—Step-by-step procedures for its use.

WHAT'S NEXT—Expected outcomes and possible next steps.

A CASE IN POINT—A real-life example of its use, when appropriate.

If you decide to make the actual transition in your organization, techniques such as those in this section will be invaluable to your progress toward self-direction.

EMPLOYEE INVOLVEMENT: ALTERNATIVES TO SELF-DIRECTION

WHAT

Employee involvement refers to the degree to which employees in a given organization or department stay informed and make decisions about their work. Employee involvement is influenced by an organization's (or group's) culture, management style, and employee preferences. Employee involvement levels range from very little to almost total involvement, with self-directed work teams calling for a high level. Although to some extent descriptions of this sort are arbitrary, they can provide a baseline to compare with employee involvement in your own organization. With this understanding, determination of what must be done to increase this level can begin. This section of the book describes six levels of employee involvement. Two additional levels (limited and total self-direction) are not covered here.

WHEN

As part of your feasibility study, you may want to get a sense of how much employee involvement exists in your organization.

Or, after completing the feasibility study, you may decide your organization is not comfortable with the amount of employee involvement work teams require. Even so, you may still feel that your present level of employee involvement no longer fits your organization's needs or objectives, and you might want to explore ways of increasing it.

WHO

The steering committee should be involved in initial explorations. If it decides to include the issue in the feasibility study, it may want to ask a representative sample of employees to estimate the level of involvement in their department. In some cases, someone from outside these groups may need to be brought in to provide perspective and facilitate discussions.

HOW

There are no hard-and-fast, step-by-step procedures for this exploration. One approach would be to ask the steering committee to read a description of employee involvement levels, and then ask the committee as a group to agree on the highest level of employee involvement that now characterizes their organization (or a group within it), and identify a higher form or forms of involvement that might fit better with the organization's evolving needs and intentions.

SIX LEVELS OF EMPLOYEE INVOLVEMENT

The following six levels of employee involvement begin at the minimum level seen in organizations today, and stop just short of the level at which self-directed work teams operate. Keep in mind that these are not developmental stages that an organization must go through in sequence to reach self-direction. Nor are higher levels automatically better. It's up to each organization to find the level that works best.

LEVEL 1. MANAGERS MAKE DECISIONS ON THEIR OWN, ANNOUNCE THEM, AND THEN RESPOND TO ANY QUESTIONS EMPLOYEES MAY HAVE

At this level, employee involvement is defined as listening and asking questions; employees are involved neither in making nor approving decisions. Typical activities include (1) the regularly scheduled meeting in which managers bring employees up to date on regular operations, (2) the special meeting in which managers announce new developments, and (3) the "press conference" meeting in which employees can voice their concerns and/or request information about events.

Example:
The plant manager calls a general all-hands meeting to announce the new safety procedures.

Management expectations. Managers expect that this level of involvement will produce conformance to decisions made by them.

Employee needs. This level of involvement meets employees' need for information concerning their work.

Advantages. This level of involvement is a fairly speedy and efficient way to disseminate information, and it keeps employees from wasting energy ferreting out rumors. Also, if employees believe managers are being honest and open, it develops a sense of trust between the two groups.

Pitfalls. It can fail to uncover—and can often cause—employee alienation and even rebellion, and it places the entire burden of decision making on managers, without any input from employees.

Level 2. Managers Usually Make the Decisions, but Only after Seeking the Views of Employees

If Level 1 is typified by a press conference type of meeting, a typical Level 2 activity is a round-table discussion. The key difference is that managers seek the views of employees on problems and issues before making a decision, although they do not necessarily agree to act on these views.

Example:
A sales manager calls her sales people together once a month to get their ideas on ways to increase sales in their region.

Management expectations. Managers expect that this level of involvement will give them information they can use in making management decisions, and will reassure them that employees accept these decisions.

Employee needs. This level of involvement satisfies employees' need for a limited degree of interaction with the decision makers in the organization (versus involvement in the decision-making process itself).

Advantages. The advantages are (1) managers have access to the opinions and views of employees (including technical experts with special expertise), and therefore can make better decisions; (2) employees tend to feel more involved in the decision-making process than they do in Level 1, and they are therefore more likely to accept and endorse management decisions wholeheartedly without having to take responsibility for them when they don't work out; and (3) decisions can still be made quickly since employees have no vote in the decision-making process itself.

Pitfalls. Because at this level of involvement there is no specific purpose beyond getting employees' concerns and ideas on the table, the dialogue can turn into time-wasting gripe sessions. Employees may also resent having their ideas taken over and carried out by others. This level of limited, two-way communication can also be misconstrued as "total employee involvement," guaranteeing that no further levels will be explored.

Six Levels of Employee Involvement

Level	Advantages	Pitfalls
1. Managers make decisions on their own, announce them, and then respond to employee questions.	• Enhances efficient decision making	• Can cause employee alienation • Requires management to make all decisions alone
2. Managers make decisions, but only after seeking employees' views.	• Permits input from employees • Helps employees feel more involved • Speeds up decision-making process	• Can waste time and blur focus • Can create employee resentment
3. Managers create temporary employee groups to recommend solutions to particular problems.	• Helps avoid use of outside consultants • Permits application of just the right mix of expertise to problem	• Can conflict with employees' "regular" work • Can become substitute for taking action
4. Managers meet with groups of employees on regular basis to identify problems and recommend solutions.	• Taps employee creativity • Requires no alteration of existing management system	• Can lack enough clout to get things done
5. Managers establish and participate in cross-functional problem-solving teams.	• Helps managers/employees gain understanding of other departments, and of the overall organization	• Can trigger "turf" conflicts among departments
6. Ongoing work groups assume expanded responsibility for a particular issue, like cost reduction.	• Greater employee commitment and involvement	• Approach can threaten supervisors and managers

LEVEL 3. MANAGERS CREATE TEMPORARY EMPLOYEE GROUPS TO RECOMMEND SOLUTIONS TO PARTICULAR PROBLEMS

Level 3 represents an increase over Level 2, with selected employees (often from more than one department) formally assigned to come up with solutions to particular predefined problems, rather than simply offering their ideas. Task forces are typical of Level 3. The key elements of this level are: (1) the problem has been predefined, (2) employees carry out this assignment in addition to their regular work, and (3) once the group makes its recommendations, it is disbanded.

Example:
The vice president appoints a task force consisting of one plant manager, one market analyst, and one product designer to come up with ways of reducing the time it takes a new product to reach the marketplace.

Management expectations. Managers expect real commitment—in the form of expert and effective contributions toward the solution of a specific problem—from the employees in these special groups.

Employee needs. This level of involvement provides employees with opportunities to receive recognition for their efforts, and perhaps to move up in the organization.

Advantages. The advantages of this level are that (1) because managers can use the expertise of their own employees, they can avoid having to pay for outside help, and (2) management can bring just the right combination of expertise to solve a problem.

Pitfalls. Employees can be squeezed between the demands of their jobs and those of the problem-solving group. Appointing a special group can become a substitute for taking action, because the group itself has no authority to act upon its recommendations. When their assignment is finished, employees can feel disappointed and let down.

LEVEL 4. MANAGERS MEET WITH GROUPS OF EMPLOYEES ON A REGULAR BASIS TO IDENTIFY PROBLEMS AND RECOMMEND SOLUTIONS

Level 4 is like Level 3, with two important exceptions: groups are permanent, and they identify problems as well as recommend solutions. Quality circles typify this kind of involvement. Groups operating at this level are usually led by the employees' supervisor; employee participation is, for the most part, voluntary and is perceived as an add-on to regular work. While this type of involvement is still outside the regular management structure, the organization often appoints facilitators to train these groups and to serve as a link between teams and managers with the authority to implement employee recommendations.

Example:
Employees in the shipping department of a tubing company sign up to meet with their supervisor for an hour Tuesday afternoons to identify improvements they would like to make in their work.

Management expectations. Managers expect real employee commitment to seek out and solve productivity, quality, safety, and quality-of-work-life problems.

Employee needs. The primary employee need met by this level of involvement is the opportunity to play a real part in identifying and solving problems of concern to them.

Advantages. Employee creativity unleashed by this greater level of involvement can result in superior problem-solving efforts. Also, the organization need not alter its traditional management system.

Pitfalls. Because groups at this level are outside the traditional management system, they may not have enough clout to make much of an impact. Also, to remain in existence, they constantly need to find new problems. If the problems disappear, they have nothing left to do but disband.

Level 5. Managers Establish and Participate in Cross-Functional Problem-Solving Teams

This level combines the cross-functional aspect of Level 3 (typified by the task force) and the permanence of Level 4 (typified by the quality circle). Often members will be "peak performers" from several departmental quality circles. They form a permanent, cross-functional group that typically meets less frequently but for longer sessions than a quality circle. The group may have enough people from different departments to be able to break into subgroups to work on specific problems.

Example:
One employee from each department in a finishing plant (operators, mechanics, instructors, parts handlers, cleaning, and safety) meet all day once a month to work on an agenda of problems for the whole plant.

Management expectations. At this level, management expects to see interdepartmental cooperation throughout the organization, and improved coordination and productivity organization-wide as a result.

Employee needs. This level of involvement meets employees' need to have some influence on policies and procedures that go beyond their own departments.

Advantages. Managers and employees can begin to understand the issues and concerns of other departments, and of the organization as a whole.

Pitfalls. As more people from different parts of the organization work together, "turf issues" can flare up, strengthening barriers between departments instead of eliminating them.

Level 6. Ongoing Work Groups Assume Expanded Responsibility for a Particular Issue, Like Cost Reduction

At this level, problem solving is integrated with employees' daily job responsibilities, or rather, one aspect of them, such as service quality or job safety. The traditional management structure hasn't changed, but within it employees have more responsibility to find ways to improve how they do their jobs. The rationale is that when it comes to their jobs, employees are the experts and, given a specific focus for their improvement efforts, can come up with the best solutions.

Example:
An apparel manufacturing plant decides to concentrate on on-time shipments in order to achieve a competitive edge in the marketplace. All employees are expected to stay constantly alert to opportunities to meet that goal.

Management expectations. Managers expect that a top-priority issue or problem will receive concentrated attention. Managers expect employees to take the initiative for this process, leaving managers to function as coaches.

Employee needs. Whereas in Level 5 employees had a measure of influence over organization-wide policies and procures, in Level 6 they have the opportunity to exert total control in the smaller arena of their jobs.

Advantages. With control, employees have the chance to make small but critical improvements in their work that can pay off in productivity increases and real quality improvements. Furthermore, being held responsible for their efforts tends to increase their commitment and level of contribution. Finally, this level offers organizations an opportunity to get a flavor of what self-direction feels like without having to make extensive changes in their existing management structure.

Pitfalls. This approach can seriously threaten those supervisors and middle managers who are not equipped by either temperament or training to take a less directive, more facilitative approach with their employees.

WHAT'S NEXT?

Once you have reached agreement on your present level of employee involvement, and the level you think you would like to move to, you need to consider the steps to make this shift possible. These could involve new procedures, training, and other less direct efforts to create a more supportive organizational environment.

THE STEERING COMMITTEE

WHAT

The initial team established by the leader or champion of self-directed work teams is called the *steering committee*. Its purpose is fourfold:

- Learn about self-direction.
- Determine if work teams are appropriate for a given site (or sites).
- Organize the design team or teams.
- Oversee the transition to work teams.

One of the first assignments of the steering committee is to conduct site visits to organizations that have been successful and unsuccessful in implementing teams. Analyzing the results of these site visits is the first step in a multistage steering committee assessment, which determines the applicability and benefits of work teams for the organization, and the organization's readiness to make the transition to teams.

Before making the commitment to teams, it is critical to decide if this is indeed the best direction for the organization. What has happened to other organizations that have shifted to teams? Will a shift to self-directed work teams provide the same results in this organization? Site visits conducted by steering committee members provide the means for addressing these questions and exploring alternatives.

WHEN

When an organization or company champion becomes interested in the potential of self-directed work teams, it is time to establish a steering committee to carry out the initial investigation. Steering committee site visits precede the more visible, high-profile feasibility study and allow the low-key gathering of information upon which the organization's initial decision to go ahead with the feasibility study will be based. (See "The Feasibility Study," pages 265–272.)

If the possibility of change becomes common knowledge in the organization, unnecessary questions and insecurities can be raised, even before a commitment is made. The steering committee, however, can address the question of self-directed work teams without high-profile visibility, and thus avoid widespread speculation among employees and later disappointment if anticipated changes are not forthcoming.

WHO

The steering committee works best when it consists of from 4 to 12 members who have the expertise to explore the following concerns:

1. How will the transition to self-directed work teams affect overall productivity?
2. What will the probable impact of teams be on the people in the organization, and what impact will the people have on the transition to teams?
3. Can systems and work processes in the organization be successfully modified to fit self-directed work teams?

The individuals selected for the steering committee should be high-level executives (such as vice presidents) who are responsible for and knowledgeable about the major functional areas of the company. The overall champions for self-direction may not always be the best choice for steering committee membership, because their commitment can easily bias the team's assessment.

Individuals who should be considered for selection to the steering committee include:

- A high-level executive who fully understands the company's product or service. In a manufacturing company, this person would be the vice president of manufacturing, who is knowledgeable about products and manufacturing processes. In a service company, the vice president in charge of services would fill this position.

- The vice president of human resources or a high-level individual who understands the people needs of the organization and can be the advocate of the people. The human resources person is most likely to have contacts outside the organization—contacts that will be important in providing resources for site visits.

- A high-level corporate finance or management information systems executive, someone who understands organizational systems. This person is often the one most responsible for systems in the organization.

- The vice president of organizational development (OD) or another high-level person with an OD background.

- Other department executives who must support the change if it is to be successful.

The members of the steering committee will have different primary assignments that will take advantage of their individual areas of expertise. Some organizations have more than four people on the steering committee, but at this early stage of low-profile investigation, it is probably advisable to keep the committee small and to gain input from nonmember executives.

HOW

The steering committee will carry out visits and interviews at sites that have been both successful and unsuccessful in the transition to teams. Each steering committee member should interview the individuals who can supply information from his or her area of expertise. For example, the vice president of manufacturing should solicit information about the manufacturing operation; the human resources person should ask about the impact on people.

Once steering committee members have been selected, they will need training to prepare them for their role in the initial gathering of information and its analysis. Attending a seminar and reading articles and books on self-directed work teams is a good place to start. (See "Suggested Reading List for Steering Committee," page 264.)

With this background information, steering committee members are ready to work with the self-directed work-team consultant to develop interview questions to ask during site visits. Four major issues should be covered in these interviews:

1. What were the major hurdles the site-visit organization had to overcome in terms of production and delivery, people, and systems?
2. What memorable actions were taken to overcome these hurdles?
3. What are the major driving forces for success?
4. What significant strategies were built on these driving forces?

For the steering committee members, the key to the success of the interviewing process is to probe for detailed answers to these questions—answers that will be heavily used in the analysis process conducted at the completion of site-visit activities.

With interview questions in hand, the steering committee is ready to begin its data-gathering visits. It is ideal for all steering committee members to visit a site simultaneously, but busy schedules often make this difficult. As an alternative, members should visit the sites in pairs. A partner can be of considerable help in conducting a better interview.

The visitation process should continue as long as necessary, until sufficient information is gathered on which to base the decision to shift to teams (as much as six months). It is critical to identify any possible pitfalls that the organization might face during the transition to teams.

When site visits and interviews have been completed, the steering committee meets as a team to analyze and discuss the findings. They usually spend two or three days off site to analyze data, to evaluate the organization's readiness for teams, and to determine whether a feasibility study should be done.

The analysis should focus on several areas:

1. The present state of the organization with regard to participation. (See "Employee Involvement: Alternatives to Self-Direction," pages 247–256.)

2. The changes which will accompany the transition to work teams.

3. The positive or negative results of each change.

4. The impact on the present organization if each of the changes were to occur. (This step is called an "impact analysis." An example of how to do an impact analysis follows under "A Case in Point.")

5. Negative results that might be sufficient to block a move to self-directed work teams.

6. The resources or alternatives that exist inside or outside the organization to counter any such negative result.

7. The go or no-go recommendation to proceed with a feasibility study.

After identifying the positive and negative results, the steering committee analyzes their impact on the organization. If a major negative result is identified, the data gathered from other organizations becomes especially valuable. Considering what other organizations have done, the committee determines whether a negative impact can be overcome.

Based on this analysis, the committee decides on a go or no-go recommendation for a feasibility study. Once a recommendation to proceed is put before executives, the project takes on a higher profile, with increased levels of expectation and concern.

WHAT'S NEXT?

The steering committee confers with the champion of self-directed work teams regarding its analysis and recommendation. With the champion's approval, the committee then presents its recommendation to the executives who decide whether to go any further with the investigation. If the feasibility study is approved by these executives, the steering committee helps decide the specific operating unit in which the study will be made, and initiates the feasibility study.

A CASE IN POINT: Jet Engine Components Manufacturing Facility

A steering committee was formed at a small plant that manufactures critical jet engine components. This plant was one of several within a large division; the division president was championing the shift to self-directed work teams. Because all plants within the division were suppliers and customers to other plants in the division, the president recognized that team implementation could have a major impact on the entire division.

The steering committee consisted of the division director of human resources, the vice president of manufacturing, the director of management information systems, and the director of quality assurance.

Awareness training for the steering committee was conducted by the corporate organizational development specialist, who had a strong background in self-directed work teams. He had implemented teams at several other locations within the corporation.

The steering committee took the following steps:

1. Developed interview questions with a strong focus on gathering information about the impact of teams on quality, cost, and productivity.
2. Identified specific concerns that would have a major impact on the transition to teams, including a concern regarding government-required inspection regulations.
3. Developed additional questions that specifically addressed the inspection issue and other concerns—questions designed to solicit information valuable in seeking possible solutions.
4. Conducted site visits and interviews both within the corporation and at other high-technology organizations outside the corporation.
5. Met as a group following visitations and interviews to discuss findings and carry out an impact analysis of changes that would result from a shift to work teams.
6. Based on the results of the impact analysis, made a recommendation to the division president to proceed with a feasibility study.

The impact analysis conducted by the steering committee included identification of proposed actions and potential positive and negative results of these actions. One proposed action the committee had identified prior to analysis was to make inspection the responsibility of everyone on the work team, rather than of quality assurance. Here is the impact analysis done by the committee on the effect self-directed work teams would have on the inspection activity.

IMPACT ANALYSIS

Current Situation. Government regulations stipulate that products must be tracked and inspected by government-certified quality professionals at every step of production, from incoming raw materials to the shipping of the final product. In this organization, inspections are conducted by the quality assurance department.

Positive Results	Negative Results
a. Everyone on the team operates under known standards.	a. Everyone will need to be trained.
b. Becoming certified in QA is a valuable skill for employees to have.	b. There will be a loss of status for QA people.
c. Throughput of products will be more efficient if all employees can do inspections.	c. The government will have to approve certification procedures.

Proposed Action 1.   Make inspection the responsibility of everyone on the work team.

Of the identified results, the team was most concerned about the third negative item: having to get government approval for in-team inspection. Here is where the information collected in interviews came into play. Committee members had learned from their visits at two sites, which were both high-technology companies with government contracts, that these organizations had received government approval for in-team inspection within one year of implementing work teams.

Because committee members were able to get similar reassuring data for their other concerns, the steering committee recommended a "go" for a feasibility study to the division president.

SUGGESTED READING LIST FOR STEERING COMMITTEE

1. Paul S. Goodman and Associates. *Designing Effective Workgroups*. San Francisco: Jossey-Bass, Inc., 1986.

2. J. Richard Hackman and G. R. Oldham. *Work Redesign*. Reading, Mass.: Addison-Wesley Publishing, 1980.

3. Edward E. Lawler III. *High Involvement Management*. San Francisco: Jossey-Bass, Inc., 1986.

4. William A. Pasmore and John J. Sherwood. *Sociotechnical Systems*. San Diego, Calif.: University Associates, 1978.

THE FEASIBILITY STUDY

WHAT

A feasibility study is a systematic exploration undertaken to determine if the organizational climate and business conditions favor self-directed work teams or an alternative level of employee involvement. A work-team feasibility study covers the organization's potential payoffs, the potential costs involved, any special problems or opportunities, and recommended action steps (usually presented as a series of options for the steering committee to choose from). A feasibility study may also recommend those sites most ready to implement self-directed work teams.

WHEN

A feasibility study is initiated after the steering committee has conducted its site visits and has made a recommendation to management to continue exploring work teams. (See "The Steering Committee," pages 257–264.)

WHO

A feasibility study for self-directed work teams is conducted under the auspices of the steering committee, which has been commissioned by the executive who is the work-team champion. The study is often carried out by a consultant to the steering committee—someone who can ask hard questions and maintain an objective attitude. The people who provide the data can include any or all of the following: everyone in the organization, specific groups of employees (or a representative sample), and people outside the organization with expertise in the organization's industry or market.

HOW

There are four steps in a feasibility study: (1) designing the study, (2) collecting the data, (3) analyzing the data, and (4) presenting the results of the analysis. These steps are usually carried out by the consultant.

1. *Designing the study.*   The most critical aspect of the design from the point of view of the steering committee is to make sure the study will generate a fair sampling of data and opinions.

2. *Collecting the data.*   Information needs to be collected in the following six areas:

Are the work processes compatible with self-directed work teams? Is the organization's present technology so automated that increased employee motivation and involvement would do little to increase productivity? Can people be cross-trained in a reasonable amount of time to perform more than one job? Can performance results be documented and communicated?

Are employees willing and able to make self-direction work? What is the literacy level of the work force? Is the present and/or potential work force capable of learning new technical, administrative, and interpersonal skills? What is the employees' attitude toward involvement in their work? Do union and/or seniority policies give the organization the right to select and train team members? Are potential team members willing and able to train other team members in technical and administrative skills?

Can managers master and apply the hands-off leadership style required by self-directed teams? Historically, how have the organization's managers responded to change? Is there a history of encouraging and supporting employee participation and development? Are managers skilled in reinforcing positive actions and redirecting negative actions? Do managers have strong technical competencies? How do managers respond to being challenged by employees? Disagreements with employees? Do managers establish and meet objectives and performance standards? Will managers yield authority to teams when the teams are ready to receive it?

Is the market healthy or promising enough to support improved productivity without reducing the work force? Is the market stable, shrinking, or growing? Will improved quality, cost, and delivery result in increased demand? Will the ability to respond to special orders increase profitability? Will increased productivity result in a market glut, with reduced prices and no payoff? Are upcoming changes in the market likely to open up new opportunities for the organization's product or service? If employees strive to improve their productivity and quality of work, can they enhance the organization's product or service?

Will the organization's policies and culture in both corporate and field locations support the transition to teams? Do corporate documents like employee handbooks and policies and procedures manuals encourage trust? Are manager-employee relationships characterized by an "us-them" attitude? Are productivity and job satisfaction expectations in balance? Are strategic plans communicated to those who need to know about them? Are strategic plans related to operational plans? Are support departments willing to give and receive suggestions for change? Are channels for communication established, known, and used? What are the expectations and attitudes towards self-direction at corporate headquarters? In the field? Is consulting assistance available and affordable?

Will the community support the transition to teams? Is the community supportive, neutral, or hostile? Do local training and educational institutions offer the potential for help? How do employees' families and friends perceive and influence a move to self-direction?

This information is collected through a combination of a review of organizational documents, personal observations and interviews, group interviews, and pencil-and-paper questionnaires.

3. *Analyzing the data.* The data analysis should indicate clearly the steps being suggested and why. The cost for each of these steps (e.g., dollars, time, training, change in attitudes/approach) should be balanced against the anticipated payoff (e.g., increased productivity, responsiveness to new or changing markets, improved quality of work life, organizational survival).

Although the analysis need not—and in fact should not—include a detailed plan for enacting the recommendations, it probably should include general recommendations for any first steps towards self-direction, such as possible pilot sites and types of team members. Normally, a company compares data from several sites to determine the best site for self-directed teams.

4. *Presenting the analysis.* Some consultants present their findings in the form of final recommendations. Many, however, make a preliminary presentation of general findings to the steering committee, and then, after getting feedback from the committee, make a final presentation of recommendations or possible options. This two-phase process helps stimulate discussion. It also permits committee members to form their own recommendations and, in so doing, develop ownership of the study. Whatever approach is taken, the presentation should emphasize the costs and payoffs of several options.

In addition, feasibility studies often serve to help sell a particular course of action, form the basis for initial planning (including selection of a pilot site), and spark discussion of other forms of employee involvement.

While feasibility studies bring together information and suggest directions, they are by no means the final word. For example, a committed and enthusiastic CEO—someone who wants self-direction, no matter what—can offset a host of negative indicators.

WHAT'S NEXT?

In most cases, the next step is to make the go/no-go decision regarding self-direction. If the decision is go, the next step will be the process described in Chapter 3 of this book. If it is no go, the steering committee should (1) begin discussions of what can be done to make the organization more receptive to and compatible with self-direction and/or (2) consider other, more limited forms of employee participation. (See "Employee Involvement: Alternatives to Self-Direction," pages 247–256.) Unless the possibility of moving to self-direction has been kept securely under wraps, deciding to do nothing at all could be demoralizing.

A CASE IN POINT: Industrial Heating and Air Conditioning Company

The CEO of an industrial heating and air conditioning company headquartered in the Midwest was determined to set up self-directed work teams. The only question in his mind was, Where to start in the organization? Branch office managers? An entire regional office? A maintenance crew in one branch office? A district sales force?

The CEO formed a steering committee and commissioned an outside consultant to conduct a feasibility study. The consultant reviewed company documents; conducted interviews with employees at corporate, regional, district, and branch office sites; and sent out opinion surveys to all employees.

Here is the sequence of activities the consultant carried out:

1. She conducted one-on-one interviews (based on the questions above listed under "How") with key people in the company.

2. She conducted cross-functional group interviews in the branches, each group consisting of one representative from

Exhibit 3-1.

Organizational Environment	Yes	Somewhat	No
An inspiring vision has been developed		X	
The vision has been communicated		X	
People development is a high priority	X		
Developmental programs are in place		X	
Productivity data is available	X		
Productivity data is widely shared		X	
Standards of performance are known		X	
Rewards match performance excellence		X	

construction, sales, maintenance, and modernization (upgrading previously installed equipment). The consultant asked group members to talk about how they did and did not communicate with each other. She used information from the first round of interviews to probe for potential problem areas.

3. She distributed an opinion survey to all employees through their managers. (About 10 percent responded.)

4. She prepared a "trait analysis," a broad-brush summary of the data she had collected, organized in three categories: organizational environment, leadership, and work force. The trait analysis for the organizational environment looked like Exhibit 3-1.

5. She prepared a series of start-up options based on her assessment of the organization's readiness to move to self-direction. (Each of these options was a starting point for a broader, longer-term implementation of teams.) The options included the following:

Option 1. Start by working with the maintenance mechanic group only. Don't change the structure of their jobs, but have them form into groups of five or six. These groups would support each other to handle complex jobs and emergencies. Make some minor improvements in communication and training, and change the compensation system to reward the mechanics for their performance.

Option 2.   Start with the maintenance mechanic group, but do a major restructuring of their jobs. Create a team in which mechanics take assignments based on their skills and interest levels (equipment specialties, concentration on electronic versus mechanical systems, interest in troubleshooting), rather than on the customer's location.

Option 3.   Take a broader approach and develop cross-functional construction, maintenance, and sales/service teams in each branch.

6   The consultant presented the options to the steering committee at a preliminary meeting. At the meeting she led the committee through an analysis of each option. Committee members listed the positives and negatives under four categories: cost/profitability, quality, customer-vendor relationships, and organizational climate/job satisfaction.

The results of this session, together with individual conversations with steering committee members, convinced the consultant that despite the CEO's initial enthusiasm, neither he nor members of the steering committee had the commitment required to make self-direction a success. Furthermore, there were some significant organizational factors indicating that at this time, a full-scale move to self-direction would not be a good idea.

7.   She presented her final recommendation: not to move to self-direction at this time, but instead to work on improving the areas identified by the trait analysis chart.

DEVELOPING A MISSION STATEMENT

WHAT

A mission statement summarizes the objectives that a company or organization plans to achieve through change—its vision for the future. The statement suggests the organizational structure that will be created to meet objectives, motivate people, and achieve excellence. It targets goals such as high-quality products, customer satisfaction, competitive edge, reputation for quality and service, and the like. The purpose of the mission statement is to stimulate and focus the energies of everyone involved with changes in company structure. In making the long and often difficult transition to self-directed work teams, the organization will rely on its mission statement to help clarify the reasons and provide the incentives for change.

WHEN

After the steering committee determines the feasibility of shifting to self-directed work teams and, with company executives, makes the commitment to change, it is time to draft a mission statement.

WHO

The steering committee, plus any other key people they need to involve, construct the mission statement. Usually the work-team consultant serves as a facilitator for this process.

HOW

The steering committee and company executives, working with a facilitator, will need to consider various factors in drafting the mission statement:

1. Decide the overall purpose of the organization's transition to self-directed work teams. What goals does the organization hope to realize from the change?

2. Consider the methods that will best encourage employee involvement in reaching company goals and identifying areas for change. What do employees perceive as possible and desirable?

3. Determine which of the six focuses best suit the organization and its people (see Chapter 3, page 52). A mission statement may use any one or more of these focuses.

4. Strive for a general, strategic statement. Mention of self-directed work teams is not usually necessary.

5. Make the statement as long or short as is necessary to clarify goals and motivate change.

Sample mission statements follow in Exhibits 4-1 through 4-3.

In putting together the mission statement, be aware of the following pitfalls:

- Statements that are too global may lack the focus needed to provide clear incentives for change.

- If the statement expresses an executive vision not held companywide, it won't serve its function as an incentive for change.

EXHIBIT 4-1. Manufacturing Organization

[Company Name] is dedicated to the production and maintenance of top-quality weighing and measuring devices for industry. To ensure that quality, we pledge to
Encourage open communication among all levels of the company;
Reward effective employee actions, decision making and innovation;
Maintain a safe, clean, and up-to-date plant;
Solicit feedback from our customers and the community to meet their needs more responsively.

EXHIBIT 4-2. Technology Organization

As a customer-oriented company serving a global, multi-industry market, [Company name's] goal is to be a recognized leader in the community in which we work.

We will achieve our goals by providing top-quality products and services to create customer satisfaction and by developing the strengths and skills of all our employees, with everyone working together in an environment of mutual trust and respect.

EXHIBIT 4-3. Service Organization

[Company name] will provide a full range of services that is continuously expanded and updated. To insure customer satisfaction, we will establish a cooperative internal environment that projects our company's dedication to serving its customers and the community. We will provide for our employees
Opportunities to participate in making decisions;
Rewards for contributions to company goals;
Opportunities for personal and professional development;
Programs to enhance the level of work satisfaction.
We will provide for our customers
Rapid response time to inquiries or orders;
Timely follow-up procedures;
Assistance in determining the service level appropriate to their needs.
We will provide for the community
A site that enhances its surroundings;
A responsiveness to community concerns, activities, and programs;
Practices that support the environment, including recycling, an energy-efficient building, and a company transportation plan.

- If the statement is introduced too early, employee expectations for widespread change may be raised too soon, causing frustration and disillusionment.

- If the statement is not made public, employees won't have a clear expression of the context for change and the expected results.

WHAT'S NEXT?

After drafting the mission statement, identify actions top-level managers can take to demonstrate their commitment. For example, if the company vision targets equality, separate employee and executive facilities like parking areas or exercise rooms should be eliminated.

The mission statement will become the crucial foundation for the transition to self-directed work teams and will need to be communicated to the organization. Round-table meetings are one vehicle that allows employees to react to the mission statement. In addition, the design team will use it in developing a preliminary plan in preparation for implementing the shift to teams.

DESIGN-TEAM TRAINING

WHAT

The select group of individuals that maps out the first version of a full-scale implementation plan for self-directed work teams is designated the *design team.* Empowered by the steering committee, the design team researches the day-to-day staffing and operational questions that must be answered prior to implementation and then designs the organization's plan for the transition to teams.

Initially, classroom training provides the design team with the skills it needs to draft its implementation plan. The training includes an intensive program, which can last up to four months, that prepares team members to become both explorers of the possibilities teams offer and teachers of those who will participate in the implementation of teams.

Thereafter, training addresses the ongoing transition and deals with any concerns that are the focus of the design team's attention when the training occurs.

To ensure a smooth transition from theory to practice, the design team needs detailed knowledge of the procedures critical to establishing work teams. Without the strong background provided by training, the design team will lack the confidence to function independently or to provide the critical planning and guidance needed for successfully implementing teams. Preparing the design team for its task involves informal coaching by the steering committee, visits to sites using teams, classroom training, extensive reading, and regular interaction with the internal or external work-team consultant. (See "Suggested Reading List for Design-Team Training," page 284.)

WHEN

The design team is established after the feasibility study has been completed, the mission statement and parameters clarified, and the pilot sites selected. (See "The Feasibility Study," page 265–272 and "Developing a Mission Statement," pages 273–276.) Once design team members have been selected by the steering committee, design team training begins. Foundation training must be completed before the design team can draft its preliminary plan.

WHO

The design team is made up of a "diagonal slice" of from 8 to 15 executives, managers, and supervisors. Some companies later include members from the actual work teams on the design team. (See "Establish and Prepare the Design Team," Chapter 3, page 56.)

The design team should represent a wide range of knowledge and talent from every area of the organization that will be affected by self-direction. Often to ensure greater continuity and improved communication, the design team includes one or two members from the steering committee. Training for the design team is conducted both by the steering committee and by an internal or external consultant, one who is well-acquainted with self-directed work teams.

If the organization has implemented work teams at other sites, the company will most likely have a qualified internal consultant who can help in making a similar shift at new sites. In most companies, the same consultant who does the feasibility study also conducts the design team training. Working with the same consultant throughout the transition to teams provides consistency and ensures that the consultant is familiar with the organization and any special problems or pitfalls it may face. If an outside consultant is needed, take time to locate one with the necessary expertise. (See "On Consultants," Chapter 2, page 39.)

HOW

Design-team training falls into three general areas: meetings with the steering committee, classroom training, and site visits.

After design-team members are selected, one or more members of the steering committee should meet with the newly established design team to clarify its role and to briefly explain the guidelines used in selecting people for design-team participation. The design-team trainer/consultant may also invite individual steering committee members to talk about their areas of expertise during classroom training sessions.

The steering committee will continue to meet with the design team throughout planning and early implementation. Interaction with the steering committee provides opportunities for design-team members to discover and understand the organization's underlying philosophy, to review research, to share ideas, and to monitor progress.

Classroom training lays the foundation for the design team's role in implementing teams. It proceeds in three phases:

- An initial two- to four-day intensive workshop.
- Half- or whole-day sessions held once a month for six months.
- Two-day workshops held once or twice a year after work teams are established and evolving toward maturity.

FOUR-DAY FOUNDATION TRAINING

Foundation training provides the design team with background information on the decision to implement teams. The first half of training concentrates on steps already taken by the organization and the effects that can be expected once teams are in place.

The second half of training includes hands-on experience and concentrates on identifying the kinds of training that work-team members will need.

The specific objectives to be addressed in this four-day training include:

1. Design-team members will understand the current organizational environment in relation to self-direction (with regard to operations, work processes, and previous or existing self-directed efforts).

2. Design-team members will understand the organization's strategic goals for productivity (in terms of cost, quality, and delivery of goods or services) and the overall organizational climate.

Here is a sample training for the four-day foundation training:

Foundation Training, Day 1.   Two basic areas should be addressed:

1. Background information on the current competitive condition of the organization, including financial conditions, productivity, economic considerations, and overall organizational information, such as climate and environment.

2. A review of the steps already taken toward implementing teams:
   - Steering committee findings and data from site visits.
   - Feasibility study and its implications for teams.
   - Executive vision and the mission statement, particularly as related to organizational goals.
   - Parameters or boundaries established for the implementation of teams.
   - Design-team selection process and the team's role in implementation.

Foundation Training, Day 2.   Topics critical to implementation should be covered:

1. Eight levels of employee involvement (see Chapter 2).

2. Definition of self-directed work teams, including structure and functions.

3. Payoffs and pitfalls of work teams.

4. Experiences of other organizations, as covered in a panel discussion given by a design team or work team from another organization or site.

5. The five stages of work-team evolution as a conceptual framework for design-team planning (see "Adopt a Framework for Planning," Chapter 3, page 60).

6. New roles and responsibilities resulting from teams, including social and technical changes.

7. Brief overview of compensation, job classification, hiring, discipline, and performance reviews in the context of changes resulting from teams.

Foundation Training, Day 3. Practice in handling changes should be provided: A hands-on exercise that simulates what happens when work is redesigned. This can be a commercially available or a custom-designed program.

Foundation Training, Day 4. Topics should address the design team's upcoming tasks:

1. Short versus long teams (see Chapter 3, page 65 for an explanation of short versus long teams).

2. Guidelines for selection of pilot sites.

3. Criteria for selection of work-team members.

4. Preparation of people and systems for the transition to teams, including training topics for work-team members, supervisors, and managers.

5. Components of the preliminary plan.

6. Design-team planning for implementation of teams.

The initial design-team training should also include site visits. Site visits are extremely useful for the design team and fulfill the following functions:

1. Stimulate discussion.

2. Yield information about how actual work teams operate.

3. Build a sense of shared history with others making the transition to teams.

4. Provide opportunities for learning not only *what* was done, but *how* it was done.

5. Reveal the results of procedures followed by other design-team planners.

6. Convert team members who are skeptical.

If at all possible, it would be ideal to extend the foundation training to five days and have the entire team spend one day on an all-day site visit. This could be done after day three or day four of the foundation training. (For additional information on site visits, see "The Steering Committee," pages 257–264.)

When foundation training is complete, the design team is ready to begin its initial task of drafting the preliminary plan (see Chapter 3, page 63) that will provide the basis for the transition to teams. Later, the preliminary plan will be modified in response to information and feedback gathered by the design team from throughout the organization.

In addition to the up-front training design-team members receive, a second phase of classroom training occurs in full- or half-day sessions held once a month through the first year. The consultant uses these sessions to lead the design team in hands-on activities to help the team solve practical problems.

Topics are introduced on an "as needed" basis and can cover a variety of concerns. Typically, these educational sessions help team members put their experience in perspective with organizational theory as well as with the experiences of other companies.

The consultant who provided foundation training should also provide ongoing training. A long-term relationship helps the team and the consultant to maintain consistency from one training phase to the next.

The link that the consultant provides to the outside world is essential. Among other things, the consultant provides the design team with contacts for sharing information, with resources for training materials and problem solving, and with a context for developing a wider perspective.

The following are some typical topics to be included in ongoing training:

- Group dynamics (best when scheduled for an all-day session during the first month).
- Workplace analysis. (See "Workplace Analysis," pages 291–296.)
- Socio-technical concepts, including background on what has historically happened with teams.
- Organizational development issues related to work teams (presented as brief lectures followed by questions or discussion).
- Reward systems and compensation.
- Job classification.
- Hiring.
- Discipline.

WHAT'S NEXT?

When work teams are in place and more or less mature, design-team activity drops to a less intensive schedule and continues as follows:

1. The team carries out its task of managing the transition to teams and providing training as needed for managers and work teams.
2. The team participates in a third phase of classroom training, with sessions once or twice a year to stay in touch with new developments and organizational progress.

In an organization where work teams and design teams are functioning at several sites, design teams can get together once a year for two-day workshops to share what they have learned, discuss progress, and bring each other up to date on new developments. If a meeting with other teams is not appropriate, a two-day workshop can be scheduled for a single design team.

A mature design-team workshop can be structured according to the following plan:

Day 1, Information Sharing

Morning session: Discussion covers the progress of work teams and any problems encountered, along with any solutions attempted and their results, both successful and unsuccessful.

Afternoon session: Presentations from internal and external consultants on issues that are key to the success of work teams; topics should relate to the current stage of development in the transition to teams. (Consultants include the primary training consultant plus any subject-matter specialists brought in to address specific issues or areas of expertise.)

Day 2, Hands-On Problem Solving

Typical issues include getting middle-level management involved in teams, the transition roles for supervisors, compensation, recognition and rewards, transfer of decision-making power, and the strategic framework of the five-stage shift to teams.

SUGGESTED READING LIST FOR DESIGN-TEAM TRAINING

1. Brian Dumaine. "Who Needs a Boss?" *Fortune,* 7 May 1990, 52–53, 58, 60.
2. Paul S. Goodman, Elizabeth C. Ravlin, and Linda Argote. *Designing Effective Workgroups.* San Francisco: Jossey-Bass, Inc., 1986.
3. J. Richard Hackman and G. R. Oldham. *Work Redesign.* Reading, Mass.: Addison-Wesley Publishing, 1980.
4. John Hoerr. "The Payoff from Teamwork." *Business Week,* 10 July 1989, 56–62.

DESIGNING AND IMPLEMENTING AWARENESS TRAINING

WHAT

The transition to self-directed work teams demands that all employees, from management, to team members, to those not involved in work teams, understand the process and the reasons for the shift to teams. Awareness training is the means for reaching that understanding.

Presentations, discussion, visual aids, and question-and-answer sessions are targeted to specific levels of people within the company. Training varies in content and format for each level. The content also depends on the anticipated involvement of the attendees. For example, if the attendees are potential team members, they will receive more training than people who will not be part of a team, at least initially.

WHEN

Once initial planning is complete, awareness training begins. After the steering committee has completed its tasks and the design team has drafted its preliminary plan, it is time for the design team, in conjunction with the steering committee, to prepare executives, managers, and employees for the shift to self-directed work teams.

WHO

The design team has responsibility for designing, organizing and implementing awareness training.

HOW

Each level provides training for the one just below it. Accordingly, executives conduct training for managers, managers for supervisors, and supervisors for first-line employees. Often a top executive will participate in all levels to show top-level commitment.

The content and format of this training should be tailored to those receiving training. Using the same participant materials, visual aids, and session format, however, will ensure that a consistent message is delivered to everyone.

The following guidelines will help determine the content and format of each training session.

EXECUTIVE LEVEL

The steering committee leader should conduct the awareness session for other executives. Several areas are appropriate for the agenda at this level:

- Background on the decision to shift to teams.
- Competitive and economic advantages to be gained.
- Presentation of the feasibility study and mission statement.
- Executive role.
- Definition, structure, and function of self-directed teams within the company (based on factors identified in the feasibility study).
- Eight levels of employee involvement.

- Five stages of team evolution: how teams will develop throughout transition.
- New roles and responsibilities.
- Overall roll-out of the implementation plan.
- Awareness training plan for managers and supervisors.
- Criteria for the selection of team members.
- New processes and procedures for work teams.
- Compensation and recognition plans for work teams.
- Questions.

MANAGERIAL AND SUPERVISORY LEVELS

Awareness-trained executives should be prepared to lead training sessions for middle managers, who in turn will train supervisors. The training agenda for managers and supervisors might include the following items:

- Background on the decision to shift to teams.
- Competitive and economic advantages of teams.
- Presentation of feasibility study and mission statement.
- Role of executives and their plans to demonstrate commitment.
- Definition, structure, and function of self-directed teams within the company (based on factors identified in the feasibility study).
- Benefits to individuals and the organization.
- Eight levels of employee involvement.
- Five stages of team evolution: how teams will develop throughout transition.
- New roles and responsibilities.
- Possible concerns and obstacles; organizational support and available resources.
- Overall roll-out of the implementation plan.
- Criteria for selection of team members.

- Compensation and recognition plans for work teams.
- Hiring and job security issues.
- Special training for managers and supervisors (including topics such as delegation, recognizing team efforts, and communication).
- New processes and procedures for work teams.
- Questions.

Non-Work-Team Employees

For employees not working at a pilot site, awareness training will be less intensive and can usually be covered in a one-hour session. Supervisors conducting the training might cover the following agenda items:

- Background on the decision to shift to teams.
- Competitive and economic advantages.
- Presentation of the mission statement.
- What executives, managers, and supervisors will do differently.
- Overall plan for the transition to teams.
- How the plan will affect workers.
- Questions and concerns.

Prospective Work-Team Members

Employees at probable pilot sites for work teams should receive full awareness training from their supervisors. Agenda items might include the following:

- Background on the decision to shift to teams.
- Competitive and economic advantages of teams.
- Presentation of feasibility study and mission statement.
- Executive, management, and supervisory roles.
- Definition, structure, and function of self-directed teams within the company (based on factors identified in the feasibility study).

- Benefits to individuals and the organization.
- Eight levels of employee involvement.
- Five stages of team evolution: how teams will develop throughout transition.
- New roles and responsibilities, both inside and outside the team.
- Possible concerns and obstacles; organizational support and available resources.
- Overall roll-out of the implementation plan.
- Selection of team members.
- Compensation and recognition plans.
- Hiring and job security for team members.
- Future training for team members (exact curriculum to be determined by the teams).
- New processes and procedures for work teams.
- Questions and concerns.

Awareness training at all levels should clarify the reasons for shifting to teams and should address issues of concern to the group receiving the training.

WHAT'S NEXT?

Awareness training sets the stage for educating the work force about the details of the transition to teams as well as the selection of work-team members. Next, the design team will be responsible for managing the team member selection process.

WORKPLACE ANALYSIS

WHAT

A workplace analysis is a method for examining in depth both the current condition of productivity and the level of employee satisfaction in a department or work operation. The process looks at productivity in terms of quality, standards, delivery, cost, flexibility, and efficiency. Analysis of employee satisfaction yields information on people's sense of accomplishment, level of self-esteem, perception of opportunities for development, sense of control over the job, and opinions regarding safety hazards.

Data gathered in a workplace analysis becomes the basis for revising the design team's preliminary plan for implementing self-directed work teams. It also helps identify areas to concentrate on when training team members. By providing an in-depth evaluation of work operations and the people who do them, the workplace analysis helps the design team refine the implementation plan. It provides critical information for expanding the team concept and reveals what is needed to promote work-team procedures and attitudes among employees.

WHEN

Workplace analysis begins after the selection of work teams has been made, and awareness training for employees has been completed. (See "Designing and Implementing Awareness Training," pages 285–290.) Analysis is the next step in gathering specific information for the revision of the design team's preliminary plan.

WHO

At the request of the design team, the internal or external consultant (already working with the organization) conducts the workplace analysis by questioning employees in the targeted work operation or department.

The consultant also talks with direct support people, including internal suppliers and/or customers of the target operation and any support services, such as accounting (receivables and payables), human resources, shipping and receiving, or other departments that work closely with or provide products or services to the target operation.

HOW

Employees are brought together in groups of three to four, with each group usually containing a mix of team members, support group people, supervisors, and managers. Each group gathers around a table that holds a large diagram of the building floor plan or of the space occupied by the organization.

The consultant conducts the process by following these steps:

1. Orient people to the diagram of the building floor.
2. Ask everyone to point out something that relates to the diagram, such as the location of where they work or sit, and the traffic and work-flow patterns.
3. Explain that the analysis will examine how effectively the product flows from one work site to the next and how people feel about what happens in the work process.
4. Let people know that notes will be taken and answers recorded; show everyone the form for recording information. Emphasize the openness of the process.

5. Begin discussion by asking questions that address the following topics:
    Employee Satisfaction
    • Sense of accomplishment.
    • Opportunities for development.
    • Level of self-esteem.
    • Sense of control over the job.
    • Perception of safety hazards.
    Quality and Standards
    • Work schedule and delivery deadlines.
    • Costs (of materials, products, services, etc.).
    • Efficiency of layout and work flow.
    • Flexibility of layout and work operation.

6. The consultant asks questions and leads discussions to determine what currently happens and what employees believe should happen. Topics for examination include the following:
    • Existing and perceived standards.
    • Common deviations from those standards.
    • Causes and effects of the common deviations.
    • Potential solutions to work-flow problems.
    • Current strengths to be maintained.

7. The consultant takes notes on the discussion and records employees' comments using the following procedure:
    • The first time a comment is made, record it under the appropriate heading.
    • If the same comment is made by another employee, place a check next to the first comment in order to determine later the frequency of the response.
    • If any responses seem to evoke high levels of emotion, note that information when recording the response.

8. After meeting with all work-team members and support group personnel, the consultant sorts the data by frequency of response, listing the category with the most responses at the top of the list, followed by the one with the next largest number of responses, and so on. While analyzing data for frequency of response, the consultant also looks for other concerns that surfaced regularly, such as supervisory or

management practices. Those concerns should also be ranked by frequency of response.

9. Using information collected, the consultant develops recommendations for planning that include the following:
   • What should be maintained?
   • What should be changed?
   • What solutions are possible based on information provided by those interviewed?

The consultant's report and recommendations are submitted to the design team for further evaluation.

WHAT'S NEXT?

Following the workplace analysis, the design team reviews the consultant's recommendations and may then meet with the work team to consider the ideas of team members and agree on amendments to the operational aspects of the preliminary plan. These amendments can include reorganizing the team to include other functions and equipment. Once the implementation plan is amended and adopted, training for work-team members begins.

A CASE IN POINT: Large Insurance Company

A workplace analysis was done with a group of clerical workers at a large insurance company. The clerical workers were regularly in direct contact with hospital billing departments. The purpose of the analysis was to ascertain how best to proceed in establishing a work team in the clerical department.

Small groups of clerical workers, along with support people from such departments as claims and payables, met with the consultant to evaluate the clerical operation. In each group, participants gathered around a large table that held a complete diagram of the building layout where the employees worked.

With the layout before them, employees responded to questions asked by the consultant. The discussion focused on topics and information relevant to the workplace analysis, particularly the interactions with internal and external customers and suppliers, like hospital billing departments.

The consultant's questions addressed the issues of employee satisfaction and work quality and standards. During each analysis session, the consultant asked questions from among the following:

- Where do you work? Put a marker on the diagram.
- What materials, paperwork, instructions, etc., come to you that require your action, processing, decision, or involvement?
- Where do the materials, paperwork, etc., come from?
- Describe what this product or paperwork is like when it comes to you in good shape.
- Describe what it is like when it comes to you in bad shape.
- What has been done prior to your receiving it that causes it to be in good or bad shape?
- Who or what most strongly influences those conditions or results?
- How do you give feedback to this person or department (your internal or external supplier)?
- Is the feedback process helpful and/or satisfying to you? Is it helpful and/or satisfying to your supplier?
- What do you do to the product, paperwork, etc., once it comes to you for action or processing?
- What can you do presently to influence the cost of the product positively or negatively? The quality of the product? The delivery time for the product?
- What could be done by you to make your work more effective? What could be done by the organization? What could be done by your co-workers?
- What could be done by you to make your work more satisfying? What could be done by the organization? What could be done by your co-workers?
- What is your final product for this department or process (goods or services)?

- What makes your product good or bad?
- Where does your product go when you are finished with it?
- What feedback do you get from the person or department to which you send the product (your internal or external customer)?
- Where do you currently have the chance to self-manage in your job?
- Where do you believe you should be able to do more self-managing?
- What needs to be changed most to improve productivity for this operation or process?
- What needs to be changed most to improve the quality of your work life? Of your work environment?
- What positive aspects of your work life and/or work environment should be maintained? Which positive aspects should be enhanced or strengthened?
- What ideas do you have for solutions to work-flow or quality problems?

Responses to questions were recorded by category and then ranked according to frequency. The results showed a high number of negative responses in the self-esteem category.

Based on the employees' identification of factors that contributed to low self-esteem and their suggestions for solutions, the consultant made recommendations to the design team. Taking the consultant's recommendations into consideration, the design team modified the preliminary plan to include specific steps to increase employees' self-esteem, including a custom computer program to match billings with services, a training program for employees in negotiation skills, and job evaluations including interpersonal skills, in addition to technical skills.

TEAM MEMBER TRAINING

WHAT

Team members need training in work-team awareness, technical skills, interpersonal skills, problem solving, and administrative procedures. They continue to need training—more of some types at the beginning and more of other types later on—as long as their team continues to grow, to diversify, to add new members, and to acquire members with new or enhanced skills.

WORK-TEAM AWARENESS TRAINING

Usually presented just before work teams get under way, awareness training gives employees an overview of what self-directed work teams are all about, why the organization is adopting them, and how employees can benefit personally from team membership. (For more information, see "Designing and Implementing Awareness Training," pages 285–290.)

TECHNICAL TRAINING

The focus of this training is on the actual tasks the team is responsible for: operating a piece of equipment, processing a claim, repairing a machine, and so forth. Since team members should continually be adding to their technical skills, technical training goes on throughout the life of a team. The specific training programs—and who takes them—grow out of the team's need for certain technical skills and out of individual members' abilities and interests. (See "Team Member Role Expansion Plan," pages 321–324.) Technical training usually is a mix of formal classroom instruction, on-the-job training, and, when the team is mature, member-to-member tutoring. Basically, technical training varies according to the specific tasks of each team.

INTERPERSONAL SKILLS TRAINING

Without conventional channels for giving and receiving orders, work-team members need to talk with, explain to, agree or disagree with, listen to, and convince more people more often than they probably ever have before. Moreover, they will also be doing many of these things in groups. In other words, they need to be skilled communicators both one-on-one and in groups.

To analyze the problems they run into, and to come up with good solutions as a group, team members need to learn a basic approach to problem solving that helps them zero in on the problem area, gather facts, analyze the cause, and select the best solution. The approach should be used by everyone in the organization; having the same set of problem-solving concepts and terminology will help team members work together—on their own team and with other teams in the organization. (See "A Group Problem-Solving Process," pages 339–344.)

Basic interpersonal skills training begins before the work teams begin; more advanced topics are introduced as they are needed, at various stages of team development. Since interpersonal skills are challenging, team members will need as much training in interpersonal topics as they do in technical topics.

ADMINISTRATIVE TRAINING

In the absence of supervisors, team members need to know how to perform those administrative tasks that supervisors used to do—for example, filling out request forms from other departments and keeping records. Administrative training, although often focused on forms and procedures, boils down to learning how to deal directly with other parts of the organization—purchasing, payroll, engineering, accounting, and so forth—tasks once performed by supervisors and managers.

SPECIAL TOPICS TRAINING

These include peer performance appraisal training (see "Peer Performance Appraisal," pages 349–356), interviewing and selection training, peer coaching, work process analysis, and business economics. Not all teams will have an immediate need for training in all these topics.

WHEN

The process of training team members should begin during the start-up stage, after the preliminary plan has been revised and the workplace analysis completed.

WHO

Training is the responsibility of a training coordinator—either someone from the training department or a knowledgeable ex-supervisor who has been trained as a team facilitator.

HOW

The key to an effective training program is to put together a long-term plan that is comprehensive enough to meet all short- and long-term training needs and flexible enough to change as team needs change and as teams themselves become more knowledgeable about the specific training they need. The ideal is just-in-time training which gives team members the training they need, exactly when they need it.

The first step is for the training coordinator or team facilitator to work with the design team to find out what overall training the work teams will require. Then sources for each training segment need to be identified. There are several sources: modules purchased from outside training companies, or internally developed with help from the design team and/or team members.

It is important to offer enough training to give team members the skills they need, but not so much that they become overloaded. Using the five stages of development as a structure, the schedule might look something like this.

Stage 1: Start-Up

The challenge of this stage is to get everyone committed to the plan and to prepare selected employees to participate. The training focus for team members:

- An awareness of what work teams are, why they're important, and how team members can benefit.
- Basic interpersonal skills (giving and receiving feedback).
- Basic administrative procedures (completing attendance records, ordering materials).
- Technical training overview of all team tasks.

Stage 2: State of Confusion

The challenge of this stage is to help people work through their confusion and personal anxiety without getting so frustrated they give up. The training focus for team members:

- Learning how to do things together—communicating expectations, taking on a new assignment, setting job standards, and requesting help.
- Developing administrative abilities, such as tracking production flow against performance standards.
- Expanding technical training to enable team members to begin learning other team members' tasks, so they can function in a back-up capacity.

Stage 3: Leader-Centered Teams

The challenge of this stage is to encourage further team growth without giving up gains in productivity. The training focus for team members:

- How to lead and participate in problem-solving sessions.
- How to conduct peer performance appraisals.
- How to master advanced technical skills, such as preventative maintenance.

Stage 4: Tightly Formed Teams

The challenge of this stage is to broaden work teams' goals to include the organization as a whole without destroying team spirit. The training focus for team members:

- Learning how to work across team lines by building collaborative relationships, winning support, and resolving conflicts.
- Applying administrative training in computing the cost of quality and working with vendors to establish specifications.
- Making use of technical training to perform support group tasks.

Stage 5: Self-Directed Teams

The challenge of this stage is to avoid complacency by working towards new goals. The training focus for team members:

- Managing customer-supplier relationships, both internal and external; understanding customer expectations; dealing with the dissatisfied customer.
- Understanding the economics of the marketplace.
- Learning accounting procedures, such as how to read financial reports or calculate return on investment.
- Applying administrative training in reviewing and responding to customer feedback.

WHAT'S NEXT?

Training in one form or another is a continuous process and should be provided in response to the growing and evolving responsibilities of team members.

MANAGER AND SUPERVISOR TRANSITION TRAINING

WHAT

Transition training for supervisors and managers provides the information and skills they need to take on their new roles in the transition to self-directed work teams. These workshops and training sessions can be held both on-site and off-site. Content is geared to the evolutionary level of the work teams and the corresponding roles of managers and supervisors.

WHEN

During the start-up period and throughout the evolution of teams, managers and supervisors participate in training that meets their evolving roles at each stage of development.

WHO

Managers and supervisors involved with self-directed work teams participate in this training. The internal or external work-team consultant works with executives, steering committee members, and design-team members to provide training. Some or all of these individuals may participate as presenters, trainers, or facilitators.

HOW

The issue of new roles and skills for managers and supervisors is first introduced during awareness training. (See "Designing and Implementing Awareness Training," pages 285–290.) Design-team members and awareness-trained executives provide this initial information, which is then explored in more depth in the training sessions that follow the selection of pilot sites and work teams. Since each stage in the evolution to work teams requires specialized training, topics and approaches for the training sessions need to cover a variety of skills and strategies.

Stage 1: Start-Up

Managers and supervisors meet with the consultant to discuss how their roles will change. This session should concentrate on general guidelines but should also provide time for the managers and supervisors to create their own individual action plans.

Activities for this session include the following practices and subjects:

- Begin with general discussion that refers to information first presented in awareness training.
- If possible, have as speakers one or more managers who have gone through the transition period with teams and can give firsthand accounts of how their roles changed.
- Ask someone from the steering committee to present a perspective of how the roles of managers and supervisors will change, and what the new roles will or can be.
- Teach the key skills for guiding start-up teams. These skills include the following:
    1. How to build trust within teams, and between teams and managers.

2. How to work with teams to establish their new performance expectations and criteria.

3. How to develop a hand-off plan that outlines a step-by-step transfer of responsibilities to teams, including what responsibilities should be transferred to teams and how teams should prepare to take on these responsibilities. (See "Hand-off Plans for Supervisory and Support Groups," pages 309–320.)

- Allow time for managers and supervisors to practice these new skills and strategies. A "dry run" in the safe environment of the classroom with constructive feedback from peers can help managers feel more comfortable when they use these new skills with their teams.

- Follow the skills practice with individual planning and goal-setting activities to prepare managers and supervisors to carry out their new roles. (For more on first-stage topics, see "A Case in Point," which follows this section.)

- Encourage participants to express concerns they have about the transition to teams, but keep the workshop from becoming a gripe session by continually pointing out how the training will help them deal with those concerns.

After start-up activities, training sessions for managers and supervisors continue throughout the evolution of teams. After each stage is reached and its special set of problems and adjustments mastered, training begins for the next stage.

Several topics need to be covered in the stages that follow the start-up period.

Stage 2: State of Confusion

To function well, managers and supervisors need to continue using skills already learned and also learn how to:

- Encourage teams to reorganize for self-management.
- Monitor team performance against clear standards.
- Work with teams when expectations are not being met.

- Manage group dynamics.
- Lead and participate effectively in meetings.
- Solve problems in cooperation with teams.
- Coordinate efforts among teams and facilitate communication between teams and the organization.
- Recognize team efforts.
- Hand off new responsibilities for teams and for their support groups.
- Clarify roles and responsibilities for teams and for their support groups.
- Decide when it is appropriate to lead the team.

Stage 3: Leader-Centered Teams

To function well, managers and supervisors need to build on using skills already mastered and also learn how to:

- Train teams in group problem-solving techniques.
- Master coaching skills for use with teams.
- Infuse teams with a sense of their own identity.
- Help teams choose their own leaders.
- Monitor and assess peer performance appraisals. (See "Peer Performance Appraisal," pages 349–356.)
- Monitor and assess the peer discipline process. (See "Peer Disciplinary Review Committee," pages 325–330.)

Stage 4: Tightly Formed Teams

To function well, managers and supervisors need to develop the skills to:

- Help the team expand their responsibilities.
- Foster innovation in teams.
- Monitor team loyalty and competition to prevent overzealous behaviors.
- Refocus teams when necessary on cross-functional goals.

Stage 5: Self-Directed Teams

To function well, managers and supervisors need to be able to:

- Coach new team members and leaders in mastering their roles within the team.
- Help teams understand the rationale behind important management decisions.
- Continue seeking new ways to foster commitment and trust among team members and between teams.

A CASE IN POINT: Heavy Equipment Manufacturer

A heavy equipment manufacturing company that had made the commitment to self-directed work teams brought managers and supervisors together for a three-day workshop. The training would prepare them for their roles in the start-up phase of implementing teams.

Training sessions used discussions, case studies, videotaped demonstrations, and skills practice exercises to teach the managers and supervisors the skills they would need to feel comfortable with and to carry out their new roles.

Topics covered in the three-day session included:

- Changing expectations for managers and supervisors in a self-directed work-team environment.
- Specific demands on managers and supervisors at each phase of the transition to teams.
- Ways to assess personal leadership style and evaluate strengths and weaknesses in relation to teams.
- Identification of which responsibilities to shift to teams and the steps to prepare teams for them.
- Strategies for building employee commitment to teams.

HAND-OFF PLANS FOR SUPERVISORY AND SUPPORT GROUP TASKS

WHAT

A hand-off plan is a systematic process for deciding which tasks in the work unit will be transferred to the team. It's called a hand-off plan, because tasks are "handed off" to team members as they demonstrate their ability to perform them. Hand-off plans include a list of specific tasks to be handed off, as well as specific standards, training, and/or experience required to perform each task.

There are usually two hand-off plans: one for the work performed by the supervisor, and another for the work performed by support departments like shipping, quality control, human resources, and purchasing.

WHEN

Developing a hand-off plan is a multistep process that takes several weeks. It should start at or before Stage 1, after team sites have been chosen and employees have been selected as team members. So they can get fully involved in these discussions, team members should already have received training in how to participate in meetings.

WHO

The facilitator has primary responsibility for seeing that the hand-off plan gets developed. Others who play a part in the process are team members, supervisor(s), and members of support departments. Executives need to encourage and recognize supervisors for their willingness to participate in handing off tasks.

HAND-OFF PLAN FOR SUPERVISORY TASKS

HOW

To design a hand-off plan for supervisory tasks, the following steps need to be carried out:

1. The team facilitator asks supervisors and employees to keep an activities analysis log for one week of all the activities or tasks that make up their day. (See "Activities Analysis Log," Exhibit 10-1, page 312.) This assignment can be given at a general team meeting held soon after team sites have been selected.

2. Based on the logs, the facilitator works with the team and the supervisors to develop a list of tasks required to get the work of the team done. This list should be compiled at a special meeting of supervisors and team members. The tasks are recorded on flipchart paper so that everyone can see them. Time is allowed to explain and add to the lists, but tasks are not "weeded out" at this point.

3. These tasks are categorized according to the following six categories:

a. This task should become an immediate team responsibility.

b. This task should eventually become a team responsibility.

c. This task should become the responsibility of a team leader or specialist.

d. This task should remain or become a management responsibility.

e. A formal procedure should be developed to handle this task.

f. This task is unnecessary; no one needs to do it.

4. The facilitator helps the team members and supervisor(s) agree on final disposition of each of the tasks. The end result should look something like Exhibit 10-2.

Although team members should give individual thought to how they think the tasks should be categorized, final discussions and decisions should take place in the group.

5. For the tasks in categories **d** (management), **e** (a formal procedure), and **f** (nobody), the facilitator makes sure the team's recommendations are acceptable to and followed up by those outside the team.

6. Each task in categories **a** (team now), **b** (team later), and **c** (team leader) is assigned to an individual or pair for further work outside of the meeting. These individuals or pairs determine a standard of performance for each task and decide what training or experience the team needs to perform that task. The team then meets again and considers the recommendations of the subgroup. The upshot should look something like Exhibit 10-3.

WHAT'S NEXT?

Tasks are handed off as indicated in the plan: some to team members when they demonstrate the ability to perform them, some to team leaders, and some to management. Other tasks will be handled by procedure once the procedure has been written, or done away with altogether. It is a joint responsibility of the team, a manager, and facilitator to draw up a project management plan—with accountabilities and time frames—to carry out this process.

EXHIBIT 10-1. Activities Analysis Log (with Directions)

ACTIVITIES ANALYSIS LOG

		EVALUATION									
			STRATEGICALLY IMPORTANT			ROUTINE, BUT NEEDS TO BE DONE BY:			NOT NEEDED, BUT PRESSURES TO DO IT FROM:		
	SATISFACTION		SELF	OTHER		SELF	OTHER		SELF	ABOVE	BELOW
TIME	ACTIVITY	+	−		▼ ▶ ◀			▼ ▶ ◀	▼	▲	▼

EXHIBIT 10-1. (Continued)

How to Complete Each Column in the Log:

Time. Record the time you begin and end each activity (e.g., "8:10–8:23").

Activity. Describe the activity briefly (e.g., "Talked on phone to Jim Brown from Receiving").

Satisfaction. Put a check in the plus (+) or minus (–) column to record whether the activity was satisfying or not.

Strategic Importance. If (and only if) you think the activity is strategically important to the future of a project or function, put a check in the column indicating who you think should perform the activity:

Self - you

▲ - someone above you in the organization

▼ - someone below you in the organization

◀ - someone at your level

Routine, but needs to be done by. If, instead, you think the activity is routine but necessary, put a check in the column indicating who you think should perform the activity.

Self - you

▲ - someone above you in the organization

▼ - someone below you in the organization

◀ - someone at your level

Not needed, but pressures to do it from. If you think the activity is unnecessary, put a check in the column indicating the source of the pressure to do it:

Self - you

▲ - someone above you in the organization

▼ - someone below you in the organization

Note: It can be enlightening to ask other people (like your boss and/or subordinates) to evaluate your activities.

EXHIBIT 10-2. Disposition of Supervisory Tasks

TASK	(A) TEAM NOW	(B) TEAM LATER	(C) LEADER	(D) MANAGEMENT	(E) PROCEDURE	(F) NOBODY
			RESPONSIBILITY OF:			
Work assignment	X					
Job training		X				
Reviews		X	X			
Special assignments			X	X		
Monitor breaks					X	
Inventory control						X

EXHIBIT 10-3. Skills/Training/Experience Needed to Perform Supervisory Tasks

TASK	RESPONSIBILITY TEAM NOW/LATER LEADER	STANDARD OF PERFORMANCE (KNOWLEDGE/SKILL REQUIRED)	TRAINING/EXPERIENCE TO BE ARRANGED
Work assignments	Team/later	Coordinate staffing to equal capacity requirements	Knowledge of individual member skills
		Make Daily adjustments to accommodate emergency requirements	Knowledge of priorities of total department
		Replace overtime schedules if anticipated components are not available	Procedure of capacity planning and review
		Group to make weekly and daily assignments (staggered rotation suggested)	
Inventory control	Team/now	95% just-in-time production (within 4 hrs.)	MRP certification
		Below 1% shrinkage	Level 2 computer operation
			Components configuration test passed

315

HAND-OFF PLAN FOR SUPPORT GROUP TASKS

Once the supervisory plan has been completed and the tasks handed off, it's time to design a hand-off plan for the tasks support groups perform.[1] Exhibit 10-4 provides examples of support groups and functions. Deciding which support functions get handed off, and in which order, depends on individual team needs.

A hand-off plan for support tasks includes the following steps:

EXHIBIT 10-4.   Examples of Support Groups and Functions

Accounting/Finance	Human Resources	Production Services
Cost accounting	Benefits	Supervision
Accounts payable	Compensation	Manufacturing
Accounts receivable	planning	engineering
Payroll	Training and	Maintenance
Credit management	education	Machine programming
Tax accounting	Health services	Tool design/repair
Cash management	Employee	Clerical support
	representation	Materials handling
	Office services/	
	supplies	
	Security forces	
	Interviewing/selection	
Product Flow	**Marketing**	**Quality Services**
Purchasing	Market analysis	Quality engineering
Ship/receive store	Market development	Production inspection
Production control	Sales	Process control
Order entry/scheduling	Product development	Metrology
Customer service	Customer relations	Reliability engineering
Invoicing	Field service	Vendor education
Product Engineering	**Information Services**	**Legal Services**
Research and	Data processing	Liabilities protection
development	Hardware	Government
Special design	maintenance	compliance
Documentation	Software management	Proprietorship
Value analysis	Procedure monitoring	Lobbying

1. The facilitator secures top management support for the hand-off process. No matter how willing people think they are to give up tasks, when it comes right down to it, they can resist the process. Without top management encouragement, the process can stall.

2. The facilitator helps the team identify the support groups they need to work with. These will vary according to team responsibilities and needs. For example, if a team decides that it needs more authority to make personnel decisions, it might want to take over the interviewing/selection functions from human resources.

To help the team identify the support group(s) it needs to work with first, the facilitator takes members through several exercises (see Exhibit 10-5, "Which Support Groups Does the Team Work With?," page 317, and Exhibit 10-6, "Support Function Analysis," page 318), which help them analyze the

EXHIBIT 10-5. "Which Support Groups Does the Team Work With?" Worksheet

Directions: Label the circles to identify support groups or people who (a) do something for, (b) do something with, or (c) get something from the team. Consider team supervision/management as a support function.

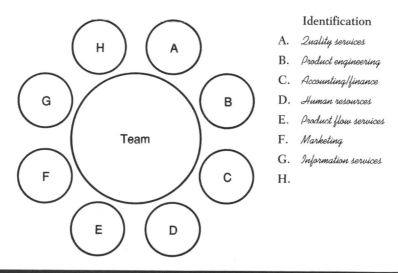

Identification

A. *Quality services*

B. *Product engineering*

C. *Accounting/finance*

D. *Human resources*

E. *Product flow services*

F. *Marketing*

G. *Information services*

H.

Exhibit 10-6.   Support Function Analysis

Directions: For each support group you identified on the "Which Support Groups Does the Team Work With?" worksheet, categorize the activities of that group as follows:

Support function or person _____*Human Resources*_____

		RECOMMENDATION		
Now done for the team	Within	Outside	Shared	When?
a. *Interviews applicants*	✓			
b. *Select new members*	✓			
c. *Decide training needs*			✓	
d. *Arrange training*			✓	
e. *Manage pay system*			✓	
f. *Counsel discipline cases*	✓			
g. *Administer discipline*	✓			
h. *Manage benefits plan*		✓		
i. *Manage EEO/AAP compliance*		✓		
j. *Administers*				
k.				
l.				
m.				
n.				
Now done with the team				
a. *Plan picnic/social affairs*			✓	
b. *Sponsor safety committee*	✓			
c.				
d.				
e.				
f.				
g.				
h.				
i.				
j.				
Team now does for support group				
a. *Report attendance*			✓	
b.				
c.				
d.				
e.				
f.				
g.				
h.				
i.				
j.				

support tasks they now rely on and decide how they want to handle them in the future.

3. The facilitator arranges for a series of meetings between one or two team members and the appropriate support groups to discuss which tasks should be handed off. These sessions should not go too far too fast. A conscious effort may be needed to keep support staff people from feeling resentful, defensive, and intruded upon.

Working together, the support groups and representative team members should develop an analysis for all the tasks and processes the team and support group share. (See Exhibit 10-7, "Recommended Disposition of Support Groups Tasks," page 320.)

WHAT'S NEXT?

The support group, team member representatives, manager, and facilitator need to draw up an implementation plan to hand off these tasks.

NOTE

1. In a greenfield site, the disposition of support tasks would have been included in the initial plan. In a retrofit situation, the hand-off of these tasks probably should not begin until later, probably at Stage 3, *Leader-Centered Teams*.

Exhibit 10-7. "Recommended Disposition of Support Group Tasks"

Support Group: Tasks Human Resources Does Now	In the future, this task should be:		
	Done by the Team	Done by the Support Group	Shared between Team and Support Group
Support group performs the following tasks for the team:			
1. *Interviews/hires*	1. ✓	1.	1.
2. *Plans training*	2.	2.	2. ✓
3. *Administers pay and benefits*	3.	3.	3. ✓
4. *Counsels/disciplines*	4.	4.	4.
5. *Administers EED/AAP compliance*	5.	5. ✓	5.
Support group performs the following tasks with the team:			
1. *Plans social affairs*	1.	1.	1. ✓
2. *Sponsors safety committee*	2. ✓	2.	2.
3.	3.	3.	3.
4.	4.	4.	4.
5.			
The team performs the following tasks for the support group:			
1. *Keeps attendance reports*	1. ✓	1.	1.
2.	2.	2.	2.
3.	3.	3.	3.
4.	4.	4.	4.
5.	5.	5.	5.

TEAM MEMBER ROLE EXPANSION PLAN

WHAT

The role expansion plan lists the skills and responsibilities that an individual team member has agreed to master over a specified period, usually six months. The plan includes how and when this mastery will occur. It formalizes the individual's developmental commitment to the team just as the hand-off plan formalizes the team's developmental commitment to the larger organization. The plan is keyed to the categories in the peer performance appraisal format that will eventually replace this role expansion planning process.

WHEN

The role expansion planning process is completed at or just prior to the start-up stage, when team members need to clarify which skills they must learn to function effectively.

WHO

A team member's first role expansion plan is prepared jointly by the team member and his or her supervisor or manager. The second plan, six months later, is prepared by the team member and the facilitator or the team leader. By the third or fourth time, this process will become the foundation for the performance planning component of the peer performance appraisal process. (See "Peer Performance Appraisal," pages 349–356.) At that point, the individual is preparing the plan in concert with other team members.

HOW

Typically, role expansions plans are prepared during the course of two one-hour sessions: The first session is devoted to specific job performance skills, and the second to interpersonal skills and work habits.

There are steps for both the team member and the supervisor or manager (or, eventually, the team leader) to carry out. Also, before teams can start this process, the organization should develop a standardized role expansion worksheet. (See Exhibit 11-1, page 323, for an example of a worksheet developed by one organization.)

1. The team member should schedule the job performance skills session with his or her supervisor or manager (if it is the first plan) or with the facilitator or team leader (if it is the second or third plan). To prepare for this meeting the team member should review the specific job performance skills categories in the organization's role expansion worksheet and think about the types of skills he or she needs or wants to learn in each category.

The supervisor, manager, or team leader should review the same categories with the team member in mind, and identify specific skills that would (a) advance the team member's career growth, (b) improve the balance of skills and responsibilities on the team, (c) enable the team to improve its production process, and (d) help the team exceed customer expectations.

2. During the session, the team member and supervisor (or manager or team leader) should discuss their ideas and arrive at

EXHIBIT 11-1. Role Expansion Worksheet

ROLE EXPANSION WORKSHEET

AREA I—SPECIFIC JOB PERFORMANCE

WHAT I NEED TO DO	HOW	BY WHEN
Additional Skills		
• Learn to operate station 6	OJT with Dean	1/21
• Level 1 electronic gauging	2-day course	5/15
• MRP data terminal	4-hr. MIS workshop	2/15
Production responsibilities		
• Learn to operate station 6	Study manual/OJT with Jane	1/15
• Improve tool usage on 3	Workbook and OJT	3/31
• Rework below 5% on 1	OJT with Dean	4/15
Teamwork responsibilities		
• Train two people on 3	Sign-up sheet	6/15

ROLE EXPANSION WORKSHEET

AREA II—NONTECHNICAL DEVELOPMENT

WHAT I NEED TO DO	HOW	BY WHEN
Work Habits		
• Improve priority planning	Video/workbook	2/10
•		
•		
Communication		
• Assertive meeting contribution	Join Toastmasters	join 1/15
		demonstrate 6/1
•		
•		
Leadership		
• Develop production report form	Consult with support group	4/20
• Volunteer to be team leader	See facilitator	immed.
•		
•		

agreement on the specific skills to be learned. On the worksheet they should list these skills.

During this session the supervisor or manager/team leader's role is to focus the team member on what makes sense for both the team and the individual. This means helping the team member think through such questions as, If your team is going to be as effective as it can, what new responsibilities do you need to take on? What skills do you need to learn? What tasks do you need to master?

When agreement has been reached, both people should decide how the team member will learn these new skills, and indicate their decisions in the worksheet's "How" column. Some possible training resources are:

- On-the-job training.
- In-house or outside training sessions.
- Video- or audiocassettes.
- Workbooks.
- Equipment manuals.

3. At a second session, the team member and supervisor (or manager or team leader) should review the "communication" and "leadership" portions of the worksheet. The process followed is the same as for discussing specific job performance skills.

4. The team member presents his or her plan to the team. The team discusses the impact of each member's plan on the total team's responsibilities. During the early stages of this process the manager should make sure that the interesting and critical new skills are being evenly distributed among team members.

WHAT'S NEXT?

These plans represent a commitment, not a rigid restriction. The facilitator, the team, and the individual share the responsibility for activating all the individual plans, and for altering them as necessary.

PEER DISCIPLINARY REVIEW COMMITTEE

WHAT

Whenever an employee wants to challenge his or her termination or any severe disciplinary action taken by management or through an intra-team disciplinary procedure, the Peer Disciplinary Review committee is convened to review the complaint. The committee is made up of from four to six employee representatives who, as committee members, are empowered to conduct a full investigation and to recommend a course of action directly to the top local executive.

Establishing a Peer Disciplinary Review committee broadens the application of the work-team concept within an organization. The committee extends the decision-making capacity of work teams into personnel issues, communicating the organization's intent to deal fairly and to expand the team concept into areas that affect employees' rights and performance.

When peers are given authority to review disciplinary decisions, the company benefits with improved morale. Employees no longer see job security as dependent on relationships with individual managers. In addition, discipline enforced by peers is more often accepted without resentment.

WHEN

As self-directed work teams become more mature—typically during Stage 4, Tightly Formed Teams—and are accepted within the organization, a Peer Disciplinary Review committee can be initiated. The committee can be established at any time during the later stages of the transition as long as the orderly shift to teams is not disrupted or undermined.

Once established, the committee is convened whenever a disciplined employee believes that due process has not been followed. The employee initiates the review action and agrees to submit to the committee's inquiry and judgment. Management can neither initiate nor prevent a committee review.

WHO

The sponsoring group within the organization, whether management or the design team, establishes the committee, and makes its purpose and procedures known to all employees. The committee's purpose and procedures should be permanently and prominently posted, and the right of review should be communicated to each employee at the time of the original disciplinary action. Typically, because human resources will be involved in a consulting role to the committee, a human resources manager will take the lead role in establishing the committee and its procedures.

HOW

The design team (or management) determines criteria for the selection of employee representatives. The committee should be formed in accordance with the following plan:

1. Six responsible employees are recruited for the initial committee. Half will serve for one year; the other half for two years. At the end of the first year, half the members are re-

placed by vote, with the other half replaced the following year.

2. Thereafter, members will serve two-year terms, with new members elected to half the positions each year.

3. A human resources development specialist serves as consultant to the committee to ensure that legal requirements and procedures are followed and to act as recorder/communicator. The specialist is a nonvoting committee member.

An employee facing termination or disciplinary action can initiate the review process either by written or oral request to any committee member or to the human resources specialist. The committee reviews the request according to the following guidelines:

1. Only four committee members will hear any one case. If a committee has more than four members, those hearing the case should be selected as follows: The employee selects one member, the disciplining party selects one member, and the selected members select one additional member each. Committee members have the right to refuse to hear any given case.

2. The committee of four interviews first the employee and then the discipliner.

3. Next, the committee of four interviews other interested parties—those recommended by either of the involved parties and/or those sought out by committee members.

4. Any information or opinions offered by those interviewed is held in strictest confidence by the committee. To that end, deliberations are conducted privately. Open court style proceedings, with confrontation and cross examination, are not permitted.

5. The committee reaches a decision and drafts its recommendation. In the case of an employee who has been terminated, the committee's recommendation could include one of the following:
    - Full support of the termination without further recourse for the employee.

- Approval of discipline only, with termination deemed inappropriate, and the committee's suggested, alternative disciplinary action and its rationale.
- A finding that the employee has been unfairly judged, and that termination and/or discipline is unwarranted, with suggestions for follow-up action.

6. The committee's recommendation and the process used in reaching it are written up by the human resources specialist and delivered to the top local executive. The executive may accept or reject the recommendation or seek further clarification.

7. The committee and involved parties are notified of the final decision.

Committee members, who may be neither prolific nor proficient readers or writers, need to feel competent and comfortable with their roles. A cumbersome review process or one that relies heavily on paperwork can hamper their effectiveness.

Rejection of committee recommendations should be made only for the best and clearest of reasons, and those reasons must be clearly communicated both to committee members and to the involved parties. Committee members must not be made to feel ineffective. If their recommendations are not seriously considered, their trust of company executives and their commitment to the peer review process will diminish.

The peer review process can threaten both managers and discipliners. Committee members will need training to feel comfortable with their roles and to function effectively. Managers, too, will need help learning how to avoid "lose-lose" situations, and how to cope with what they may see as a loss of position, power, or prestige.

WHAT'S NEXT?

Once the Peer Disciplinary Review committee has been established, care must be taken to ensure that all team members accept the process and feel comfortable with their part in it. Committee members may also need help fitting into their new roles.

Procedures for electing new committee members also need to be determined and communicated to all employees. While the review process is gaining acceptance, committee procedures and elections may need to be monitored to prevent controversies or problems.

RECOGNITION AND REWARD TECHNIQUES

WHAT

Organizations making the transition to teams need to provide recognition for work teams and their accomplishments. Such recognition activities should (1) recognize that the team, rather than the individual, is the critical entity in the organization, and (2) reward the team as a whole for its accomplishments.

Positive reinforcement motivates effort, dispels confusion, and eases anxiety for employees making the transition to teams. Recognition promotes a sense of team identity by allowing the team to take pride in its progress and accomplishments. Recognition reassures team members that they are performing well, thus encouraging continued effort toward the success of the team.

WHEN

Recognition is an ongoing process that should adapt to the team's changing needs. Early in the shift to teams, recognition is needed to create a positive environment for self-direction and to encourage team members. As teams continue to evolve, recognition lets them know they are on track and performing well.

WHO

Recognition is provided to teams as a whole by managers, supervisors, executives, and customers. The team itself provides recognition to its own members, but only after it is firmly established and ready to develop its own internal recognition system.

HOW

Typically, recognition is given verbally or through modest team gifts, icons, or awards. The specific methods of recognition are set up initially by the steering committee and design team, in conjunction with the organization's consultant and the managers of operations or departments where work teams have been implemented.

It is critical to understand the difference between recognition that is constructive, and rewards that foster resentment and isolation. Most organizations intentionally stay away from monetary rewards. Recognizing a team with money or bonuses puts it in competition with other departments or individuals in the company. Monetary awards give the team a special status that invites jealousy and may result in attempts by others to sabotage the efforts of the team. (For more on monetary reward systems, see "Compensation Systems that Support Teams," pages 229–241.)

Recognition techniques that draw attention to the formal establishment of teams include:

- Setting aside a display wall that emphasizes team activities with announcements, banners, certificates, schedules, and so forth.
- Providing special T-shirts, hats, mugs, jackets, or similar team items that the team has selected.
- Displaying a plaque in the work area to identify the team.
- Holding celebrations to mark key events in the development of the team, such as anniversaries of the team, first-time activities, and special team accomplishments.

- Initiating activities that identify the team as an entity, such as adopting a team color or choosing a team logo to use on all team communications, uniforms, and so forth.
- Painting equipment in the team color.
- Competing as a team in company athletic events.

Techniques that recognize a team for its accomplishments include:

- Establishing a "Team of the Week" award, with gifts presented by the organization to each team member or to the team as a whole.
- Conducting a team trip to visit customers whose product or service has been improved by the team.
- Holding public ceremonies or displays to point out team accomplishments.

WHAT'S NEXT?

As teams evolve through the various stages of development, the need for recognition of individual efforts will increase, and the team will need to develop ways to recognize its individual members. Recognition of individuals can still be done publicly, but it must be done by the team itself, not by managers or the organization.

Recognition is an ongoing process that continues and evolves with the teams and the organization. It may change to meet the changing needs of the team, but it never becomes obsolete.

A CASE IN POINT: MANUFACTURING ORGANIZATION

A manufacturing company devised a method for rewarding teams that met team objectives of productivity and interactions with other teams. Points were awarded each quarter, based on performance in these two areas. Teams that earned 500 or more points could select items from a gift catalog that offered everything from decorative items for the workplace to coffee makers and microwave ovens.

Points were earned for the following accomplishments:

- If the team's replacement and rework costs were less than 2.5 percent of the market value of their output, the team earned up to 200 points.
- If the team met or exceeded its production objectives, based on a computerized system that tracked materials into the department and output from the department, the team earned up to 200 points.
- If the team's interpersonal interactions with another team met standards identified on a cross-team rating form, the team earned up to 200 points.

Every team was encouraged to participate in the award system. Whenever enough points were earned by a team and gifts were selected, the information was posted on a company bulletin board outside the cafeteria and announced in the company newsletter.

MATURE TEAM– NEW TEAM COACHING SESSION

WHAT

Mature team members make good coaches because they have "been there." Often new teams in trouble will listen to these men and women when they won't listen to anybody else.

A coaching session between a mature team and a new team consists of a four- to six-hour meeting between two to four members of a mature team, and all the members of a new team. The meeting is usually held in a meeting room at the job site. (A mature team is defined as one that has been functioning for at least one year and is at either the Tightly Formed or Self-Directed stage.) The purposes of this session are to accomplish one or more of the following:

- Help the new team resolve specific issues they are struggling with.
- Give the new team access to information "from the horse's mouth."
- Allow the new team to see what a mature team looks and acts like.
- Reassure new team members that the prize is worth the struggle.

- Enable mature team members to recognize how far they have come.
- Enable mature team members to practice coaching skills, and to build bridges to other teams.

WHEN

A coaching session of this type may be needed when:

- A new team is about to start and wants guidance from a mature team's perspective.
- A team is demoralized and ready to give up.
- A team needs help developing systems, procedures, and work practices to support the transition.
- A leader of a new team may be so dominant that the team does not feel it is making progress toward self-direction.
- A new team is experiencing the same problems that a mature team experienced—and solved.

WHO

The facilitator usually takes responsibility for determining when a new team needs one of these sessions. The facilitator also sets up and facilitates the meeting. Managers are usually not invited, partly because they could hinder frank discussion, and partly because teams need to recognize their own competence.

HOW

The following steps should be performed by a facilitator.

1. Determine if a coaching session is needed (see "WHEN").
2. Identify members from a mature team to do the coaching. The selection criteria should include:

- Has the mature team experienced—and already re-solved—a situation similar to the new team's?
- Do these team members have good coaching skills?
- Are they good "role models" for new team members to emulate?

3. Prepare an agenda. Although the facilitator should consult with the new team, preparing the agenda is his or her re-sponsibility. The agenda for a session might look like this:
   - *How to do peer performance reviews.*
   - *How to create a self-discipline system.*
   - *How to do self-scheduling for your team.*
   - *Future team development issues.*

4. Handle logistics. Arrange a time when work can be shut down for four to six hours, and all concerned can attend.

5. Facilitate the meeting. The format for the meeting might be 15- to 20-minute presentations by mature team members, followed by questions from the new team, and then a work-shop session. In the workshop, the facilitator and mature team members can roll up their sleeves and help the new team members work on procedures, or forms, or whatever the problem is.

6. Follow up after the session by supporting the new team's ef-forts to carry out what they learned in the session. If it seems appropriate, encourage the "coaches" to follow up on their own with the new team.

WHAT'S NEXT?

If the session worked, the new team has gotten back on track, and has also developed a new resource for getting help in the fu-ture.

A CASE IN POINT: MACHINE REPAIR COMPANY

A new team in a machine repair company was engaged in con-stant argument with its supervisor, who was having a hard time living up to the spirit of the hand-off plan. In addition, team members were having difficulty keeping track of their action plans.

With help from a mature team, which had encountered a similar situation, the new team developed a procedure and a form for tracking tasks delegated by the supervisor. The success of the form was twofold. First, it made the supervisor feel more confident about handing off important tasks. Second, it gave the team a clear method for following through on these tasks.

A GROUP PROBLEM-SOLVING PROCESS

WHAT

A problem-solving process is a set of procedures for identifying a problem, determining its cause(s), deciding on a solution, and developing a plan to carry it out and monitor results.

A complete problem-solving approach for work teams includes the following elements:

- A logical, easy-to-remember set of problem-solving steps.
- A set of tools and techniques to help team members deal with complex or difficult problems.
- Procedures for using the process effectively in team sessions.
- A method for training team members in all of the above.

WHEN

Problem-solving skills become critical during Stage 3, Leader-Centered Teams. Because these skills empower the team to solve problems and take action, they promote team identity at a crucial point in the team's development.

WHO

Selecting a problem-solving process is the responsibility of the design team. However, for maximum effectiveness, everyone in the organization needs to learn and use the same process. It's a little like using computers. If everyone operates on the same system, they can do more and have a greater impact than if they use two or three different and incompatible systems.

HOW

There are many problem-solving approaches to choose from. The organization can choose a commercially packaged one that appears suitable for its needs, or it can design its own. In any case, the following guidelines will apply.

Keep the Process Simple and Easy to Use

Some problem-solving processes have many steps, use many complicated tasks, and call for fairly advanced computational skills. They are often more trouble than they're worth for any but the most complex problems. To be effective, all that's really required is a process that helps people (1) identify the problem, (2) determine the cause or causes, (3) choose a solution, and (4) plan action steps and follow up.

Augment the Basic Process with Special Tools and Techniques That Help Individuals and Groups Work through Tough Problems

Here are some situations when people require special help:

- When there are multiple possible causes to a problem.
- When people are strongly polarized on an issue.
- When the problem is unlike any other they have dealt with before.
- When the team has run out of creative solutions.

To help with these difficult situations, team members need to have access to tools and techniques that are easily explained and suitable for group as well as individual use. Some especially useful techniques include:

- Brainstorming and its variations.
- Nominal group process (for generating and prioritizing ideas).
- Checksheets.
- Flowcharts.
- Questionnaires.
- Interviews.
- Diagrams.
- Planning charts.
- Force field analysis.
- Fishbone diagram.
- Pareto chart.
- Histogram.
- Control chart.

DEVELOP GROUND RULES FOR USING THE PROCESS IN TEAM PROBLEM-SOLVING SESSIONS

Work teams—and in fact most employees in today's organizations—solve more and more problems in teams. Ground rules for members of a problem-solving session could include:

- *Stay focused on the problem.* A problem-solving session can sometimes get off track, and it's natural for team members to feel angry and frustrated. Although people tend to blame the session leader, team members can do their part to refocus discussion and keep the team moving toward a solution.

- *Contribute ideas and information.* The full potential of team problem-solving is achieved only if people contribute freely during the session. When they do, the entire group benefits from the knowledge and experience of individual team members.

- *Encourage others to contribute.* In every team, some members are less vocal than others—even though the quiet ones may have much to contribute. To take advantage of the resources of the entire team, team members need skills in helping one another contribute to the problem-solving process.

- *Help the team agree on a follow-up plan.* An effective solution requires both a good idea and a plan of action. By actively promoting agreement on action steps, schedule, and accountability, every team member can encourage mutual commitment to make the solution work.

- *Make sure everyone understands the assigned tasks.* Before leaving the problem-solving session, individual team members need to be absolutely clear about their part. When people take initiative to clarify their assigned tasks, the plan has a much greater chance of success.

Steps for the leader of a problem-solving session could include:

- *Focus the team for efficient problem solving.* Sessions that wander off the topic are frustrating for both leader and participants. The session leader needs to help the team chart a course, stay on course, and set ground rules that allow for light moments and useful digressions.

- *Reinforce constructive contributions.* Team members need to be reminded that their contributions are the backbone of group problem solving. When the session leader encourages constructive comments, team members feel more confident about volunteering ideas.

- *Encourage balanced participation.* The leader needs to make sure that no view predominates until all relevant views are considered.

- *Maintain an appropriate pace.* When a problem-solving session either drags or races, people can lose interest or get confused. An appropriate pace allows for adequate discussion and clear transitions between the phases of the problem-solving process.

- *Make sure follow-up activities are planned.* An effective solution requires more than a good idea; it also requires team involvement in planning its implementation. Without the individual commitment of team members to carry out their part in the plan, the solution may never get off the drawing board.

DESIGN A PROGRAM TO TRAIN ALL TEAM MEMBERS IN TEAM PROBLEM SOLVING

The design should take into consideration the numbers of people to be trained, who will train them, and how this program fits into the overall team-member training plan. In organizing the training, different organizations follow different options:

- Team members can go through all the steps of the process at one time or can learn them over a period of six to ten weeks.
- Training usually begins with the basic problem-solving process.
- Training in the tools and techniques is often conducted on a just-in-time basis.
- Leader training usually follows training in the basic process.

REINFORCE LEARNING

Managers need to be trained in the problem-solving process in order to reinforce its use. They can best reinforce it by following it themselves and asking team members the right questions: What causes have you examined? What's your back-up data? What symptoms have you observed? What solutions were considered? Many organizations redesign their forms to reflect the problem-solving terminology and also use the steps in the problem-solving process to structure meetings.

WHAT'S NEXT?

As the teams mature and team members become comfortable with the problem-solving process and the basic tools and techniques, they will eventually be ready for more advanced procedures, such as statistical process control (SPC).

CLUSTER MEETING

WHAT

A cluster meeting is a twice weekly, 15-minute stand-up meeting in which the team "clusters" with the area manager, and/or someone from a support group that the team needs to talk to. Its purpose is to deal with issues before they become problems, and to prevent the isolation that can occur when teams are not connected with the rest of the organization.

The stand-up format underscores the need to be quick and efficient: These meetings are for sharing information, not solving problems.

WHEN

Many organizations initiate cluster meetings toward the end of Stage 1, although to work well they need a strong team leader (who usually appears during Stage 3).

WHO

All team members should attend, along with the area manager and anyone else the team has invited. The meeting should be led by a team leader. The manager needs to understand that he or she is not in charge; it's the team's responsibility and the team leader needs to lead the meeting.

HOW

1. The team leader sets up a flipchart in a meeting room with a brief agenda in the form of questions like, What's happening with the team? What does the team need to know? Is anything going wrong?

2. The team leader convenes the meeting and leads a discussion with the team on each of the questions on the agenda.

3. Key ideas are recorded on a flipchart.

4. Action items are assigned, if necessary. Cluster meetings are not intended to be problem-solving meetings; it may be possible to deal with some questions on the spot, but issues that need further work should be dealt with outside the meeting. Some teams keep blank action plan worksheets where they have their cluster meetings so immediate action can be initiated on any problems that surface during the meeting. (See Exhibit 16-1 for a sample of an action plan form.) Typically, the team leader fills out an action plan form and a volunteer from the team agrees to take responsibility for that issue. Follow-up can be conducted at the next regular team meeting or on the job. Completed action plans can be posted on the team's bulletin board.

A CASE IN POINT: DRILL BIT MANUFACTURER

The engineering department was thinking about making a change in the design of a large drill. The team responsible for manufacturing this tool was afraid that the new design would be incompatible with their manufacturing processes.

To head off this problem, the team invited the engineering manager to a cluster meeting and presented these concerns. As a result, the engineering department went ahead and redesigned the tool, but with the needs of production clearly in mind.

EXHIBIT 16-1. Action Plan Form

ACTION PLAN

TEAM_____	DATE_____

ISSUE RAISED

NEED TO WORK/KNOW

	SUBTASKS (WHAT)	ACTIONS (HOW)	RESPONSIBILITY (WHO)	TIME (WHEN)
a.				
b.				
c.				

ACTION PLAN FOLLOW-UP

WHO	WHAT	HOW	WHEN
•			
•			
•			
•			

PEER PERFORMANCE APPRAISAL

WHAT

The peer performance appraisal is a once-a-year, formal written document (supplemented by discussion) that is conducted by members of the team to evaluate an individual member's performance during the year. Annual objectives established both by the individual and the team are the basis for the evaluation. The procedure focuses on the technical, administrative, and interpersonal skills that the team has agreed are essential for successful team membership. These objectives are initially developed by the design team and agreed upon by the work team. As work teams mature, they take more responsibility for determining objectives and standards.

For mature work teams, the peer performance appraisal replaces the traditional performance review typically conducted by the employee's supervisor or manager.

WHEN

Peer reviews should not be initiated before a work team reaches Stage 3, Leader-Centered Teams. At this stage, the teams are already choosing leaders within the team. Assuming the function of team member review is a logical next step.

WHO

Two members of the work team, one picked by the person being reviewed and one picked by the rest of the team, conduct and deliver the performance appraisal.

HOW

Before entering into the review process, all team members receive training on developing performance plans and conducting peer reviews. This training usually includes two two-hour modules and a four-hour practice session as outlined below.

- Setting and writing performance standards (two hours).
- Conflict resolution skills (two hours).
- Skills practice exercises (four hours).

The actual peer performance appraisal process typically proceeds as follows:

1. The work team develops an annual performance plan—the set of objectives and standards that the team agrees to achieve during the year. Prior to the Leader-Centered Stage in the evolution of the team, this plan will be provided by the design team and agreed to by the team.

2. Based on the overall team objectives and standards, an individual performance plan is negotiated by the two designated team members (see "WHO," above) and the employee. These designated members will later become the reviewers for this employee.

3. The employee performance plan is submitted to a manager or to human resources for review and approval. Human resources is involved both because of legal requirements and because HR people coach the committee in this process.

4. During the year, the team participates in ongoing coaching and review sessions, with guidance from supervisors or

managers and the design team. These informal reviews keep team members informed of their progress so that the formal review holds few, if any, surprises.

5. Three to four weeks before an employee's review date, the two designated team members begin gathering input from other team members on the employee's performance.

6. The reviewers' formal appraisal is written up on the performance appraisal form and reviewed by human resources.

7. The reviewers are coached on effective performance appraisal techniques by human resources and/or the work-team consultant.

8. The employee also fills out a performance appraisal form, rating his or her performance for the year. This form may be used for comparison or clarification during the discussion with the reviewers.

9. The two designated reviewers deliver the performance review to the employee. The delivery takes the form of a two-way conversation covering expectations, results, strengths, and areas for improvement. The appraisal should be thorough, open, honest, and solidly based on fact.

10. Following delivery and discussion, the employee signs the appraisal form and also any action proposed in response to a superior or unacceptable performance rating.

11. If any action has been recommended by the team, the form is referred to human resources for approval.

12. The form is returned from human resources with the proposed action approved or modifications suggested.

13. The employee and two reviewing members develop a new performance plan for the following year, incorporating any agreed-upon actions previously identified. (After the first year, when the process is more widely understood, the employee and the team should pick one or two new people to be the reviewers.)

14. In cases of proposed actions that are severe or involve discipline or termination, the employee may request a further evaluation by the peer disciplinary committee. (See "Peer Disciplinary Review Committee," pages 325–330.)

Typical performance standards addressed in a review of technical, administrative, and interpersonal skills might include criteria such as:

- Understands a number of jobs performed by the team.
- Performs tasks correctly and on time.
- Completes paperwork or procedures accurately.
- Meets production schedules.
- Uses time efficiently.
- Helps out where additional effort is needed.
- Leads or participates constructively in team meetings.
- Contributes to team problem solving and production efforts.
- Cooperates readily with team members.
- Shows commitment to the idea of self-directed work teams.
- Maintains good relationships with teammates, managers, and other teams or support services.

WHAT'S NEXT?

In some organizations, the employee's compensation is based on the results of the performance appraisal. In this case, the next step would be to use the results of the appraisal to determine adjustments to the employee's salary.

However, in the pay-for-performance system often embraced by organizations using teams (see "Compensation Systems that Support Teams," pages 229–241), a separate formal testing and observation process rates employees according to specific criteria used to determine compensation.

In a self-directed work-team environment, the performance appraisal is more often separate from the compensation process and is used as a developmental tool. As such, it can help employees achieve expected performance standards, identify and overcome weaknesses, solve problems, and improve performance. It can also identify strengths, recognize outstanding performance, acknowledge superior skills or contributions, and identify new directions for team members to follow.

A CASE IN POINT: PERFORMANCE APPRAISAL FORM

One example of a performance appraisal form follows. Organizations will need to draft or adapt a form specifically suited to their needs. Generally, this task is best addressed through human resources.

EXHIBIT 17-1.

Name		Team

Reviewer(s)	Review Period	Return to HR by (date)

Purpose:

All of us are entitled to know what is expected of us on the job and to receive regular feedback on our performance. The performance appraisal should be a two-way conversation covering performance expectations, performance results, strengths, and areas for improvement. Periodic informal reviews and coaching should have kept us informed of progress, so the formal review should contain no big surprises. The review should be a thorough, honest, open and fact-based assessment of our performance along all the dimensions covered.

PERFORMANCE PLANNING AND APPRAISAL PROCESS

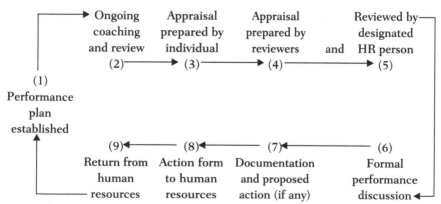

Exhibit 17-1. *(Continued)*

I. **Performance Plan:** List below objectives and standards set for this period.
   Objective = general statement of major accomplishments planned.
   Standards = observable results that show progress or achievement.
   Objective #1—
   Standards
   a.
   b.
   c.
   Objective #2—
   Standards
   a.
   b.
   c.

II. **Technical Knowledge and Skills:**
   In this section individual and reviewers should discuss the *job-specific skills and knowledge* required to meet this particular job's responsibilities.
   A. List the specific knowledge and skills needed to do your current job.

   _____   _____
   _____   _____

   B. Select and discuss one or two key *strengths* from the above list.
      1.
      2.
   C. Select and discuss one or two *areas for improvement* from the above list.
      1.
      2.

III. **Work Habits:**
   In this section individual and reviewers should discuss the importance of each *work-related behavior* and how well each is being done. Add or delete as needed.
   A. Habits or attitudes considered to be important on the job.

Comes to work on time	Handles responsibility well	Concerned about cost
Productive on the job	Maintains well organized work area	Follows safety rules
Committed to quality		Meets time schedules
		Has a "can do" attitude

   _____   _____   _____
   _____   _____   _____

   B. Select and discuss one or two *strengths* from the above list.
      1.
      2.

EXHIBIT 17-1. *(Continued)*

   C. Select and discuss one or two *areas for improvement* from the above list.
     1.
     2.

IV. **People Skills:**
   In this section individual and reviewers should discuss skills and attitudes needed to *work with others* to do the job and to create a productive climate. Add to or delete from the list as needed for the job.

   A. Listens well to others   Gives credit for   Treats all with
      Makes own ideas   ideas   respect
        known   Leads toward   Has team-player
                       solutions   attitude

    _____   _____   _____
    _____   _____   _____

   B. Select and discuss one or two *strengths* from the above list.
     1.
     2.
   C. Select and discuss one or two *areas for improvement* from the above list.
     1.
     2.

V. **Performance Rating Summary:**
   Overall performance should be summarized by checking one of the categories listed below. This summary rating should consider both the objectives met and the manner in which they were met.

   ☐ 1. Consistently *exceeds most* of the requirements of the position. Performance goes well beyond reasonable but demanding standards of excellence in terms of quantity, quality, delivery, and cost consciousness, as well as work habits and people skills.

   ☐ 2. Consistently *meets all* the requirements of the position. It is the good, solid performance expected of those who have the skills, training, and experience needed. Although minor deviations may occasionally occur, the overall performance meets or may slightly exceed normal job requirements.

     3. Performance *meets most* of the job requirements. The individual:
      ☐ A. Is new to the company or is in a significantly different assignment, requiring further *experience and development.*
      ☐ B. Has the necessary experience and has performed well in the past, but has shown *unacceptable performance* in one or more areas this period.

EXHIBIT 17-1. *(Continued)*

VI. **Plans to Maintain or Improve Performance:**
     (Specific objectives will become part of the next *Performance Plan* period.)
     •
     •
     •

VII. **Individual's Comments:**

VIII. **Signatures and Reviews:**

Individual Reviewed   Date
(Signature means only that this appraisal was reviewed and discussed with you.)

Reviewing Team Members   Date

Reviewed and Approved by   Date

REPOTTING WORKSHOP

WHAT

Teams, like potted plants, can become root-bound; to continue to flourish they need repotting to the next size larger pot, along with some revitalizing care and feeding. A repotting workshop is a one-and-a-half-day workshop for a mature team. The purpose is to generate a new wave of enthusiasm that will move team members off the plateau of complacency that mature teams can get stuck on. To be successfully "repotted," a work team may need to do the following:

- Rededicate itself to the beliefs and practices of work teams.
- Deepen its understanding of the organization's future plans.
- Renew its sense of purpose and team identity.

WHEN

A team is ready for its first repotting workshop once it reaches Stage 5, usually from three to five years after start-up. It should repeat the process about once every two years after that.

WHO

In an organization with multiple team sites, a repotting work-shop can have as many as 50 people: the work teams, the design

Exhibit 18-1.

AGENDA
DAY 1

Morning and Afternoon:

A series of 20-minute presentations from the executive team and outside experts, each sesion followed by a 25-minute discussion. At the end of the day, a panel discussion by all presenters. Possible presentation topics:

Progress towards achieving mission and philosophy of self-direction.

Reports on other kinds of employee participation in the organization.

Team progress toward product and market objectives

Team achievements in quality and reliability.

Team impact on financial health of organization.

Evening:

Celebratory social event

DAY 2

Morning:

Skills training session, such as leadership skills

---

team, and selected executives, support staff, managers, consultants, and guest experts. The design team plans and schedules the workshops. Executives, consultants, and guest experts are presenters and/or responders. Team members, support personnel, and managers are participants.

HOW

Members of the design team should carry out the following steps:

1. Design the workshop. The design team should work closely with the work team and the team facilitator. A typical workshop design could have the agenda in Exhibit 18-1.

2. Run the workshop. Keep the focus on the work team—their past accomplishments and future directions.

3. Publicize the event, and the results. A repotting workshop is evidence the organization is making progress with its work

teams. Knowing they have this kind of experience to look forward to can also motivate other work teams.

WHAT'S NEXT?

The design team can plan subsequent half-day seminars for work-team members that follow up on the skills session, for example, or go into depth on topics raised during the workshop.

DIFFUSION STRATEGIES

WHAT

Diffusion strategies are ways to establish new work teams within the organization, either by increasing the number of work teams at an existing facility or by installing work teams in a new facility.

WHEN

You should use diffusion strategies when (1) teams have been going well at one site; (2) the people, time, and money are available to set up new teams; and (3) a new location or group shows a serious interest in and capacity for moving to work teams.

WHO

The design team—local or corporate—is always responsible for team diffusion strategies. At the plant site it is the local design team for that site; at the corporate level it is the corporate design team.

HOW

To install more work teams in an existing facility, the local design team should follow these steps:

1. Identify the potential for new work teams by asking existing teams, facilitators, and internal and external consultants for their views.

2. Hold an information meeting or meetings to discuss self-directed work teams with potential new members. Discuss what is involved in making the shift, and the pros and cons for the organization and individual employees. Be upbeat, positive—and honest; if the benefits are oversold now, there may be regrets later. Team members are often invited to help in the presentation. Their views carry a lot of weight with the audience.

3. Ask employees to make the decision. If possible, employees should decide for themselves by secret ballot if they want to be members of work teams.

4. Set up the new teams. Two strategies to help new teams take root and grow are first, transfer one or more team members from mature teams to each new team; second, establish a group of existing team members to act as advisers to the new teams.

To install work teams in a new physical location within the organization, the corporate design team should carry out the following steps:

1. Identify potential sites for work teams. Indications of potential sites include (a) employee interest, (b) strong local management support, (c) a production process improvable with work teams, and/or (d) a site with a work process similar to those in existing work-team sites. Unless your organization already has a healthy track record with teams, be careful about considering facilities that are having major problems; work teams can't solve all problems, and a failure at a new site could unfairly tarnish the whole concept.

2. Generate support for work teams at the new site or sites. There are several strategies to generate support:
   • Enlist a senior manager who has been a champion of work teams to head up the effort at the new site.

- Encourage senior managers from the potential new site to attend public information seminars about self-directed work teams.
- Arrange for key people at the potential site to visit existing work teams.
- Pay for the work-team consultant to spend time talking with key people at the potential new site.
- Bring in mature teams to make presentations to the top management at the potential new site.

3. Select final sites.

WHAT'S NEXT?

If there is a lot of interest, the next step would be to install work teams in the new site(s) following the same procedures as for existing sites. If interest is low, hold off installation until you can create a more favorable climate.

A CASE IN POINT: TRW's PRODUCTIVITY CONSULTING GROUP

Managers from other parts of the organization initially feared that work teams were impractical and unrelated to "real world" business concerns. They were convinced otherwise after attending one of the productivity consulting group's semiannual, two-day workshops for its design team, where they witnessed three mature teams reporting on successes and problems, reports from consultants on installing new compensation and tracking systems that demonstrated their concern for the bottom line, a "help-needed" session demonstrating that help is available when it is needed, and the CEO's commitment and depth of understanding.

BIBLIOGRAPHY

Abernathy, W. J., K. B. Clark, and A. M. Kantrow. *Industrial Renaissance.* New York: Basic Books, 1983.

Akin, Gib, and David Hopelain. "Finding the Culture of Productivity." *Organizational Dynamics,* Winter 1986, 19–32.

Bacas, Harry. "Who's in Charge Here?" *Nation's Business,* May 1985, 57–60, 62, 64.

Bassin, Marc. "Teamwork at General Foods: New and Improved." *Personnel Journal* 67 (May 1988):62–70.

Bean, Audry E., Carolyn Ordowich, and William A. Westley. "Including the Supervisor in Employee Involvement Efforts." *National Productivity Review* (Winter 1985–86): 183–196.

Beehr, Terry A., and Nina Gupta. "Organizational Management Styles, Employee Supervisory Statute and Employee Response." *Human Relations* 40, no. 1 (1987):45–58.

Berglind, Bradford I., and Charles D. Scales. "White Collar Productivity." *Management Review,* June 1987, 41–46.

Bernstein, Aaron, and Wendy Zellner. "GM May Be Off the Hook." *Business Week,* 28 September 1987, 26–27.

Bernstein, Paul. "The Learning Curve at Volvo." *Columbia Journal of World Business* 23 (Winter 1988): 87–95.

Birch, David L. *Job Creation in America.* New York: Free Press, 1987.

Blank, Sally J. "Organizing the Future." *Management Review,* July 1986, 18–21.

Blinder, Alan S. "Want to Boost Productivity? Try Giving Workers a Say." *Business Week,* 17 April 1989, 10.

Block, Peter. *The Empowered Manager: Positive Political Skills at Work.* San Francisco: Jossey-Bass, Inc., 1987.

Blumberg, Melvin. "Job Switching in Autonomous Work Groups: An Exploratory Study in a Pennsylvania Coal Mine." *Academy of Management Journal* 23, no. 2 (1980):287–306.

Brossy, Roger, and Douglas G. Shaw. "Using Pay to Implement Strategy." *Management Review,* September 1987, 44–48.

Buchanan, David. "Job Enrichment Is Dead: Long Live High-Performance Work Design!" *Personnel Management* (UK) 19 (May 1987):40–43.

Burck, Charles G. "What Happens When Workers Manage Themselves." *Fortune*, 27 July 1981, 62–69.

Carnall, C. A. "Semi-Autonomous Work Groups and the Social Structure of the Organization." *Journal of Management Studies* 19 (July 1982): 277–94.

Carnevale, Anthony P., Leila J. Gainer, and Ann S. Meltzer. *Workplace Basics. The Essential Skills Employers Want.* San Francisco: Jossey-Bass, Inc., 1990.

———. *Workplace Basics Training Manual.* San Francisco: Jossey-Bass, Inc., 1990.

Carnevale, Anthony P., Leila J. Gainer, and Eric Schulz. *Training the Technical Work Force.* San Francisco: Jossey-Bass, Inc., 1990.

Casey, Mike. "Quality in the Works: Is the Valley Turning Out the Best?" *Dayton Daily News*, 24 April 1989, 11–12.

Chelte, Anthony F., Peter Hess, Russell Fanelli, and William P. Ferris. "Corporate Culture as an Impediment to Employee Involvement: When You Can't Get There from Here." *Work and Occupations* 16 (1989): 153–64.

Cherns, Albert. "Principles of Sociotechnical Design Revisited." *Human Relations* 40, no. 3 (1987): 153–62.

Clipp, F. Paul. "Focusing Self-Managing Work Teams." *Quality Digest*, April 1990, 20–22, 24–29.

Coates, E. James. "Employee Participation—a Basic Link in the Productivity Chain." *Industrial Management* 31, no. 3 (1989):2–4.

Cotton, John L., David A. Vollrath, Kirk L. Froggatt, Mark L. Lengnick-Hall, and Kenneth R. Jennings. "Employee Participation: Diverse Forms and Difference Outcomes." *Academy of Management Review* 13 (1988):8–22.

Cox, Allan. "Managing without Hierarchy. Even 'Flat' Companies Need Leaders." *The New York Times*, 20 August 1989, sec. 3, p. 3.

Cummings, Thomas G. "Self-Regulating Work Groups: A Socio-Technical Synthesis." *Academy of Management Review* 3 (1978): 625–33.

Cummings, Thomas G., and W. H. Griggs. "Workers' Reactions to Autonomous Work Groups—Conditioning for Functioning, Differential Effects, and Individual Differences." *Organization & Administrative Sciences* 7 (Winter 1976–1977):87–100.

Cummings, Thomas G., and E. S. Molloy. "Autonomous Work Groups: Theory and Change Strategy." In *Improving Productivity and the Quality of Work Life.* New York: Prager, 1977.

Dalton, Gene W., Paul H. Thompson, and Raymond L. Price. "The Four States of Professional Careers—A New Look at Performance by Professional." *Organizational Dynamics*, Summer 1977, 19–42.

Dalziel, Murray M., and Stephen C. Schoonover. *Changing Ways. A Practical Tool for Implementing Change within an Organization.* New York: Amacom, 1988.

Davies, Kent R. "Is Individual Responsibility a Radical Idea in American Business?" *Training,* November 1988, 63–65.

Denison, Daniel R. "Sociotechnical Design and Self-Managing Work Groups: The Impact on Control." *Journal of Occupational Behavior* 3 (October 1982):297–314.

Donovan, Michael. "Employees Who Manage Themselves." *Journal for Quality and Participation,* March 1989, 58–61.

———. "Redesigning the Workplace." *Journal for Quality and Participation,* December 1989, 6–8.

———. "Self-Managing Work Teams—Extending the Quality Circle Concept." *Quality Circles Journal* 9 (September 1986):15–20.

Dulworth, Michael, Delmar Landen, and Brian Usilaner. "Employee Involvement Systems in U.S. Corporations: Right Objectives, Wrong Strategies." *National Productivity Review* (Spring 1990): 141–56.

Dumaine, Brian. "Who Needs A Boss?" *Fortune,* 7 May 1990, 52–53, 58, 60.

Elden, Max. "Sociotechnical Systems Ideas as Public Policy in Norway: Empowering Participation through Worker-Managed Change." *The Journal of Applied Behavioral Science* 22 (August 1986):239–55.

Farrell, Christopher, and John Hoerr. "ESOPs: Are They Good for You?" *Business Week,* 15 May 1989, 116–23.

Feuer, Dale. "Paying for Knowledge." *Training,* May 1987, 57–66.

Fisher, K. Kim. "Management Roles in the Implementation of Participative Management Systems." *Human Resource Management* 25 (Fall 1986): 459–79.

Fotilas, Panagiotis. "Semi-Autonomous Work Groups: An Alternative in Organizing Production Work?" *Management Review,* July 1981, 50–54.

Galagan, Patricia. "Work Teams That Work." *Training and Development Journal,* November 1986, 33–35.

Galbraith, Jay R. "Organization Design: An Information Processing View." *Interfaces* 4 (May 1974):26–36.

Garcia, Joseph E., and Carla Haggith. "OD Interventions That Work." *Personnel Administrator* 34 (June 1989):90–94.

Garvin, David. "Quality Problems, Policies and Attitudes in the U.S. and Japan: An Exploratory Study." *Academy of Management Journal* 29 (December 1986):653–73.

Geber, Beverly, "Quality Circles: The Second Generation." *Training,* December 1986, 54–61.

———. "Teaming Up with Unions." *Training,* August 1987, 24–30.

Gilbert, G. Ronald. "Building Highly Productive Work Teams through Positive Leadership." *Public Personnel Management* 14 (1985):449–54.

Glaberson, William. "An Uneasy Alliance in Smokestack U.S.A.: How the Motor Division of G.E. Forged Its Deal to Pay Less but Preserve Jobs." *The New York Times*, 13 March 1988, sec. 3, pp. 1, 11.

Goodman, Paul S., Rukmini Devadas, and Terri L. Griffith Hughson. "Groups and Productivity: Analyzing the Effectiveness of Self-Managing Teams." In *Productivity in Organizations*, edited by John P. Campbell, Richard J. Campbell, and Associates, 295–327. San Francisco: Jossey-Bass, Inc., 1988.

Goodman, Paul S., Elizabeth C. Ravlin, and Linda Argote. "Current Thinking about Groups: Setting the Stage for New Ideas." Chapter in *Designing Effective Work Groups*. San Francisco: Jossey-Bass, Inc., 1986.

Grayson, C. Jackson, Jr., and Carla O'Dell. *American Business, A Two-Minute Warning: "Ten Changes Managers Must Make to Survive into the 21st Century."* New York: The Free Press, 1988.

Greco, Gail. "Teams Score Victories at Work." *Nation's Business*, April 1988, 38–40.

Gulowsen, Jon. "A Measure of Work Group Autonomy." Chapter in *Selvstyrte Arbeidsgrupper*. Oslo: Tanum, 1971.

Gummer, Burton. "Post-Industrial Management: Teams, Self-Management, and the New Interdependence." *Administration in Social Work* 12, no. 3 (1988):117–32.

Gupta, Nina, G. Douglas Jenkins, Jr., and William P. Curington. "Paying for Knowledge: Myths and Realities." *National Productivity Review* (Spring 1986):107–23.

Hackman, J. Richard. "The Design of Work Teams." *A Set of Methods for Research on Work Teams. Technical Report #1, Group Effectiveness.* Research Project, School of Organization and Management, Yale University, 1982.

Hackman, J. Richard, ed. *Groups That Work and "Those Who Don't." Creating Conditions for Effective Teamwork.* San Francisco: Jossey-Bass, Inc., 1990.

Hackman, J. Richard, and G. R. Oldham. *Work Redesign.* Reading, Mass: Addison-Wesley, 1980.

Hanna, David. *Designing Organizations for High Performance.* Reading, Mass: Addison-Wesley, 1989.

Harmon, Roy L., and Leroy D. Peterson. *Reinventing the Factory Productivity Breakthroughs in Manufacturing Today.* New York: Free Press, 1990.

Henry, Lori. "Reorganization at McCormack and Dodge: Getting Everybody in on the Act." *Personnel*, November 1987, 48–52.

Herman, Stanley M. "Participative Management Is a Double-Edged Sword." *Training,* January 1989, 52, 55–57.

Hess, Karen, ed. *Creating the High-Performance Team.* New York: John Wiley and Sons, 1987.

Hillkirk, John. "Everyone Weaves Ideas into Milliken." *USA Today,* 26 December 1989, sec. B, p. 5.

Hills, Frederick S. "The Pay-for-Performance Dilemma." *Personnel,* October 1979, 24–31.

Hoerr, John. "Is Teamwork a Management Plot? Mostly Not." *Business Week,* 20 February 1989, 70.

———. "The Payoff from Teamwork." *Business Week,* 10 July 1989, 56–62.

———. "Workteams Can Rev Up Paper-Pushers, Too." *Business Week,* 28 November 1988, 64, 68, 72.

Hoerr, John, Michael Pollack, and David Whiteside. "Management Discovers the Human Side of Automation: Companies Are Finding That Workers Are the Key to Making Technology Pay Off." *Business Week,* 29 September 1986, 70–75.

Hoglund, William E. "Saturn: An Experiment in People Management." *Survey of Business* 21 (Spring 1986):12.

Holpp, Lawrence, and Richard S. Wellins. "The Role of HRD in World-Class Manufacturing." *Training,* March 1989, 50–55.

Holusha, John. "Beating Japan at Its Own Game." *The New York Times,* 16 July 1989, sec. 3, pp. 1, 8.

———. "Corning: The Search for Flexibility on the Line." *The New York Times,* 16 July 1989, sec. F, p. 8.

Imai, Ken-Ichi, Ikujiro Nonaka, and Hirotaka Takeuchi. "Managing the New Development Process: How Japanese Companies Learn and Unlearn." In *The Uneasy Alliance,* edited by K. B. Clark, R. H. Hayes, and C. Lorenz. Boston: Harvard Business School Press, 1985.

Imai, Masaaki. *Kaizen.* New York: Random House, 1986.

Jackson, Susan E. "Participation in Decision Making as a Strategy for Reducing Job-Related Strain." *Journal of Applied Psychology* 68, no. 1 (1983):3–19.

Johnson, Robert L. "The Power of Participation." *Quality* 24 (February 1985):49–50.

Kamien, Morton, and Nancy Schwartz. *Market Structure and Innovation.* Cambridge: Cambridge University Press, 1982.

Kanter, Rosabeth Moss. *Change Masters.* New York: Simon and Schuster, 1983.

———. *When Giants Learn to Dance.* New York: Simon and Schuster, 1989.

————. "Increasing Competitiveness without Restructuring." *Management Review,* June 1987, 21, 23.

————. "The New Managerial Work." *Harvard Business Review,* November-December 1989, 85–92.

————. "Quality Leadership and Change." *Quality Progress,* February 1987, 45–51.

Keller, Robert T. "Predictors of the Performance of Project Groups in R&D Organizations." *Academy of Management Journal* 29 (December 1986):715–26.

Kelly, John E. "A Reappraisal of Sociotechnical Systems Theory." *Human Relations* 31, no. 13 (1978):1069–99.

Kemp, Nigel J., Toby D. Wall, Chris W. Clegg, and John L. Cordery. "Autonomous Work Groups in a Greenfield Site: A Comparative Study." *Journal of Occupational Psychology* 56 (1983):271–88.

Klein, Janice A. "The Human Costs of Manufacturing Reform." *Harvard Business Review,* March-April 1989, 60–66.

Kochanski, James. "Hiring in Self-Regulating Work Teams." *National Productivity Review* 6 (Spring 1987), 153–59.

Koenig, Richard. "Quality Circles Are Vulnerable to Union Tests." *The Wall Street Journal,* 28 March 1990.

Kolodny, Harvey F., and Barbara Dresner. "Linking Arrangements and New Work Designs." *Organizational Dynamics,* Winter 1986, 33–51.

Lawler, Edward E. III. *High Involvement Management.* San Francisco: Jossey-Bass, Inc., 1986.

————. *Pay and Organizational Effectiveness: A Psychological Approach.* New York: McGraw-Hill, 1971.

————. "The Multitrait-Multirater Approach to Measuring Managerial Job Performance." *Journal of Applied Psychology* 60 (1975): 550–55.

————. "The New Plant Revolution." *Organizational Dynamics,* Winter 1978, 3–12.

————. "Today's Leaders Look to Tomorrow." *Fortune,* 26 March 1990, 49–50.

Lawler, Edward E. III, G. E. Ledford, and S. A. Mohrman. *Employee Involvement in America: A Study of Contemporary Practice.* Houston, Texas: American Productivity & Quality Center, 1989.

Lawler, Edward E. III, and Susan A. Mohrman. "Quality Circles after the Fad." *Harvard Business Review,* January 1985, 65–71.

Lawler, Edward E. III, and Lee Ozley. "Winning Union-Management Cooperation on Quality of Worklife Projects." *Management Review,* March 1979, 19–24.

Lee, M. S. "Alienation and Control Among 'Semi-Autonomous Work Groups' in the Non-unionized Residential Sector of the Construction Industry." *Dissertation Abstracts International* 45 (November 1984):5a.

Levin, Doron P. "U.A.W.'s Challenge from Within." *The New York Times,* 18 June 1989, sec. F, p. 5.

Likert, Rensis. *New Patterns of Management.* New York: McGraw-Hill, 1961.

Lord, Robert G., and Paul J. Hanges. "A Control System Model of Organizational Motivation: Theoretical Development and Applied Implications." *Behavioral Science* 32 (1987):161–78.

Majerus, R. E. "Workers Have a Right to a Share of Profits." *Harvard Business Review,* September-October 1984, 42, 44, 50.

Mann, Eric. "Work Teams Muffle Labor's Voice." *The New York Times,* 11 June 1989, sec. 3, p. 2.

Manz, Charles C., and Harold Angle. "Can Group Self-Management Mean a Loss of Personal Control: Triangulating a Paradox." *Group & Organization Studies* 11 (December 1986):309–34.

Manz, Charles C., and Henry P. Sims, Jr. "Leading Workers to Lead Themselves: The External Leadership of Self-Managing Work Teams." *Administrative Science Quarterly* 32 (1987):106–28.

———. "The Potential for 'Groupthink' in Autonomous Work Groups." *Human Relations* 35, no. 9 (1982):773–84.

———. "Searching for the 'Unleader': Organizational Member Views on Leading Self-Managed Groups." *Human Relations* 37, no. 5 (1984):409–24.

———. "Self-Management as a Substitute for Leadership: A Social Learning Theory Perspective." *Academy of Management Review* 5, no. 3 (1980): 361–67.

Margulies, Newton, and Lora Coleflash. "A Socio-Technical Approach to Planning and Implementing New Technology." *Training and Development Journal,* December 1982, 17–29.

Markham, S. E. "Pay-for-Performance Dilemma Revisited: Empirical Example of the Importance of Group Effects." *Journal of Applied Psychology* 73, no. 2 (1988):172–80.

McCaskey, Michael B. "An Introduction to Organizational Design." *California Management Review* 17, no. 2 (1974):13–20.

Meglino, Bruce M., and William H. Mobley. "Minimizing Risk in Organization Development Interventions." *Personnel,* June 1977, 23–31.

Michaels, Marguerite. "Hands Across the Workplace." *Time,* 26 December 1988, 14, 17.

Moran, Linda, and Ed Musselwhite. *Self-Directed Workteams: A Lot More Than Just Teamwork.* San Jose, California: Zenger-Miller, Inc., 1988.

Moskal, Brian S. "Lessons from the Shop Floor." *Industry Week,* 1 May 1989, 15, 18–19.

———. "The Sun Also Rises on GM." *Industry Week,* 5 September 1988, 100–02.

Mossop, Mary Walsh. "Total Teamwork: How to Be a Leader, How to Be a Member." *Management Solutions,* August 1988, 3–9.

Musselwhite, W. Christopher. "Knowledge, Pay, and Performance." *Training and Development Journal,* January 1988, 62–65.

Nichols, Don. "Taking Participative Management to the Limit." *Management Review,* August 1987, 28–32.

Nicklas, Greg. "Self-Managing Teams and Unions." *Quality Circles Journal* 10 (June 1987):36–40.

Nora, John J., C. Raymond Rogers, and Robert J. Stramy. *Transforming the Workplace.* New Jersey: Princeton Research Press, 1986.

Ouchi, William G. "A Conceptual Framework for the Design of Organizational Control Mechanisms." *Management Science* 25 (1979):833–48.

Pasmore, William A., Carole Francis, Jeffrey Halderman, and Abraham Shani. "Sociotechnical Systems: A North American Reflection on Empirical Studies of the Seventies." *Human Relations* 35, no. 12 (1982):1179–1204.

Pasmore, William A., and John J. Sherwood. *Sociotechnical Systems.* San Diego, California: University Associates, 1978.

Patten, Thomas H. *Pay: Employee Compensation and Incentive Plans.* New York: Academic Press, 1965.

Pava, Calvin. "Redesigning Sociotechnical Systems Design: Concepts and Methods for the 1990s." *The Journal of Applied Behavioral Science* 22, no. 3 (1986):201–21.

Pearce, John A. II, and Elizabeth C. Ravlin. "The Design and Activation of Self-Regulating Work Groups." *Human Relations* 40 (November 1987):751–82.

Pearson, Peg, and Jake Baker. "Seattle Workers' Brigade: History of a Collective." *Puget Consumers' Co-Op Newsletter* 54 (June 1977): 279–89.

Persico, John, Jr. "Team Up for Quality Improvement." *Quality Progress,* January 1989, 33–37.

Peters, Tom. *Thriving on Chaos.* New York: Harper and Row, 1987.

———. "The Issues in Quality: Making Quality America's Job One." *Quality Anniversary Issue,* 1987, Q58–Q65.

Peters, Tom, and Nancy Austin. *A Passion for Excellence.* New York: Warner Books, 1985.

Peterson, Donald. "Three Management Challenges to High Tech Manufacturing." *Supervision,* July 1989, 14–16.

Piore, Michael, and Charles Sabel. *The Second Industrial Divide*. New York: Basic Books, 1984.

Poza, Ernesto J. "Twelve Actions to Build Strong U.S. Factories." *Sloan Management Review*, Fall 1983, 27–38.

Poza, Ernesto J., and M. Lynne Markus. "Success Story: The Team Approach to Work Restructuring." *Organizational Dynamics*, Winter 1980, 3–25.

Proctor, Barcy H. "A Sociotechnical Work Design System at Digital Enfield: Utilizing Untapped Resources." *National Productivity Review* (Summer 1986):262–70.

Ranney, Joyce M. "Bringing Sociotechnical Systems from the Factory to the Office." *National Productivity Review* (Spring 1986): 124–33.

Redburn, Tom, and James Flanigan. "U.S. Firms Regain Competitive Edge." *The Los Angeles Times*, 2 August 1987, sec. 1, pp. 1, 22.

Rehder, Robert R., Robert W. Hendry, and Marta Medaris Smith. "Nummi: The Best of Both Worlds?" *Management Review*, December 1985, 36–41.

Reiker, Wayne S. "Where Are We Headed?" *Journal for Quality and Participation*, December 1987, 32–36.

Rock, Milton L. *Handbook of Wage and Salary Administration*. New York: McGraw-Hill, 1984.

Rosen, Ned. *Teamwork and the Bottom Line*. New Jersey: Lawrence Erlbaum Associates, Inc., 1989.

Rubenstein, Sidney P. "Don't Fear the Team—Join It." *The New York Times*, 11 June 1989, sec. 3, p. 2.

Rumelt, Richard P. *Strategy, Structure, and Economic Performance*. Cambridge, Mass.: Harvard University Press, 1971.

Samuel, Howard. "A Labor Perspective on Participative Management." *Quality Progress*, February 1987, 38–39.

Schellhardt, Timothy D., and Carol Hymowitz. "U.S. Manufacturers Gird for Competition: Foreign Inroads Demand Changes in Methods, Management." *The Wall Street Journal*, 2 May 1989, sec. A, pp. 2, 9.

Schoonover, Stephen C., and Murray M. Dalziel. "Developing Leadership for Change." *Management Review*, July 1986, 55–60.

Schuster, Michael H. "Gainsharing: Do It Right the First Time." *Sloan Management Review*, Winter 1987, 17–25.

———. "Gainsharing: The State of the Art." *Compensation and Benefits Management*, Summer 1986, 285–90.

Schuster, Michael H., and Christopher J. Miller. "Employee Involvement: Making Supervisors Believers." *Personnel*, February 1987, 24–28.

Selznick, Phillip. *TVA and the Grassroots*. Berkeley: University of California Press, 1949.

Sherman, Stratford P. "The Mind of Jack Welch." *Fortune,* 27 March 1989, 38–50.

Simmons, John, and Geri Blitzman. "Training for Self-Managing Work Teams." *Quality Circles Journal* 9 (December 1986):18–21.

Sims, Henry P., Jr., and James W. Dean, Jr. "Beyond Quality Circles: Self-Managing Teams." *Personnel,* January 1985, 25–32.

Sims, Henry P., Jr., and Charles C. Manz. "Conversations within Self-Managed Work Groups." *National Productivity Review* (Summer 1982):261–69.

Smulsky, Suzanne. "At Ford. Teamwork Pays Off." *The Secretary,* January 1989, 18–20.

Storey, Greg. "American Worker." *Fortune,* 11 November 1985, 91–98.

Tichy, Noel M. "When Does Work Restructuring Work? Organizational Innovations at Volvo and GM." *Organizational Dynamics,* Winter 1976, 63–80.

Tomasko, Robert M. "Running Lean, Staying Mean." *Management Review,* November 1987, 32–38.

Tosi, Henry, and Lisa Tosi. "What Managers Need to Know about Knowledge-Based Pay." *Organizational Dynamics,* Winter 1986, 52–64.

Townsend, Patrick L., and Joan E. Gebhardt. *Commit to Quality.* New York: John Wiley and Sons, Inc., 1986.

Trist, Eric. "Collaboration in Work Settings: A Personal Perspective." *The Journal of Applied Behavioral Science* 13, no. 3 (1977): 268–78.

Trist, Eric, and K. W. Bamforth. "Some Social and Psychological Consequences of the Long Wall Method of Coal-Getting." *Human Relations* 4, no. 1 (1951):3–38.

Usilaner, Brian, and John Leitch. "Miles to Go—Or Unity at Last." *Journal for Quality and Participation,* June 1989, 60–67.

Varney, Glenn H. *Building Productive Teams.* San Francisco: Jossey-Bass, Inc., 1989.

Von Hippel, E. "Users as Innovators." *Technology Review* 80 (January 1978):1–11.

Wall, Toby D., Nigel J. Kemp, Paul R. Jackson, and Chris W. Clegg. "Outcomes of Autonomous Workgroups: A Long-Term Field Experiment." *Academy of Management Journal* 29 (June 1986):280–304.

Walton, Richard E. "Establishing and Maintaining High Commitment Work Systems." In *The Organizational Life Cycle: Issues in the Creation, Transformation, and Decline of Organizations,* edited by J. R. Kimberly, 208–90. San Francisco: Jossey-Bass, Inc., 1980.

———. "From Control to Commitment in the Workplace." *Harvard Business Review,* March-April 1985, 77–84.

Walton, Richard E., and J. Richard Hackman. "Groups Under Contrasting Management Strategies." *Designing Effective Work Groups,* September 1984, 168–200.

———. "Innovative Restructuring of Work." Chapter in *The Worker and the Job: Coping With Change.* Englewood Cliffs, N.J.: Prentice-Hall, 1974.

Walton, Richard E., and Leonard A. Schlesinger. "Do Supervisors Thrive in Participative Work Systems?" *Organizational Dynamics,* Winter 1979, 25–37.

Waterman, Robert H. *Adhocracy: The Power to Change.* Knoxville, Tenn.: Whittle Communications, 1990.

———. *The Renewal Factor.* New York: Bantam Books, 1988.

Weik, Karl E. "Organization Design: Organizations as Self-Designing Systems." *Organizational Dynamics,* Autumn 1977, 31–46.

Weisbord, Marvin R. *Productive Workplaces: Organizing and Managing for Dignity, Meaning and Community.* San Francisco: Jossey-Bass, Inc., 1987.

———. "The Flying Starship Factory." *Industry Week,* 3 April 1989, 60–64.

———. "Participative Work Design: A Personal Odyssey." *Organizational Dynamics,* Spring 1985, 4–20.

Whitsett, David A., and Lyle Yorks. "Looking Back at Topeka: General Foods and the Quality-of-Work-Life Experiment." *California Management Review* 25 (Summer 1983):93–109.

Worthy, Ford S. "You're Probably Working Too Hard." *Fortune,* 27 April 1987, 133, 136, 140.

Yankelovich, Daniel. "The Work Ethic Is Under-Employed." *Psychology Today,* May 1982, 5–6, 8.

Zemke, Ron. "Sociotechnical Systems." *Training,* February 1987, 47–57.

INDEX

ABOUT THE AUTHORS

Jack Orsburn, president of Phoenix-based Orsburn Team Works, Inc., is recognized as a highly successful OD consultant. His preference is to work with designated internal people in a mentoring role—to transfer the technology—rather than developing a dependent relationship.

Orsburn Team Works has worked with business, industry, education, government, and public service organizations since 1966, in situations where there had been a decision to involve a broader range of members in the effort to achieve excellence. Although Jack has become most known for his work with hundreds of self-directed work teams, he continues to emphasize that teams are a means to the end of organizational excellence, not an end in itself.

For those of you who have a feeling that things need to change toward broader involvement in and ownership of your organization's customer satisfaction objectives, several services are available from Orsburn Team Works. An initial service is a readiness assessment to determine what strengths and weaknesses exist in terms of building a high-involvement environment. Customized consulting is available to work to reduce any weaknesses that are surfaced in an assessment.

We offer design team consultation and facilitation for those who know they want to work toward a team-based organization and demonstrate a readiness to move in that direction right now. Assistance and advice are available for the development of team performance assessment models, which define the specific knowledge, skills, and attributes (KSAs) required to do specific tasks within teams—both production and support workers.

These models have proved to be an ideal foundation both for training and for establishing a basis for skill-based pay systems. If a client need is for assistance toward achieving a high-involvement culture, Orsburn Team Works can probably provide skilled consultants.

Jack D. Orsburn, Ph.D., President, Orsburn Team Works, Inc., 8840 W. Sequoia Drive, Peoria, Arizona 85382, (623) 566-2784.

Linda Moran, Senior Practice Leader, AchieveGlobal, has more than 15 years of experience in organizational performance improvement. She has extensive experience in large-scale organizational change, designing team-based organizations and measures, change management, work redesign, and executive coaching. She applies her knowledge in a wide range of industries and organizational levels.

Linda is the coauthor of numerous articles and books, including *Self-Directed Work Teams: The New American Challenge* (1990), *Keeping Teams on Track: What to Do When the Going Gets Rough* (1996), and *Self-Directed Workteams: A Lot More Than Teamwork* (3rd edition, Zenger-Miller, San Jose, California, 1989). She is frequently quoted in *Quality Digest, Training, Training and Development,* and the *Journal of Quality and Participation,* and has collaborated with Zenger-Miller on a number of essays.

She also is a nationally acclaimed speaker, presenting at conferences such as the International Work Team Conference (1991–1999), the American Society of Quality Control (1992, 1994), the Association for Quality Performance (1992), and the American Society for Training and Development (1989).

Her professional experience includes human resource training positions at both the Oyster Creek Nuclear Power Plant and Chubb & Sons, Inc.

She earned a B.S. degree from Pennsylvania State University and a master's degree in organizational communication from the University of Maryland. She became certified in Advanced Organizational Development through Columbia University in 1996 and currently is a doctoral candidate in organizational learning and leadership at Columbia University.

AchieveGlobal is an exciting combination of three of the world's best-known training and consulting organizations: Kaset International, Learning International, and Zenger-Miller. With offices throughout North America and in 38 countries around the world, we help organizations achieve business results through superior sales, customer services, leadership, and teamwork.

Linda Moran, Senior Practice Leader, AchieveGlobal, 8875 Hidden River Parkway, Suite 400, Tampa, Florida 33637-1034, (813) 977-8875.